WHOLEFOOD AND VEGETARIAN COOKERY

CARL WITHEY

Hodder & Stoughton

A MEMBER OF THE HODDER HEADLINE GROUP

Every effort has been made to obtain permission for the reproduction of copyright material. Any rights omitted from the acknowledgements or in the text will be added for subsequent printings following notice to the publisher.

Thanks are due to Coeliac UK, Diabetes UK, and Victoria Taylor for all their comments and suggestions.

Logos on pages 21, 36, 37: © Pedigree Masterfoods; © Soil Association; © RSPCA. Reproduced with permission.

EBLY® is a registered trade mark of Ebly SA.

All photographs (including cover images) by Steve Tanner.

Orders queries: please contact Bookpoint Ltd, 130 Milton Park, Abingdon, Oxon OX14 4SB.
Telephone: (44) 01235 827720, Fax: (44) 01235 400454. Lines are open from 9.00–6.00, Monday to Saturday, with a 24 hour answering service. Email address: orders@bookpoint.co.uk

A catalogue record for this title is available from The British Library.

ISBN 0 340804 815

First published 2002

Copyright © 2002 Carl Withey

Typeset by Dorchester Typesetting Group Ltd, Dorchester, Dorset
Printed in Great Britain for Hodder & Stoughton Educational, a division of Hodder Headline Plc, 338 Euston Road, London NW1 3BH by The Bath Press Ltd, Bath

contents

acknowledgements

To put pen to paper is a daunting task, with the project being aimed at the young and older chef alike, each of whom has their own ideas on what is good, bad and indifferent. It really isn't a one-man show, producing a guidebook like this. The book is meant as a guide through the minefield of vegetarian and wholefood cookery to help caterers build on what they already know or suspect; it is not meant as a bible, but as a means of transport to an exciting world of vegetarian and wholefood cookery.

I would never have started, let alone finished without the help of the people below. I would like to say a big thank you to Bill Farnsworth and Rob Smith from the Birmingham College of Food for their encouragement, also thanks to Ian Monger for his technical help with salt and sugar, Rodger Bradly, Rod Burton, John Bridges and Malcolm Sims for their technical help, Pam Williams for the hours spent proofreading this book.

Michael Chew and Dorothy for their help with recipes, along with Michael Leiw for the recipes he supplied. To Mark, Jackie and Andy Cleverdon from Master Foods for their information and recipes. To the Soil Association in Bristol and Hammond Communications Ltd, on behalf of the RSPCA. Thanks to Steelite for supplying all the crockery.

Thank you also to Luke Hacker for his foresight and encouragement in helping to get this project off the ground, and to Stephen Halder and Stephen Baker.

The biggest thanks of all go to my best friend and wife Ruth, who had to put up with the moods and bad temper moments that all chefs have.

introduction

In today's multicultural society, there is more variety and choice in the cuisines and dishes that are on offer to the public than there has ever been. Colleges have to adapt their programmes to provide the wide range of skills and knowledge that a young qualified chef requires on leaving for industry. In the early 1980s all the programmes were geared around European cookery, mainly French classical cuisine, which was required by industry at the time. Now there are all sorts of opportunities for young chefs other than those in hotels, for example: contract catering, off-shore catering, in-flight, hospital catering, ethnic restaurants, educational catering, fast food, pub food, coffee shops, brasserie restaurants, vegetarian restaurants. The list goes on.

This wholefood and vegetarian cookery book will benefit both students and caterers alike. As well as containing recipes for all food groups, it also explains what the commodities are, together with their nutritional importance and value; identifies what a vegetarian, vegan or none meat eater needs to have for a healthy life and diet; and shows how the chef should use the ingredients and why.

An important part in the book is the chapter on Special Dietary Considerations. With so many people nowadays suffering from reactions to certain foods, this will be of interest not only to students of catering but also to chefs in the industry employed in contract catering, nursing homes, educational catering, fast food, pub, coffee shops, brasserie restaurants, vegetarian restaurants, etc. This book will give the caterer the opportunity to understand what food they can and cannot give to their customer suffering from a food-related complaint and also gives easy-to-follow recipes.

what do we mean by wholefood and vegetarian diet?

DEFINITION

Wholefood is a general term used to describe food that has not been refined or modified, or which has been altered as little as possible and is consumed in its original or natural state. Examples are whole grain or brown rice and whole-wheat flour.

A **vegetarian** is someone who does not eat meat, fish, poultry, game, shellfish, crustacea, or slaughter by-products such as gelatine or animal fats, but lives on a diet of grains, pulses, nuts, seeds, free-range eggs, vegetables and fruits, with or without the use of dairy products.

TYPES OF VEGETARIAN

The term vegetarian can be confusing to the caterer when used to describe various vegetarian diets. The broad term 'strict vegetarian' could refer to a vegan diet, or it may simply refer to a lacto-ovo-vegetarian diet. Semi- or demi-vegetarian is sometimes used to describe people who will eat no or little meat but may eat fish. Those consuming fish but no meat are sometimes called pescetarians.

A **lacto-ovo-vegetarian** will consume both dairy products and free-range eggs. This is the most common type of vegetarian diet, whereas the **lacto-vegetarian** consumes dairy products but no eggs.

Ovo-vegetarians eat free-range eggs and egg products but not dairy products.

A **vegan** is a vegetarian who abstains from eating or using any animal products or by-products (e.g. wool, leather, silk, honey).

Fruitarian is a type of vegan diet where no or very few processed foods are eaten. The diet consists mainly of raw fruit, grains and nuts. Fruitarians will eat only plant foods that can be harvested without harming or killing the plant, i.e. organic foods.

Macrobiotic is a diet that is followed for a number of spiritual and philosophical reasons. The diet progresses through approximately ten levels that become increasingly restrictive, gradually eliminating all animal products and ending in the highest level of a brown rice diet.

VEGETARIAN FOODS

A vegetarian diet that is well balanced can provide all the nutrients required by the body without animal products. There is some scientific evidence indicating that vegetarians may be healthier than meat eaters because the diet is often low in saturated (animal) and total fat, high in dietary fibre and complex carbohydrates, and high in protective minerals and vitamins present in fresh fruit and vegetables which could be destroyed by intensive farming methods, fertilisers, pesticides and chemical sprays.

WHY BE A VEGETARIAN?

There are a number of different reasons why people become vegetarians. The majority of people do so because of their strong belief that it is wrong to slaughter animals for the consumption of food and because they are opposed to the cruelty and suffering forced upon the millions of animals reared for this purpose. Some people become non-meat eaters for religious or medical reasons, because of food cost, philosophy or because they believe in non violence.

For others it's the effect on the environment from meat production with large areas of rainforest are cut down for sheep and cattle farming, giving another reason for becoming a vegetarian or vegan. Some may become a non-meat eater simply because they do not like the taste of meat.

Another reason is the health advantages of eating a vegetarian diet, with BSE, salmonella in eggs, and foot and mouth outbreaks being well documented.

SPECIAL DIETARY CONSIDERATIONS

Catholics
Strict Catholics still value the tradition of eating fish on Friday.

Hindus
Hindus consider it is wrong to kill animals for food and are vegetarian. The cow is sacred and eating beef is strictly prohibited. Alcohol is prohibited.

Jews
Jews do not eat any meat from the pig. Jews have special rules about the killing of animals. The preparation of food is called Kosher.

Medical conditions

This could include someone who has a specific medical condition, personal intolerance or illnesses rather than nutritional problems for example, high cholesterol or seafood which could cause anaphylactic shock.

Muslims

Will not eat pork or pork products and all other meat must be bled and slaughtered according to their law and tradition. Alcohol is strictly prohibited. Adult Muslim's fast during day light in the month of Ramadan.

Rastafarian

Are vegetarian, but sometimes eat meat, except pork.

Seventh Day Adventists

Many Afro-Caribbean Christians do not eat pork or pork by-products.

Sikhs

Many Sikhs will not eat beef or drink alcohol.

Weight-reducing diet

Someone who needs to reduce the amount of animal fats and by products in their diet, due to obesity, medical reasons or for personal idiosyncracies.

BASIC NUTRITION

Many people about to take the step to becoming a vegetarian or changing to a healthy diet worry that if they stop eating meat and fish, they might be lacking some nutritional deficiency. With a well-balanced diet, this is not the case. All the nutrients needed are easily obtained from a vegetarian diet. It is in fact much healthier than that of a typical meat eater, according to research.

Most of our foods contain a number of different nutrients, but it is easier to classify them by the main nutrient that they provide. Everything you eat will give your body a wide range of essential nutrients. Animal products give you large amounts of protein, fat (cholestrol), vitamins B and minerals (mostly iron, zinc, potassium and phosphorus). Fish and shellfish in addition supplies vitamins A, D and E, and the mineral iodine. Vegetarians on a well balanced diet can easily obtain all of these nutrients from other sources, without the cholesterol. See the chapter 'Nutrition' for further information.

nutrition

FATS

Reports from the Committee On Medical Aspects of Food and Nutrition Policy (COMA) and the National Advisory Committee on Nutrition Education (NACNE) recommend a reduction of fat content in the diet by at least half, especially animal fats, but also vegetable fats. Some studies have suggested that more oily fats from fish (sardines, herrings, etc) in the diet are beneficial, in preventing heart disease and in maintaining flexible and supple joints because they contain the omega-3 fish oil. They also recommend increased intakes of complex carbohydrates and fibre and a decrease in intake of sugar and salt. In 1990 the World Health Organisation also recommended a reduction of fat and an increased consumption of complex carbohydrates, as well as increased consumption of fruit, cereals, pulses and vegetables.

Ways to reduce intake of fats include:
- using butter and margarines sparingly. Offer low-fat spreads instead
- removing any visible surface fat from dishes such as stews, casseroles, etc.
- reducing the amount of high-fat cheese and milk used. Offer low fat yoghurts, or low-fat alternatives such as skimmed milks or soya milk
- trying to use vegetable oils containing polyunsaturated fatty acids like corn oil, soya bean and sunflower oils rather than cheap vegetable oil. Avoid solid vegetable fats because they contain saturated fats
- using bean dishes as well as those containing low-fat cheese and yoghurts
- avoiding fried and glazed vegetables
- using flour-based sauces (roux with skimmed or soya milk, or vegetable stock base)
- remember crisps, chocolate and many snacks have high (animal) fat content.

Note: COMA was disbanded in March

2000 and has been replaced by The Scientific Advisory Committee on Nutrition (SACN). SACN will advise the health department and the Food Standards Agency on all matters relating to food, diet and health.

PROTEIN

Protein is a crucial component of every living cell. Blood and blood vessels, all muscles, nerves, skin and hair all contain protein along with enzymes, hormones and antibodies. Without proteins we could not digest any foods. We also depend on proteins for vital functions such as blood clotting, transporting oxygen around the body and fighting infections.

On average women need 62g of protein a day (more if pregnant, lactating or active), while men require approximately 85g (more if very active).

The amount of protein in food varies but the main sources of protein for a vegetarian or vegan are:

- Dairy products
- Eggs (with the exception of battery or intensively farmed eggs)
- Fungi
- Grains/cereals
- Nuts
- Pulses
- Seafoods
- Seeds
- Soya products

The protein structure is made up of amino acids, which in turn are made up of the compounds carbon, hydrogen, oxygen, nitrogen and sometimes sulphur.

There are only 20 different amino acids but the number in which they are sequenced is incalculable. The body can make some amino acids by converting other amino acids, but eight cannot be made, they have to be obtained from a balanced diet. These **essential amino acids** are isoleucine, phenylalanine, leucine, lysine, threonine, valine, tryptophan and methionine.

No single plant food contains all the essential amino acids that are needed in the correct amounts or proportions, but when we combine the plant foods any deficiency in one is counteracted by another. So a vegetarian or vegan who eats a variety of vegetable proteins should not be any more deficient than a meat eater. It is therefore important to mix protein foods all the time (protein combining). This is a normal way of eating; simple examples are beans on toast, or muesli. Including dairy products or free-range eggs to the diet can also add missing amino acids, e.g. macaroni cheese, quiche or porridge.

The body contains a pool of amino acids, so if a meal is deficient it can be made up from the body's own stores. It is therefore not necessary to complement amino acids all the time. If the diet is generally varied and well balanced there is no need to worry unduly. Foods low in protein will still be adding some amino acids to the body's reserves.

Reference nutrient Intake (RNI)

The RNI is the amount of nutrient which is enough for at least 97 per cent of the population. Reference nutrient intakes for protein in grams per day are as follows:

Age	RNI
0 to 3 months	12.5g
4 to 6 months	12.7g
7 to 9 months	13.7g
10 to 12 months	14.9g
1 to 3 yrs	14.5g
4 to 6 yrs	19.7g
7 to 10 yrs	28.3g
Men 11 to 14 yrs	42.1g
Men 15 to 18 yrs	55.2g
Men 19 to 49 yrs	55.5g
Men 50+ yrs	53.3g
Women 11 to 14 yrs	41.2g
Women 15 to 18 yrs	45.0g
Women 19 to 50 yrs	45.0g
Women 50+ yrs	46.5g
Pregnant women	51.0g
Lactating women	53–56g

Vegetarian or balanced vegan diets often meet and exceed the required protein levels required. They are normally lower in total intake of protein than non-vegetarian diets. A lower protein intake may well be beneficial, because a high intake of protein has often been linked to a number of conditions, like osteoporosis and in some cases attributed to aggravating poor or failing kidney functioning. However, the connection between protein levels and these medical complaints remains controversial.

PROTEIN COMBINING

Illustrated in Figure 1 are the five groups of food that are required for a balanced vegetarian diet. These combined foods will ensure that all the essential amino acids will be supplied in the diet. This will prevent the reliance upon dairy foods, which would increase the daily fat intake.

VITAMINS

Vitamins are organic substances that are needed in small amounts in the body for numerous special functions. They can be obtained by eating a balanced diet. Most of the vitamins we need cannot be made in the body and a lack of them or insufficient amounts in our diet can lead to a number of deficiencies, for example weakness, growth restriction, poor vision, mouth ulcers, malnutrition. It is rare to find vitamin deficiency today in the United Kingdom. Vitamins are essential in the body and are necessary for good health. It is also true that if your body takes too much of some vitamins they can have ill effects.

Vitamins come from a wide variety of commodities and no one food can provide all the necessary vitamins we need. Vitamins have to provide a variety of functions throughout the body. They can also be adversely affected by conditions such as light, heat and air, food storage, environmental conditions, processing and cooking. All of these can act to reduce the level of vitamin and nutritional value in food.

A well-balanced diet can provide vegetarians with all the vitamins they need.

Vitamins can be divided into two groups:

- Fat-soluble
- Water-soluble

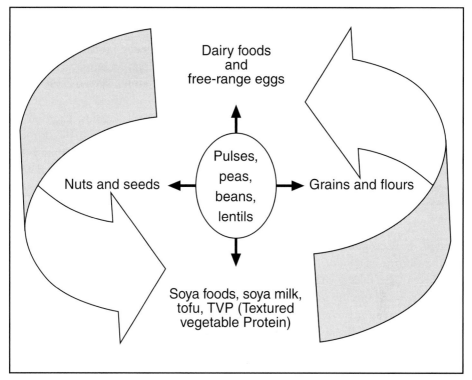

Dairy foods and free-range eggs

Nuts and seeds

Pulses, peas, beans, lentils

Grains and flours

Soya foods, soya milk, tofu, TVP (Textured vegetable Protein)

❏ Figure 1 ❏

Fat-soluble vitamins

Fat-soluble vitamins can be stored in the body and so dietary sources are not required every day.

Vitamin A (retinol)

This is found in foods from animals, i.e. milk and cheese, and also in yellow and orange fruits and vegetables such as apricots, mangos, green leaf spinach, curly kale and leeks that contain carotene or beta-carotene, which the body can convert into Vitamin A. This is an important antioxidant and is stored in the liver. This vitamin is required for maintenance of good vision. Deficiency can result in night blindness or total blindness but this is rare.

Vitamin D (cholecalciferol)

There are few foods that contain significant amounts of vitamin D, as it is made by the body through ultraviolet rays. Breakfast cereals are normally fortified with vitamin D. It is also found in dairy products, eggs and margarine.

Its main function is to help control and absorb the amount of calcium from food that is consumed. It therefore has an important role in developing and sustaining bone strength. A vitamin D supplement may be required if vegan. A deficiency of vitamin D will lead to a condition called 'rickets', and severe muscle pains and weakness in adults called Osteomalacia. Too much exposure to vitamin D can result in kidney damage.

Vitamin E

This is an antioxidant and its role is maintaining the body's red blood cell function. As an antioxidant protecting vitamins A and C and other important substances it is thought to help reduce the risk of some cancers such as cancer of the bowel and breast. It is also thought to reduce heart disease. It can be found in nuts, cereals, soya beans and green vegetables. It is extremely rare to find any vitamin E deficiency in the United Kingdom.

Vitamin K

Vitamin K is coagulant and is essential for the clotting of blood. It is found in dark green vegetables such spinach, cabbage, parsley and sprouts, and also in cauliflower. The vitamin can also be obtained from bacterial synthesis in the intestine.

The water-soluble vitamins

The body is less able to store water-soluble vitamins with the exception of vitamin B12 which is stored in the liver. A daily intake of vitamins is needed. Water-soluble vitamins are more likely to be lost during the cooking process.

Vitamin B1 (thiamin)

Thiamin is found in unprocessed foods such as grains, cereals, fruit, nuts and vegetables. A good source is brown rice and yeast. It has an essential role to play in the steady release of energy from carbohydrates; the more fats and carbohydrates that we consume, the more thiamin is required. Long cooking can destroy thiamin in food. Deficiency in vitamin B1 can cause the condition called beri-beri which causes nerve damage, muscle and eventual heart failure. Beri-beri is almost unheard of in the United Kingdom today.

Vitamin B2 (riboflavin)

Riboflavin helps the body release energy from carbohydrates, protein and fats. It is contained in high amounts in milk and its products, nuts, green vegetables, wholemeal bread, dried prunes, mushrooms, millet and avocados. There are no real deficiency diseases, but the skin can become dry and cracked around the mouth and nose if insufficient amounts are absorbed.

Vitamin B3 (niacin)

Gives energy production released from food and can be made from amino acid. It helps maintain the nervous system and a healthy skin. It is found and contained in most foods including peanuts, yeast extract, wholemeal bread, wheat bran, mushrooms, tempeh and sesame seeds. Deficiency can cause a skin rash (pellagra), diarrhoea and liver damage.

Vitamin B6 (pyridoxine)

This plays an important role in converting protein into amino acid (tryptophan) into vitamin B3 (niacin) and is required in the formation of haemoglobin for red blood cell formation. It is found in wheat bran, wholemeal flour, yeast extract, tempeh, nuts, bananas and currants. Deficiency can cause dryness and cracking of the skin, mouth and nose, but excess may cause loss to sensory nerves.

Vitamin B12 (cobalamin)

B12 is a very important and unique vitamin. The body cannot make this vitamin and requires only very small amounts. Vitamin B12 can be stored in small amounts by the body. It is required for red blood cell formation, growth and a healthy nervous system. This vitamin is exclusively synthesised by bacteria in the intestine and is found primarily in meat, eggs and dairy products.

It is produced by micro-organisms that live in soil and in the intestines. Organically unprocessed vegetables that are fresh and lightly washed in pure water are likely to contain small traces of these micro-organisms. Today's intensive sterile farming methods kill off these organisms and B12. It can also be found in free-range eggs, dairy products and fortified plant and cereal foods including soya milks, veggie burger mixes, yeast extracts, and fermented soya products. Seaweeds and algae have all been suggested as possible sources of B12.

It is suggested that vegans should supplement their diet to include food that is fortified with B12. These can include yeast extracts, veggie burger mixes, TVP, Soya milks, vegetable and sunflower margarine and fortified breakfast cereals.

B12 is important in maintaining the nervous system – the nerves are surrounded by an insulating fatty sheath made up of a complex protein called myelin. B12 is vital in the metabolism of fatty acids, which are essential in the maintenance of the myelin sheath. Long-term deficiency can lead to nerve degeneration and irreversible neurological damage.

Folate (folic acid)

Folate has a number of differing functions, one being its action with B12 in the formation of red blood cells. It is also important in the production of amino acids, DNA and in the development of a healthy nervous system.

Folic acid is the manufactured form of folate. Cooking can destroy a large proportion of folate, in some cases by to 50 per cent. It can be found in a variety of foods, for example, spinach, broccoli, nuts, soya flour, pulses, tempeh and potatoes.

Pantothenic acid

This is required to release energy from carbohydrates, protein and fats. It also helps in the production and formation of antibodies, converting cholesterol to natural steroid hormones and producing a healthy nervous system. Pantothenic acid is found in pulses, tubers, nuts, seeds, vegetables, mushrooms and cereals.

Biotin

Biotin is required for the production of healthy skin, nerves, bone marrow and hair. It is also needed to break down proteins, carbohydrates and in particular fats.

Biotin is found in wheat bran, bananas, yeast extract, pulses, nuts and most vegetables. A deficiency is very rare, but it can cause hair loss, anaemia, muscle pains, fatigue, nausea and possible high blood cholesterol.

Vitamin C (Ascorbic acid)

This vitamin has a vital role in keeping the skin, bones, teeth and gums healthy. It helps the immune system to fight against infection, aids wound healing and helps with energy production and growth. It also helps with the absorption of iron found in citrus fruits, fruits, green vegetables such as broccoli and spinach, berries and peppers. Because it is water soluble there can be a loss of some of the vitamins when cooked in water.

It has been suggested that ascorbic acid in fruit can help to prevent or decrease the chances of heart disease and the development of cells that can cause cancers, although this is subject to much debate.

Deficiencies in this vitamin can result in scurvy, a condition where bruising under the skin, bleeding gums, swollen joints, bone damage and even death occur. This condition blighted sailors of old and is very rarely seen today in the United Kingdom. Too much intake of vitamin C can result in diarrhoea and development of kidney stones.

Vitamin research
There is much research being conducted at present into the benefits of food and vitamins in the fight against cancer and heart disease. The present thought on this subject is that free radicals which are a by-product from natural cell formation and can be produced by smoking, have been linked with the development of some cancers and heart disease. Eating fruits that contain vitamins C, E, carotenes and certain minerals can help the body's defence and fight against free radical damage.

MINERALS

There are thought to be 15 essential minerals that are needed for the vital function of the body.

- Minerals help to form and build teeth and bones.
- They form an essential part in the composition of body fluids (sodium, chloride, potassium, phosphorus and magnesium).
- In conjunction with enzymes and other chemicals they are an integral part of the metabolism.

- They enable the vitamins to work and function correctly.

The main minerals required in a diet are calcium, magnesium, sodium, potassium, chlorine, phosphorus and sulphur. These must be obtained through the consumption of food. The body requires some minerals in larger amounts than others; this does not mean that the small amounts, called trace elements, are no less important. All minerals are essential to our health. Trace elements required in small quantities are copper, fluoride, iron, zinc and selenium. Taking too much of the trace elements can be toxic.

All minerals are obtained from the soil and water whether they come directly from plants or indirectly from animal foods. The quality and quantity of the minerals will be reflected in the food that is ultimately produced. Good soil means quality minerals and good water can help in good food production.

Calcium

Calcium is required for the building and maintenance of strong bones and teeth. These contain 99 per cent of the calcium in the body. The other one per cent is used in the contraction of muscles and blood clotting. Calcium is found in dairy products, leafy green vegetables, kelp, almonds, sesame seeds, dried fruit, figs, pulses and fortified soya milk.

Chromium

Chromium is necessary to help maintain the blood glucose level in the body. It is widely obtained in a variety of foods including wholemeal grain and bread, brewer's yeast, nuts and vegetables.

Copper

Copper is involved in the production of red blood cell formation, body tissue and bone maintenance. The body also needs copper to enable iron to be used correctly. Copper also has many enzyme functions. It is found in green vegetables, yeast, nuts, wheat germ, tempeh, mushrooms and seeds.

Fluoride

Fluoride helps to form and maintain the bones and teeth. The main dietary source is fluoridated water, toothpaste, seafood and tea. Too much fluoride can cause discoloration of teeth, tooth decay and changes to the bone structure.

Iodine

Iodine is essential in the making of thyroid hormones. It is also important in body metabolism for normal growth and development. Iodine is found in seaweeds and milk (it is used as a disinfectant in milk production). The amount in plant foods depends upon the amount of iodine in the soil where the plants are grown.

Deficiency in iodine can cause a goitre (swelling of the thyroid gland in the neck), weight gain or weight loss, psychiatric disturbance, constipation, dry skin and stunted growth.

Iron

Iron is required for haemoglobin, which moves the oxygen in the blood around the body. Iron in food comes in two forms – haem iron and non-haem iron.

Haem iron is found in animal-based foods (40 per cent) and is easily absorbed. All the plant-based foods contain non-haem iron and are a little harder to absorb. As citric acid and vitamin C increase absorption it is advisable for vegans to consume vitamin C and plan their diet to include this. Iron is found in fortified cereals, seeds, leafy green vegetables, pulses, wholemeal, bread, dried fruit and molasses.

Tannins in tea, soya, fibre and calcium can reduce non-haem iron absorption. Iron deficiency is a common nutritional problem in a typical British diet. Women who are breast-feeding, who have heavy periods, and people who have poor quality diet, are at risk of deficiency which may eventually turn into anaemia.

Magnesium

Magnesium is required for correct bone development and is present all the time in tissue. Its enzymes are involved in energy production. It is widely available in food such as green vegetables, brown rice, bran, tempeh, nuts, pulses and fruits. Deficiency is rare but can result in diabetes and diarrhoea.

Manganese

Manganese is required for correct bone development, muscle function, production of cholesterol and for the function of many enzymes. It is found in high amounts in tea, green vegetables, wholegrain cereals, nuts, fungi and spices. Deficiency is very rare but has been linked to diabetes, heart disease, cancer and rheumatoid arthritis.

Molybdenum

This is essential for the metabolism of proteins and fats, and also plays a part in some enzyme systems. It is found in grains, pulses and spinach, but the amount in plant food depends on the quality of the soil. Deficiency is very rare but has been linked to cancer, tooth decay, eye and nerve damage.

Potassium

Potassium is essential for nerves and cells to function correctly and plays a part in maintaining blood sugar levels. The body regulates the amount of potassium inside cells and the amount of sodium outside the cells. Potassium is widely found in plant foods, especially root vegetables, pulses, wholegrain cereals and dried fruits.

Selenium

Selenium helps to protect the body against oxidation damage, acting as an antioxidant in red blood cell function. Selenium is available from a wide range of plant foods, i.e. flour, pulses, fungi, dried fruits and nuts, but the amount in plant food depends on the quality of the soil, as intensive farming with fertilisers and chemicals has cut down on the amounts available in the diet. Deficiency is very rare in the United Kingdom, but has been linked to cancer and strokes.

Sodium (salt)

Sodium has an important role in regulating the body's fluids. It is also important in the nerve and muscle functions.

Salt (sodium chloride) is present naturally in all food. Most people consume too much sodium in their diet, which can lead to high blood pressure. Dehydration is a common condition of sodium and water deficiency. This can lead to exhaustion, nausea leading to vomiting, muscle cramps and possible shock and death.

Sulphur

Sulphur helps form part of protein and most dietary sulphur is in amino acids. Sulphur plays a role in some enzyme systems. Deficiency is linked with protein deficiency.

Zinc

Zinc plays a part in the making of proteins, growth, repair of damaged tissue, breaking down of carbohydrates, making insulin, DNA metabolism, moving of carbon dioxide and vitamin A around the body. It is found in soya foods, wheat bran, pulses, seaweeds, seeds and pasta. Deficiency is rare but can lead to infections, loss of hair and small, white spots on nails and fatigue. A vegetarian diet can contain less zinc than meat diets so careful planning is essential.

There are other mineral elements such as phosphorous, nickel, silicon vanadium, boron, and others that are present in varying amounts in the body. There is some debate as to whether they contribute to a healthy diet.

SALT

Salt consists of two elements, sodium and chlorine. Both are required in the body to maintain and balance its fluid levels. If the body maintains a high intake of salt over a long period this can increase the risk of high blood pressure, in turn leading to the possibility of strokes or heart disease.

For many centuries salt has been a very important part of our daily lives. Its uses range from preserving foods by salting (curing) fish and meats to flavouring foods. It has only been since the 1900s that the daily intake of salt has increased. Studies have shown that the body requires only 5g to 9g of salt each day, although it is suggested that the daily average is some 15g to 20g (four teaspoons). If there is too much sodium in our system, the kidneys will filter it out through urine. Some sodium is lost in sweat and if there is too little the kidneys will save it. However, if the kidneys are constantly working hard to expel excess urine then they will sooner or later begin to falter, leading to high blood pressure.

Sodium naturally occurs in meat, fish, milk and eggs. It is also present in the majority of manufactured foods.

Reducing the intake of salt

- Reduce the amount of salt during cooking. Add less than your demands require.
- Do not be tempted to use a low-salt alternative. You are replacing one chemical for another.
- Do not leave salt on the table as many customers add salt out of habit, before they even taste the food.
- Remember manufactured food contains added salt, so cut down on the a mount of these foods you offer your customers.

- Smoked fish, crisps, cheeses, salted peanuts and savoury (manufactured) products all contain high levels of salt.

As a caterer what can you do?

- Use herbs, spices and black pepper to add flavour and dimension to your food.
- Carefully measure the salt before adding it to water when cooking vegetables. Avoid putting in handfuls of salt.
- It is considered very bad manners on the part of the customer to add salt to a chef's creation. Do you leave salt out on the table or not? Is it the customer's choice or not? If you have to supply salt to the customers, then supply it in measured packets.
- Spread the high-salt foods over the week. This will help balance the intake of salt by your regular customers.
- Include more fruits and vegetables as it is thought that the potassium contained in these foods helps to balance the effects of sodium.

SUGARS

These can be described as the simplest form of carbohydrates. Green plants use the energy from sunlight to convert carbon dioxide and water into sugar. They take the carbon dioxide from the air and during the above process they release oxygen back into the air. When we take sugar into our bodies, it is converted back into carbon dioxide and water which releases energy.

There are three groups of sugars, mono-saccharides (one sugar), disaccharides (two sugars) and finally the most complex are polysaccharides.

Monosaccharides

These are galactose, glucose and fructose and they occur naturally in foods.

Disaccharides

Disaccharides are maltose (malt sugar), lactose (milk sugar), and sucrose (cane or sugar beet).

Sucrose is the name given to the little sweet white crystals that can be found in many fruits and vegetables, such as sugar cane and sugar beet. In foods refined sugar is used extensively as a sweetener and as the main ingredient in sweets, chocolates, jams, fizzy drinks and pre-serves. In manufacturing it is used in the making of cakes and biscuits.

Maltose is present in all cereal grains and is less sweet than sucrose. It is used in the making of malt beer.

Lactose is better known as the milk sugar found in varying amounts produced by lactating animals and in humans.

Polysaccharides

Polysaccharides are made up of starches like cellulose from plant cell walls and from glycogen which is an animal starch stored in the liver of animals.

There are three ways that sugars can be broken down. Naturally occurring sugars found in fruit or milk, are a part of a food and have not been processed. Processed sugars are the natural sweet by-products of insects (e.g. bees) and plants (e.g. the maple tree) which have had little process-ing and can be used as foods such as honey or maple syrup. Then there are the refined sugars such as white, brown, raw, and the commercial fructose that do not occur naturally and have been manufac-tured from sugar cane and beets. Sugar cane is a huge giant grass that grows in moist warm climates and stores the sugar in its cane. Sugar beet grows in a more temperate climate and stores its sugar in the white root.

How sugar is produced

The sugar cane juice is ground, pressed or squashed out of the cane then filtered and boiled until it becomes a syrup and is crystallised. It is then spun in a centrifuge machine to produce the raw sugar. It is the sent to the refinery to be washed, fil-tered, crystallised, dried and packed.

Beet is washed, sliced, soaked in hot water to remove the sugar juice, which is then purified and filtered, then processed the same as the cane sugar.

Sugar plays an important role in supply-ing energy to the body. It also plays a large role in culinary terms, for example:

- it sweetens an array of foods
- it preserves foods such as jams and canned fruit
- sugar prevents moulds and bacteria from growing
- it helps to balance the acidity of dish-es that contain tomatoes and vinegar-based products
- it can be used to colour cooked dishes.

Today there is a large amount of evidence

which shows that too much sugar in the diet can cause tooth decay and obesity, which in turn can lead to other more harmful illnesses such as hypertension, heart diseases and diabetes.

On average 104g of sugar per person per day is consumed. It is suggested in many government reports that sugar intake should be reduced in some cases by 50 per cent. Refined sucrose sugars can have a detrimental effect on blood sugar levels by causing them to rise and fall rapidly. Much of this sugar is hidden in everyday fizzy drinks, snacks and sauces such as tomato ketchup. Refined sugar is devoid of fibre, vitamins, protein and minerals from the sugar plant. When eaten it causes the body to draw on its own store of these essential nutrients. These are not replaced.

Caterers can easily reduce the intake of refined sugar by offering:

- artificial sweeteners (there are many on the market) for the customers' hot drinks
- un-sweetened fruit juices and cereals for breakfast
- dried compots for breakfast and fruit purée conserve instead of preserves and marmalades
- cakes and sauces made using sweeteners rather than sugar
- desserts that contain reduced sugar
- fruit salads without sugar syrups.

Be aware of convenience foods and check the labelling for sugar content. The higher up the list of ingredients, the higher the sugar content.

Starch

Food sugars are one of the two forms of carbohydrate, the major source of body fuel. The other is starch, or complex carbohydrates, such as grains, pulses, vegetables, etc. Starch is a much bigger substance (in chemical terms) than sugars. Starch has two component substances known as amylose and amylopectin and consists of large numbers of the simple sugar glucose. Starch provides useable carbohydrate over a long period, keeping the blood sugar level smooth and fairly even. As starches contain other nutrients, their digestion means that vitamins and minerals are gradually released into the bloodstream along with the sugar that provides energy. Unlike sugar, starch does not dissolve into liquids and is easier to digest when cooked. It is found naturally in a number of foods such as cereals (and cereal products) and root vegetables.

Sucrose

Brown sugar is made up of sugar crystals that are found in molasses syrup, which contain natural flavour and colour. It can also be made by blending white sugar with molasses syrup or by burning white sugar, giving it colour and flavour.

Barbados sugar is a dark brown moist sugar with a fine flavour reminiscent of rum. In the seventeenth century many tropical islands produced sugar and labelled the products after the area that they came from, and some names have remained. Barbados sugar is expensive.

Demerara sugar is from a district in Guyana from which the sugar takes its name. The crystals are a little larger than brown sugar crystals with an excellent flavour. It is expensive but in the UK you are more likely to get the white sugar mixed with molasses called "London Demerara".

Golden syrup is mainly used in the UK. It has a golden yellow colour and is thick and syrupy and looks like honey. It is often used in confectionery and baking.

Jaggery is a very crude sugar from India.

Maple syrup is the sap from maple trees of which there are two species: Sugar Maple and Black Maple. Their sap is mainly used for commercial production. Sap from Red and Silver Maples usually has a much lower sugar content and is not normally used for commercial production. After collection it is transferred to an evaporator where heat is used to concentrate the sap to develop its flavour and colour. It can take 43 gallons of sap to make one gallon of syrup, but this depends on the sugar content of the sap. Maple syrup is around 65 per cent sucrose. It can often be a suitable alternative to honey for vegans.

Molasses is a treacly, dark mass of sugars that are a by-product of sugar refining. It also contains up to 70 per cent sucrose and a number of nutrients from the plant.

Palm sugar is made by boiling down the sap of various types of palm trees. The sap is very dark and sticky. In India the syrup is known as 'gur'. It is used in many parts of the world and is called by different names in the Middle, Far East and Latin America.

Raw sugar ranges in colour from brown to a light tan and contains 98 per cent sucrose. It is the boiled sugar cane or beet juice that is shipped in bulk to the refineries. It is not normally sold to the public, but raw sugar cane juice can be purchased in the local markets of Caribbean countries and in the Orient.

Treacle is a term used to describe anything from molasses to golden syrup that is made from the cane juice.

White sugar contains 99 per cent sucrose and is a highly refined and purified sugar that is bleached turbino. Turbino is a stem cleaned raw sugar, which contains 96 per cent sucrose. The white sugar comes in a variety of differing grades, i.e.: granulated (table) sugar, caster sugar, icing sugar.

Fructose

Fructose can be described as a simple sugar (monosaccharide) and is found naturally in a variety of fresh and dried fruits and honey. Eating these foods is an excellent way to consume the natural sugar of the fruit along with the considerable amounts of vitamins, minerals and fibre that they contain. The fibre slows the absorption of the sugar into the bloodstream which will not give the highs and lows of refined sugar products such as chocolate bars and fizzy drinks.

Honey

Honey was used long before refined sugar. The ancient Greeks, Arabs and Romans used it to make bread and drinks. Honey is best described as a mixture of sugars that are formed from an enzyme, invertase, that is present in the bodies of bees. The quality and taste can differ greatly. This depends upon the types and qualities of the nectar that the bees collect and convert. If the bees collect nectar from one or two plants it will change the character, colour and flavour of the honey. For example, there are several well-known honeys like buckwheat, lavender and clover that are popular. The best honey is the one that has been taken straight from the hive; this will have all the nutrients intact. As a rule of thumb, the darker the honey the stronger the flavour.

On a nutritional level, honey contains 38 per cent fructose and 31 per cent glucose and has about the same nutritional values as sugar, but because honey is heavier it will contain a few more calories and carbohydrates.

During the filtering process the honey is heated and pollen removed. This removes the cloudiness and many nutrients from the honey, leaving it clear.

Fruit juice concentrates

Some manufacturers today use a variety of nutritive sweeteners that are taken from traditional sugar and some that are taken from fruit juice concentrates. To make a concentrate sweetener, the fruit is first crushed, then purified through heat and enzyme processing. It is then filtered to remove impurities, fibre and in some cases to remove the flavour. It is very similar to sugar syrup with almost the same amount of nutrients and calories. It is used by manufacturers in the making of canned fruits, jams, baked products and drinks.

Maltose

The two most widely known of the maltose sugars are barley malt and brown rice syrup.

Wholegrains are a source for natural sugars and they are a complex carbohydrate. Maltose sugar is taken from the grain by a natural process of enzyme activity breaking down the grain's starch molecules into maltose sugar.

Maltose sugars are generally less sweet than sucrose sugars and will, like fructose, be slowly absorbed into the bloodstream and as such will not give the highs and lows of the refined sugars.

Malt extract

Barley is usually soaked to start the germination process. This also increases the nutritional content of the grain. As the grain begins to germinate and sprout it is dried and ground, then re-soaked and boiled down to produce the maltose syrup.

Brown rice syrup

Brown rice is usually soaked to start the germination process. This also increases the nutritional value. As the grain begins to germinate and sprout it is dried and ground then mixed with cooked rice, which creates an enzyme activity in the rice which converts carbohydrates into simple sugars. It is then boiled down to produce the maltose syrup.

Alternatives to sugar

Using the more natural alternatives to sugar in recipes can be challenging and a little daunting, but the chef can be rewarded with new flavours and textures for his or her dish. The chef must take into account the flavours, textures and moisture of the alternative ingredients, such as honey or maple syrup. Also, take into account the liquid and density of syrups compared to the refined granulated sugars.

As a general rule you may have to reduce the liquid content of the dish or recipe, as most of the alternatives are syrup based.

- For alternatives such as molasses and date sugar approximately 75 per cent of the required amount of sugar should be used. There is no need to reduce the amount of liquid in the recipe.

- Alternatives such as maple syrup and honey can be substituted gram for gram with sugar but the liquid needs to be reduced in the recipe.
- Alternatives such as malt extract and rice syrup need to be twice the amount of sugar in the recipe and also require a much larger reduction in the liquid content of the recipe.

Other alternatives that can be used are sugar replacements like saccharine. When using these products it is best to follow the manufacturer's instructions.

cereals, grains and flours

CEREALS AND GRAINS

These are members of the grass family and are called a staple food in many parts of the world. They were named after the Roman goddess, Ceres. Cereals and grains are the world's most important cereal crop and have been cultivated for some 6000 years.

Wholegrains are the edible parts of the seeds; these include the bran, which is the outer layer, the endosperm which is the middle layer and the germ which is the inner layer. Wholegrains include rice, barley, wheat, corn and oats.

Cereals and grains have unique properties making them suitable for a variety of foods, and they are cheap and plentiful. When eaten in large quantities they provide an excellent source of protein. Interestingly, no country uses a wide variety. For example, in the Far East and North Italy rice is the staple, in Africa it is millet, North Europe uses rye and barley, yet in South America maize or corn-meal is used.

Cereals need different conditions to grow, for example, oats need cold climates whereas rice requires a damp climate.

The grains that are most commonly available in the UK include barley, buckwheat, corn/maize, millet, quinoa, oats, rice, rye and wheat. Buckwheat should really be classed as a seed and yet it is used as a grain.

Note: Some cereals contain gluten. Coeliacs are intolerant to the gluten and must therefore avoid wheat, barley, rye and oats, which are known to contain it.

The main concentration of nutrients is in the germ and in the outer layers of the grain. When the wheat is being milled to produce white flour there is a loss of nutrients in the refining process due to some of the bran and germ being discarded. Those that use the unrefined grain without removing any part have the highest nutritional value. There is also a loss of nutrients when rice is milled, unless the rice is parboiled. The nutrients that are lost are added at a later stage, this is known as fortification.

Refined cereals provide valuable sources of protein, yet each cereal differs affecting the final product. Cereals also provide carbohydrates; unrefined cereals contain dietary fibre, B vitamins, vitamin E and essential minerals.

All cereals can be cooked and eaten whole; lots of these cereals are processed before being prepared as food.

Bran and germ

Wheat bran contains protein, thiamin, riboflavin, niacin, fat and carbohydrates. It is an insoluble fibre and is thought to give protection against bowel cancer. Fibre-rich bran is the by-product of white flour processing. It does not keep well and can quickly become rancid. It should be stored for a maximum of 6–8 weeks in cool conditions.

Cooking grains

You must first wash the grains thoroughly to remove dust and insects. Boil the required amount of water, add the grain, stir, cover with a tight-fitting lid and simmer. Extra liquid may be required. After the required cooking time, remove from the heat and leave to stand for 5–6 minutes before taking off the lid. Use a shallow pan if possible as the weight of grains in a deep pan will compress the grains at the bottom. Any cooking water left over can be used as the base for a stock and may contain B vitamins.

Pre-soaking can reduce cooking time. It can also save around 40 per cent energy if harder grains are soaked overnight and then cooked in the soaking liquid.

Grain can also be toasted in a little oil (before cooking) to improve the flavour, although this destroys some of the vitamins. Season after cooking.

Cracked (kibbles) grains/grits

These are cut or broken pieces of cereal grain. Bulgur wheat or kibbled wheat tend to cook quicker than whole grains. Cracked grains and flours should really be used as soon as possible and within six months.

Flakes

Flakes are, for example, muesli, barley or rolled oats that have been lightly cooked then flattened between rollers, making them easier to digest, cook and even eat raw. In this process nothing is lost or removed, so all of the nutritional value is retained. Do not confuse genuine cereal flakes with commercial ones. There are numerous commercial brands of breakfast cereals that are highly refined and processed with added salt and sugars.

Flour or meal

'Meal' is almost anything that has been milled or ground. Flour is the next stage of processing after meal.

Sprouting

The sprouting of whole grains can greatly enhance their nutritional content and dramatically increases their vitamin and mineral content which doubles or triples.

Digestibility is increased. The carbohydrates and proteins change because the seeds use them for the germination process.

Storage

Any type of grain or flour must be stored in a cool, dry place. If stored in airtight containers they can keep for long periods (up to two years). They can be prone to infestation from insects. The nutritional value starts to decline the moment the grain is broken during processing.

EBLY®

Made from whole grains of durum wheat, with no additives, EBLY® is a quick cooking natural alternative carbohydrate. It is highly nutritious and contains carbohydrates (same as any carbohydrate per 100g), protein, fat, vitamin B1, niacin, sodium, phosphorus, fibre and is high in energy. It is yellow in colour and has a subtle nutty flavour.

EBLY® is a very versatile and useful ingredient in vegetarian and vegan cookery. It lends itself to a whole variety of dishes and is an ideal alternative to rice and pasta. It keeps its aroma whether cold or hot and it works well with other ingredient and flavours.

How to cook EBLY®

For 10 covers

1. Boil 2 litres water and season with five pinches of salt.

2. Take 500g grain, add to the boiling water and simmer for approximately 20 minutes uncovered.

3. When required consistency has been achieved, strain, season with pepper and a little margarine or virgin olive oil and serve.

Once EBLY® is cooked, keep refrigerated for up to three days. In its dry state keep and store in a clean, dry and well-ventilated place, where it should keep for up to 12 months.

WHOLEGRAINS

There are three parts to the whole grain, the husk or the bran, then the endosperm and finally the kernel or sprouting portion called the wheat germ.

The outer bran is where the dietary fibre is contained. This prevents constipation and aids the digestion of food. It is also thought to prevent too much sugar and fat being absorbed through the bloodstream too quickly. In the production of wholegrain flour the whole grain is used including most of the husk (or hull), which is indigestible. The husk must be removed before being processed any further. Whole grains retain all the nutritional value. The endosperm has a high concentration of starch and some protein.

The wheat germ contains the major source of nutrients such as thiamin, vitamin B6, nicotinic acid and a number of minerals such as iron, zinc, magnesium and potassium.

Sometimes you may see the term 'complete protein'. This refers to the fact that the particular grain or cereal contains all eight essential amino acids.

Item	Description and quality points	Culinary uses
AMARANTH	Ancient pseudo-grain grown originally by the Aztecs. Adds a nutty robust flavour to foods. It is called complete protein because it contains more protein, calcium, iron, lysine, potassium, phosphorus, magnesium and vitamin C, than other grains.	Ground into flour and used for breads, noodles, popcorn, cookies and pancakes. Can replace tapioca and arrowroot in recipes.
BARLEY (contains some gluten-forming proteins) Pot or Pearl	An ancient grain mentioned some 32 times in the Bible. Creamy white in colour with a nutty flavour, barley absorbs other flavours easily. High in gluten, protein, niacin, folic acid, calcium, thiamin, phosphorus and magnesium. Only the outer husk is removed. High in vitamin B3. Cook 1:3 parts water for 45–60 mins. Pearl barley is a term used to describe polished pot barley, where the bran is removed so it has less vitamin B.	A good replacement for rice and millet. Can be used for breads, soups, stews, salads, beer, barley water, whisky and barley wine.
BARLEY FLAKES	Made by heating and lightly toasting then flattening between two steel rollers making them easier to digest and cook. Sweet, nutty in flavour.	Porridge, muesli, biscuit toppings, for thickening soups and vegetarian burgers.
BARLEY FLOUR	Milled from pot barley with a sweet flavour and low in gluten. Often mixed with wheat flour for bread.	Bread, biscuits.
BUCKWHEAT (gluten free)	A relative to sorrel and rhubarb. Has a reddish triangle shape (seed) rich in protein, vitamin B3 and is good for circulation. Strong in flavour.	Bread, pancakes, noodles, casseroles, roasts and salads.

→

Item	Description and quality points	Culinary uses
→ BUCKWHEAT whole, raw, often called Groats	Not a wheat but a fruit seed. Greenish-pink colour, rich in vitamins A, E, B, fibre, sodium, calcium and carbohydrates. Has fewer calories than rice, corn or wheat. Cook 1:3 parts water for 20–25 minutes until tender. Depending on quality you may need a little longer and more liquid.	Casseroles, soups
Roasted Buckwheat (kasha)	Hulled, crushed kernels or kasha (roasted buckwheat groats). Darker reddish-brown colour and dryer texture. Cook 1:2 parts water for 8–10 minutes, leave covered for 5 minutes.	Used in soups and pilaf (instead of rice).
Buckwheat Flour	Dark speckled flour, milled from raw buckwheat. Contains protein, vitamin B6, calcium, iron, folic acid and bioflavanoid rutin. Used to make noodles called 'soba' in the Far East. Some made with wheat as well, giving an earthy flavour.	Pancakes, bread, flour for baking, buckwheat spaghetti noodles, soups, pasta dishes.
CORN/MAIZE (gluten free)	The name comes from the American Indian word 'mahiz'. Originally cultivated in America and Italy. Every part of the corn plant can be used. Husks go to make tamales, silk for medicinal tea, kernels for consumption and the stalks for animal fodder. Fermented corn is used in making Bourbon whiskey. Varieties are graded by the starch content of the grains. Low in gluten, but also contains protein, vitamin A, folic acid, lysine, potassium, calcium, phosphorus and potassium.	Soups, pasta dishes ground and made into polenta, muffins and animal feed. Corn syrup, corn oil. Corn on the cob.
Cornmeal	The varieties are graded by the coarseness of the meal. It is yellow in colour and contains 100 per cent of the wholegrain. Do not confuse with highly refined cornstarch or corn flour.	Tortillas, corn bread, muffins and cakes, pasta and noodles.
Hominy	The dried kernel from the husk. Cooked in milk, then baked or fried.	Casseroles, main dishes.
Grits	Ground Hominy. Fine whitish gritty cereal. Cooked in water.	Breakfast dish.

→

Item	Description and quality points	Culinary uses
→ Polenta	Ground semolina (durum wheat) similar to cornmeal – coarse granular texture, bright yellow. Made with water and a little salt.	Polenta and gnocchi (Italian dish).
Popcorn	Partially dried, remaining moisture expands and pops corn when placed on a high heat. Nice with maple syrup added at the end of cooking.	Snacks, salads, soups and main course dishes.
DURUM WHEAT Semolina	Gluten-rich flour produces a firm dough ideal for kneading and shaping pastas. Adding soy or millet flour to the durum wheat flour will produce noodles. Brown and white available. A grainy pale yellow flour ground from durum wheat. Higher protein and gluten content than flour produced from soft wheat. Also contains potassium, sodium, selenium and carbohydrates.	Used for making pasta and desserts and casting sugar. Noodles.
Cous cous	Cous cous is yellow granules of semolina and is part of the staple diet in Morocco, Tunisia, Libya and Algeria. Cook 1:2 parts in boiling water, keep covered with tight lid, remove from heat for 12 minutes, then fluff with fork. It has very little flavour, so requires the addition of herbs, spices and flavoursome stocks to make it a little more palatable.	Salads, soups, with dried fruits as a dessert, side dish. Pilaff (instead of rice).
MILLET (gluten free)	Protein rich cereal grass, extensively used in Africa and Asia. Tiny, round, yellow-hulled grains – light texture when cooked, bland in flavour. High in iron, protein, calcium, phosphorus, potassium, magnesium, and B vitamins. Cook 1:3 parts cold water for 15–20 minutes.	Use in place of rice, salads, and in soups risottos and stuffings.
Millet flakes	Mild flavoured flattened grains, roast to add a better flavour.	Porridge, muesli and pasta.
Millet flour	Meal or flour is gluten free.	Puddings, cakes, breads and cookies.

→

Item	Description and quality points	Culinary uses
→ QUINOA (gluten free)	This tiny bead shape pseudo-grain was the sacred grain of the ancient Incas. Lighter than rice, it cooks in half the time and is an excellent replacement. A complete protein, it contains iron, calcium, phosphorus, lysine and vitamin E. Rinse thoroughly to remove any Saponin. This is a natural sticky substance on the outer grain that repels birds and insects. It may irritate allergies and digestion in humans. Cook 1:3 parts water for 15 minutes. Quinoa can be ground into flour.	Risotto, pilaff and stuffing, soup, bread, cakes and pasta.
OATS Oat groats (low gluten)	Whole oats or oat groats are pale yellow water soluble, long and thin. Established in Britain in the Iron Age. A staple cereal crop in Scotland for centuries. Good source of carbohydrates, thiamin, iron, potassium, protein and vitamin E, riboflavin and niacin with a creamy flavour. Cook 1:3 parts water for 45 minutes. Oatmeal flour is made from ground oats.	Use in place of rice and in casseroles, soups and cakes.
Oatmeal	Raw oats milled to varying degrees of coarseness; pinhead are chopped into 3–4 pieces; medium is coarse oat flour, fine is oat flour. Adds richness to breads.	Porridge, biscuits, cakes, scones, toppings, cereal bars, oat cakes or bannocks.
Rolled oats	Whole oat groats rolled between steel rollers, partially cooked. Called quick-cooking oats.	Porridge crumbles, flapjacks and cereal bars.
Regular oats	Porridge oats rolled from pinhead (small) oatmeal.	As above.
RICE (gluten free) Short grain rice	Short grain rice is almost round in shape. The grains are soft, moist and sticky in texture and stick together during cooking. Cook 1:2 parts water for 40–45 minutes. Contains protein, carbohydrates, thiamin, niacin, folate, riboflavin, starch, and vitamins B6 and E.	Puddings and desserts.

→

Item	Description and quality points	Culinary uses
→ Brown rice	Far more nutritious than white, it retains the oil-rich germ and bran. It is chewier and has a nuttier flavour. Cook 1:2 parts water for 35–40 minutes. Contains protein, fibre, carbohydrates, thiamin, niacin, folate, riboflavin, starch and vitamin E. Low in fat. By soaking the rice overnight you increase digestibility and enhance flavour by starting the germination process. Cook in soaking water.	Side dishes, pilaffs, risotto, salads and savouries, rice wine and vinegars.
White rice (Pearl rice)	The bran and germ has been removed, but it cooks quicker and is more tender, but less nutritious than brown. Contains protein, carbohydrates, thiamin, niacin, folate, riboflavin, starch, and vitamins B6 and E. Cook 1:2 parts water for 20–25 minutes, in boiling salted water. Polished to remove bran and germ, sometimes bleached! Use good quality, e.g. Basmati.	Side dishes, pilaffs, risotto, salads and savouries, rice wine and vinegars.
Arborio (risotto) rice	Arborio rice is slightly longer and thinner than the short grain. It absorbs more liquid and is excellent for savoury dishes. Mainly imported from Italy. Contains protein, carbohydrates, thiamin, niacin, folate, riboflavin, starch, and vitamins B6 and E. Cook 1:3 parts water for 20–25 minutes.	Savoury dishes and risottos.
Rice flakes	Toasted before rolling.	Porridge.
Rice flour	Wholegrain and also white flour is available.	Noodles, puddings thickenings, desserts.
Wild rice	Actually a grass seed grain and a different species from cultivated rice. High in iron and vitamin B. It is dark (black to brown) colour with a subtle nutty flavour and has a chewy texture. Cook 1:3 parts water for 45–50 minutes until the grain splits.	Combine with other rice grains. Side dishes, good sautéed as an accompaniment.
Red wild rice (Wehani rice)	This long rice has a red bran layer and was recently discovered in the Camargue region of Southern France. Nutty flavour, smells while cooking and distinctive red (natural) colour creates excellent colourful dishes. Cook 1:2 parts water for 45–50 minutes. Contains protein, carbohydrates, sodium and fibre.	Excellent in salads, mixes well with other rices after draining.

→

Item	Description and quality points	Culinary uses
→ Jasmine rice	Polished white long grain rice originating from Thailand, similar to Basmati. Has a gentle flavour and is soft and light with a sticky texture. Cook 1:2 parts water for 20–25 minutes in boiling salted water. Contains protein, carbohydrates, sodium and fibre.	Classic with Thai cuisine and stir-fries, side dishes, pilaffs, risotto, salads and savouries.
RYE (contains small amounts of gluten-forming proteins)	Popular in the Middle Ages in Britain. Now it is mainly used in Russia and Germany. Available in thin or long greenish-grey grains. Tough, heavy, bitter and chewy. Cook 1:3 parts water, best soaked overnight. Change water and cook for 45–60 minutes. Contains protein, calcium, lysine, potassium, and magnesium. Low in gluten.	Pumpernickel, red whiskey in USA. Add to a mix of flours in making bread, pancakes, soups and stews.
Rye flakes	Toasted and flattened, quite bitter and chewy.	Breakfast cereals.
Rye flour	Contains just enough gluten for bread, heavy in texture, usually mixed with other flours.	Breads and biscuits.
SPELT (contains gluten-forming proteins)	An ancient grain from southern Europe. It has a higher protein than wheat. For those who suffer from wheat allergies it is an excellent substitute. Water soluble and easier to digest. It has a nutty flavour and contains protein, vitamin B, minerals, iron and potassium. Cook 1:3 parts water. Soak overnight, change the water, then cook for 40–55 minutes.	Excellent for bread making, spelt pasta.
WHEAT (contains gluten-forming proteins)	Wholegrain berries come in two varieties: hard red spring wheat is high in fibre protein and gluten and is used for bread. The softer lower protein white varieties are used for baking. Contains protein, vitamins B, E, potassium, iron, phosphorus and magnesium. Cook 1:3 parts water for 40–60 minutes.	Bread, salads, stews, pilaff, roasts and sprouting.

→

Item	Description and quality points	Culinary uses
→ Cracked wheat	Wheat berries that have been cracked in small pieces between rollers, then called kibbled wheat.	Added to bread and breakfast cereal to give texture.
WHEAT Bulgur wheat	Israelites called it dagan, meaning 'bursting kernels of grains'. Grains steamed before cracking. Cover grains with boiling stock, leave for 15 minutes. Add to stews and casseroles to thicken and bulk out the dish. Contains protein, carbohydrates, iron, selenium, fibre, folic acid, zinc, potassium and sodium.	Tabbouleh, meat loaf, gives texture to stews and salads.
Wheat flakes	These whole grains are toasted then flattened. Contains protein, sodium and fibre.	Porridge, breads.
Wheat bran	High in gluten and a useful source of fibre, sodium and protein.	Bread, used in breakfast cereals.

FLOUR

In the United Kingdom the most commonly used flour is wheat flour, but the nutritional value and composition may vary according to the quality of the soil, weather, chemicals, time of planting and harvesting. Flour is also made from other grains – barley, corn, oats, rice and rye – and processes.

Wholemeal flour is so called because it contains all of the grain with nothing added. By law it must contain 100 per cent of the whole wheat grain. It has a light brown appearance and contains more minerals, fibre (roughage) and vitamins than the more refined flours.

Flour can be milled from whole grains in two ways. The first is with large steel rollers and the second by hammering and grinding between two stone wheels. Stone grinding or milling is not widely used as stone particles can be found in the flour as the mill stones wear away.

The stones then need to be re-dressed every few weeks.

Wheat flour or wheat meal

This contains the germ, inner bran and the endosperm. Wheat flour or wheat meal must contain 85 per cent or more of the grain, and has therefore had 15 per cent (bran and germ) removed.

Brown flour is more refined than wholemeal flour, as some of the bran has been removed. It is often fortified.

Gluten is a mix of two insoluble proteins (gliadin and glutenin) that absorb water to form a sticky elastic material. The amount of gluten in the flour indicates the strength of the flour. When yeast or baking powder is added to leavened bread the carbon dioxide is trapped and then expands to give bread its lightness.

To make a good-yeasted bread, flour that has good gluten content, for example, wheat, barley, and rye must be used.

Although rye and barley can be used to make bread, they are often very heavy and a required taste. It is often best to use other flours with a higher gluten content to lighten them.

Malthouse or granary style flour is partially refined and has whole and milled malted grains added to give a sweet, crunchy style bread. Salt and sugar are usually added before sale.

Self-raising flour is normally made from soft wheat with the chemical agent baking powder added. When liquid is added, it reacts to slowly release the carbon dioxide which causes the mixture to expand and rise.

Soft flour is low in protein and fat, high in starch, but contains vitamins E and B6, thiamin, riboflavin, niacin and trypt. It has a low gluten content of 7–10 per cent. Soft flour is generally suitable for baking cakes, biscuits, short crust pastry and sauces.

Strong flour is often called bread flour. It is high in protein, starch and contains 10–17 per cent gluten. Strong flour is required for puff and stretch pastries, pasta, bread and other yeast goods. It also contains vitamins E and B6, thiamin, riboflavin, niacin and trypt.

White flour, when milled, has the husk, bran and wheat germ removed, an extraction rate of 70–75 per cent, and is left with only the endosperm. A good quality white flour can be defined by its fine texture and colour and is free from infestation. Sometimes chemical additives are added to give the flour its white colour. It is best to buy the unbleached flour.

Wholewheat is used and processed in commercial breakfast cereals. When made in flour it is 100 per cent unrefined wheat flour that has been ground from wheat berries.

Barley flour

Barley flour is one of the earliest cereals to be cultivated by man. It is the hardest of the cereals and makes unleavened bread, biscuits and barley cakes. It has a low gluten and protein content and requires the addition of strong wheat flour to make leavened doughs. Barley flour also contains fibre, vitamins and minerals.

Rye flour

Rye is widely used in northern Europe. It is used to mill a dark flour (white rye flour is available) to make pumpernickel and biscuits and is good for open sandwiches. Weevils and debris are difficult to spot due to its dark colour. When buying in bulk, you must discard all the rye if you spot any mould (ergot). This mould is particularly poisonous. Rye flour also contains vitamins E and B6, sodium, thiamin, riboflavin, niacin and trypt. It can be 100 per cent wholemeal or white rye flour. It has strong flavour best suited to breads, has less gluten than wheat, and is quite dense and heavy. The white rye flour is very distinctive, imparting a strong rye taste. Dark rye breads from Europe are often coloured with other ingredients such as molasses, chocolate or other colourings.

Oatmeal

Oats grow only in cold wet climates and have been around since the Bronze Age in the furthest parts of northern Europe. They have very little gluten and are not really suitable for bread making, but contain protein, vitamins E and B6, sodium, thiamin, riboflavin, niacin and trypt. There are three different grades of oatmeal – fine, medium and course – which are used in a variety of ways, for example, porridge, oatcakes, thickening of soups, whisky and sauces.

GLUTEN-FREE GRAIN FLOURS SUITABLE FOR COELIAC DIETS

Buckwheat flour

Buckwheat is from the seed of a starch plant native to Russia. It is not really a cereal as such and is from the same family as rhubarb and sorrel. It is milled from the whole raw buckwheat, it has a greyish colour with dark flecks. It is unsuitable for bread making, but is an ideal substitute for rice and breadcrumbs when used in stuffing. It can also be used to make pancakes, dumplings, cakes, biscuits, waffles, blinis, noodles, galettes and pastas. It contains vitamins A and B, sodium, fibre, calcium and carbohydrates.

Corn or maize meal

Originally cultivated by the North and South American Indians, it is ground by steel rollers and comes in varying grades of coarseness and varieties. The better cornmeal is the yellow 100 per cent wholemeal corn. The paler kind has had the germ removed, and this should not be confused with highly refined corn (flour) starch used as a thickening agent. Cornmeal is used for cornbreads, Johnny and hoecakes, tortillas, muffins, pancakes, dumplings and also polenta. It contains protein, calcium, iron, potassium, sodium and fibre.

Millet flour

Millet is not as good as wheat but it will often grow in poor soil, so the quality will vary. It is often called birdseed and is used as bird and animal feed. Millet is delicate in flavour and texture and can be used to make salads, muffins or pancakes, or cooked like semolina to make an easy porridge or pudding.

Rice flour

Gluten-free wholegrain brown rice is used to make a variety of gluten-free pastries, cakes, biscuits, pancakes, pie crusts and is added to pizzas to make them crispy. It is also used for thickening soups and sauces and contains protein, fibre, sodium and fat.

GLUTEN-FREE NON-CEREAL BASED FLOURS

Other gluten-free flours available include:

Arrowroot – this has a very fine white powder texture from the processing of the maranta root, which takes the shape of an arrow, which is where it obtained its name. It is used mainly for thickening sauces and baking, for example, biscuits. It has 80 per cent starch content. It is colour and odourless when added to sauces, and is relatively tasteless.

Banana flour – this is produced by puréeing the banana and then freeze-drying. This is then ground to a powder. It can be used to make pancakes, cakes, biscuits and breads.

Chestnut flour – this is low in protein but contains potassium, calcium, magnesium and some traces of the vitamin B group. Slightly sweeter than other flours, it is good in cakes, biscuits and breads and is becoming increasingly popular.

Chickpea (gram/besan/garbanzo) flour – this flour is high in protein, calcium, vitamins A, B, C, phosphorus, potassium and iron. Widely used in Indian cookery, it can be used to boost protein in dishes. It is good for making flat bread and pancakes, thickening sauces and it also adds lightness to deep-frying batters.

Potato flour (feculé) starch – peeled, steamed, dried and then ground this flour adds a moist texture to cakes, but is mainly used to thicken soups and sauces and make biscuits. The quality varies on the brand. Some are excellent and require only light cooking giving a clean, smooth, transparent appearance, while others are poor quality with a strong flavour. Potato flour is sometimes called feculé.

Soya flour – this is unlike most flours, in that it is high in protein and low in carbohydrates. It is often used as an enhancer and a dough improver by bakers. It can be used as an effective binding agent by replacing the albumen in eggs: dilute approximately 20ml water to 10g soya flour.

It is best purchased cooked to ensure the trypsin inhibitor has been destroyed (this prevents protein being absorbed properly). The flour should be used in a ratio of 1 part soya: 8 parts wheat flour when making bread.

dairy products

MILK

Milk has been part of the staple diet for centuries in the UK and Europe. It is one of the most complete foods, giving high nutritional value containing protein, vitamins A, B1, B2, B3, B12, C, D, iron, calcium, sodium, fat and carbohydrates. It is the main source for suckling mammals.

Milk comes not just from cows, but also from goats, ewes, buffalos, horses, asses and even camels. The main sources in the UK are from the dairy herds. The herds mainly consist from five breeds of cattle, Ayreshires, Friesians, Guernsey, Jerseys and South Devons. The richest milk, which contains the most fat, comes from both the Guernsey and the Jersey cattle, but the most milk per head is from the Friesian cattle. The nutritional value of milk is affected by the seasons. Cattle that graze in the spring and summer will produce better nutritional milk that cattle

than is fed on fodder and hay during the winter months.

Milk is a high-risk food due to its make up and as such is an ideal breeding ground for bacteria and micro-organisms, which will taint, turn milk sour and infect milk. Strict hygiene must be applied and milk should always be kept refrigerated. Milk must never be consumed untreated due to the high risk of bacterial infection from Brucellosis. Only milk from TB- or TT-free dairy herds can be sold in the UK.

Milk can take on other flavours quite easily. Milk is heat treated and then graded according to the degree to which it has been treated. The nutritional value will also be reduced according to the treatment. The coloured bottle tops or cartons in which milk is purchased show the grading. Once a British institution, the milkman is fast becoming a rare sight and so is the range of milk you can buy, shops and supermarkets will only carry the most popular grades of milk with the longest shelf life. In recent years the milks with the higher fat content, such as the gold tops, homogenised milk and even the ordinary silver tops have been on the decline with the lesser fat milks, such as semi-skimmed are increasing in popularity.

Whole milk has 3.8 per cent fat and is heated for 15 seconds at 71°C. This milk has a silver top and a visible cream line.

Channel Island milk has 4.8 per cent fat and is heated for 15 seconds at 71°C. This milk has a light yellow cream colour.

Homogenised milk has a fat content similar to whole milk and is heated for 15 seconds at 71°C. This milk has a blue top and has no visible cream line, because the cream is distributed throughout the milk.

Sterilised milk is homogenised milk and is heated for 20 to 30 minutes at 108–115°C. It has a similar fat content to semi-skimmed milk. This milk has a crown top and no visible cream line.

Skimmed and semi-skimmed milk has had most of the fat removed – semi-skimmed has 1.5 per cent fat and skimmed has 0.1 per cent fat. This milk is usually packed in waxed cartons and has no visible cream line.

UHT milk (long life) is homogenised milk and is heated to 132°C for 1–2 seconds, then rapidly cooled and aseptically packed into waxed cartons. It has no visible cream line and will keep for six months out of the fridge, but once opened should be treated like normal milk and kept in the fridge.

Evaporated milk is concentrated at low temperatures then sterilised in cans at 115°C for 15 minutes.

Condensed milk has 0.2 per cent fat and is prepared in cans in the same way as evaporated milk but with the addition of sucrose.

Raw and untreated milk is available only from Brucellosis-free herds and cannot be sold without a certificate of accreditation. This milk is bottled with green tops.

Other milks

Goats' milk has 6 per cent fat and a good protein, mineral and vitamin source which makes it ideal for making cheese and cream. It is becoming increasingly popular as an alternative to cows' milk.

Ewes' milk has 6 per cent fat and a good protein content and mineral and vitamin source.

Buffalo milk has a 7 per cent fat content and makes good cheese and butter. It is also high in protein, minerals and vitamins.

Mare (horse) milk is 1 per cent fat and protein but is high in milk sugar and is made into an alcoholic drink in the parts of Asia.

Camel milk is an essential part of the diet for many Bedouin tribesmen. It is 4.5 per cent fat and has a good protein content and mineral and vitamin source.

Some vegetarians and all vegans will not consume milk from any animal source. It is therefore important to use an alternative, for example, soya milk, coconut milk or vegetable milk, which in some south American countries such as Columbia is taken from the sap of plants and used for cooking as well as drinking.

CREAMS

Cream is the fatty top layer of the milk which, when milk is cooling, is then creamed off the top. It is more likely today to be mechanically separated. Cream is very high in fat and is best avoided for the health conscious.

It is the minimum fat content that determines the grades of cream that can be sold.

Half cream is 12 per cent fat and is the lightest. This will not whip.

Single cream is 18 per cent fat. It is light and will not whip. It is used mainly in hot beverages.

Whipping cream is 35 per cent fat and will whip up, but will not hold well.

Double cream is 48 per cent fat and is thick and creamy. It whips up well.

Clotted cream is 55 per cent fat. Milk is left in large pans or tanks for the cream to rise and then it is heated to 78°C and cooled. The clotted cream (deep yellow cream) is creamed off.

CHEESE

Cheese is made from milk or cream in which the protein called casein will coagulate to form a firm curd after it has been treated with acids, rennet, alum or even plant extract. The flavour will depend on the milk, additives, time, bacteria and mould growth.

Most cheese is unsuitable for vegetarians as it contains **rennet**. This is an extract taken from the lining of an unweaned calf's stomach and is used for curdling and setting of the curds and whey. It is also used to make junket. Rennet is also called chymosin and rennin. It is possible to extract rennet from other animal sources such as goats, rabbits and pigs. As such it is unsuitable for Sikhs, Hindus, Rastafarians and possibly Muslims and Jews, as well as vegetarians.

Vegetarian cheese is now easily available from good health food shops and supermarkets, where the rennet has been replaced with fungal or bacterial substitutes.

BUTTER

Butter has been made for thousands of years from many different milk sources, for example, milk from goats, ewes, buffalos, horses, asses, yaks, camels and even cows. It was first discovered when preserving milk, by simply churning the milk until it formed a solid fat. The techniques may vary from country to country but the principle is the same – if you shake, rotate or move it long enough, the fat will separate from the liquid.

In the UK butter must contain a minimum of 80 per cent milk fat, and no more than 16 per cent water, and 2 per cent milk solid. Up to 2 per cent of salt may be added while butter is being made but no more.

Butter milk

This is the residue liquid that is left from the churning process when butter is being made, but most of the butter milk that is sold today is made from pasteurised milk which is much more palatable and digestible.

YOGHURTS

This milk-based product from goats', sheep's or cows' milk, has been allowed to sour in warm conditions with a live bacterium called *lactobacillus bulgaricus*. Although it had been a part of the diet in many Middle Eastern countries and India for centuries, it was not until the early 1900s that it began to increase in popularity elsewhere.

It has long been linked to good health and has been advocated in many healthy diets, mainly due to the live bacteria it contains. The bacterium helps to maintain a healthy environment in the intestine by removing any harmful bacteria. The live bacteria also helps to stimulate and build up the natural intestinal flora that can be removed by modern drugs and antibiotics, and also builds up the B vitamins in the gut.

There are now a bewildering number of yoghurts, flavours, textures and makes of yoghurt. If it does not state 'Live' on the label, the beneficial bacteria is dead, even if it states that its natural. Yoghurts that are made from the low-fat milk should be used, rather than those containing dried milk powder, as they are more digestible and better for the older generation and younger children.

Many fruit versions are enhance with additives, stabilisers, colourings and high levels of sugar. Always read the labels before purchasing.

EGGS

In the United Kingdom some 26 million chicken eggs are consumed every day. This equates to 170 eggs per person, per year. But the consumption of eggs has decreased over the last 15 to 20 years.

Eggs contain protein, vitamins A, B6, B12, D and E, iron, calcium, zinc and are low in saturated fats. The colour of the eggshell is a sign of the breed of the hen, rather than its nutritional value.

There is a confusing number of different labels for eggs on sale, but what do they all mean and what are the differences?

European Union rules and regulations relating to labelling mean that all pre-packed boxes of eggs must be printed with the quantity of eggs, size, grade, best-before date and price. This is so each box, batch, producer and packing station (with a numbered code) can be traced if necessary.

The Lion Mark was used in the 1960s as an advertising tool, to help sell British produced eggs. It was re-introduced after the 1988 salmonella scare. The mark now indicates that each egg box with this stamp contains eggs that have come from a hen that has been vaccinated against salmonella enteritidis. The mark has nothing to do with the way that the hens are kept.

Eggs that are cracked should be discarded and never used. It is suggested that eggs should always be stored in the fridge below 8°C and apart from other foods. Hands should always be washed before and after touching eggs.

Battery-farmed eggs

Most vegetarians and vegans will not eat or drink anything that has been made with products made with battery-farmed eggs. This is because of the inhumane way in which the hens are treated and kept. The European Parliament in June 1999 gave egg farmers until 2012 to introduce a more humane way of producing eggs. After this date farmers will have to provide bigger areas for the hens to nest and scratch. Egg-producing hens will have to be provided with a bigger 'enriched cage', with a reduced number of hens per cage.

Farm fresh or country fresh eggs

If it does not say free range or organic on the egg box, it is likely that the eggs have been produced by battery farm hens. Do not be misled by pictures or drawings of hens out in the fields as this may be inaccurate.

Perched or barn eggs

This is a system where a hen house has a covered floor, usually of straw, with a number of feeding devices and perches at differing heights. The perch is calculated on a distance of 15cm per bird.

Free-range eggs

Birds can have the freedom of open runs, usually during daylight hours, and have access to vegetation, although this is not the case in all ranges. This is a more stress-free environment for the hens. Eggs labelled 'free-range healthier eggs' have had their feed nutritionally altered to provide an egg enriched with omega 3 fatty acids. However, because housing units are so huge and stocking densities are at times so high, most birds in units termed 'free range' are reared inside and do not stray too far. Many of them may not even reach the nearest pop holes. Those that do tend to stay close to the house and their more familiar environment, so only very few range properly.

Quail, duck and ostrich eggs are usually free-range farmed eggs, but it is best to check the label and purchase from a reputable supplier.

Organic eggs

The Soil Association has been promoting organic farming since 1946. It is the UK's leading certification body for organic food and farming.

Any egg that has been given the label 'organically farmed' will have been produced in the same way as the free-range eggs, but hens will have had their runs on land and food certified free from pesticides, herbicides or any harmful chemicals. Stock rates under the Soil Association standards for organic food and farming, 500 laying birds are permitted in any one housing unit, but occasionally permission to allow up to 2000 birds is permitted, but a 100 meter ranging distance must be supplied and birds are not allowed to be housed more than 6 per square meter. Birds must be fed with the minimum 80 per cent of their feed grown to association organic standards. The other 20 per cent must be from sources guaranteed free of genetically modified organisms and other prohibited ingredients. Beak trimming is absolutely prohibited under Soil Association standards. Antibiotics, routinely administered in intensive systems, are prohibited in organic systems. Antibiotics are used with poultry only to treat illness, during which period eggs cannot be sold.

Freedom food *(naturally farmed)* **eggs**

Certification Mark

RSPCA - committed to farm animal welfare

Freedom Food is an independent, non-profit making organisation set up by the RSPCA in 1994 to improve the welfare of some 860 million farm animals in the UK. Standards are written by the RSPCA for the following species: sheep, chickens, turkeys, laying hens, ducks, beef cattle, dairy cattle and pigs. The standards are regularly reviewed and amended according to latest research. These are based on five freedoms which are to ensure: freedom from fear and distress, freedom from pain, injury and disease, freedom from hunger and thirst, freedom from discomfort and freedom to express normal behaviour.

Under these standards hens must be given enough space and freedom to behave naturally. For example, the laying hen must be able to perch, dust bathe, stretch, flap their wings and move around as well as have a safe, comfortable resting area and a separate nesting box in which to lay their eggs.

Animals are also reared without the routine use of the array of drugs, antibiotics and wormers that form the foundation of most conventional livestock farming.

The assessors check that throughout the chain tractability and segregation procedures are in place to ensure that Freedom Foods do not get mixed up with non-Freedom Foods. They are becoming increasingly popular and sold under the trademark of Freedom Foods approved by the RSPCA.

pulses

Pulses are the dried edible seeds from the legume family that includes peas, beans, and lentils. They play a very important part in the staple diet in many parts of the world.

Pulses are incredibly cheap, healthy and nutritious. They are under-used and under-valued by today's chefs, yet they have good range colour, textures and flavours that can add excellent value to any dishes. Pulses have been around for some 3000 years.

Pulses are packed full of important nutrients such as protein, minerals (potassium, zinc, magnesium and calcium) vitamins B and E and are an excellent source of fibre. They are generally low in fat and have natural sugars.

Canned beans have often had salt or sugar added. They should be drained from the tin into a sieve and run under cold water before use.

Pulses are extremely versatile and provide excellent replacement for meat in the diet. They can be interchangeable in recipes due to the wide selection that are available. Because of the versatility of pulses they can be used and served as a vegetable like butter or broad beans, as a beverage like soya milk, as a meat replacement like chickpea or tofu from the soya bean, or as flour taken from chickpeas or soya. Pulses can be used and cooked in stews, casseroles, pastas, pâtés, salads, and soups.

By protein combining with grains, nuts, seeds and dairy products more nutritional value can be added to the dishes. For example by adding chickpea or soya flour when making a batter, or just to dust tofu for a deep fried dish, or adding yoghurt to a chickpea or mung bean curry.

When using pulses as substitutes for meat allow 50g/2oz dry weight per person as they will at least double in bulk when soaked overnight, and cooked. Pulses work well when herbs and spices are used to add more flavour to the dish. To add a little more flavour to the pulses if you intend to use them for salads, add a few bay leaves, some garlic and an onion studded with cloves to the cooking liquid.

Pulses should be carefully checked, especially the lentils, for any grit, stones and debris before cooking. They should then be rinsed to remove any dirt and dust.

SOAKING

Pulses are normally soaked prior to cooking and the length of time depends on the pulse, normally 8–10 hours. Fermentation may occur in warm conditions – in such cases, it is better to keep them in the fridge and refresh with cold running water. There are a number of exceptions to this rule: lentils, yellow split peas, mung beans and black-eyed beans. These don't need to be soaked and can be cooked from a dry state. The older and bigger the bean the longer soaking is required.

To help lessen the unsociable effects of eating pulses, it is advisable to change the soaking water several times. There are a number of alternative ways in which to counteract the problem: by cooking for a shorter time in a pressure cooker and adding bicarbonate of soda (which will then destroy any water-soluble vitamins), or by adding a strip of seaweed (Kombu), or a good pinch of aniseed or caraway seeds. Salt should never be added to pulses when soaking. After soaking it is best to peel the pulses to aid digestibility.

COOKING

Cooking times depend on the age and quality of the pulses – the older the pulse, the longer the cooking time required. Salt should never be added during cooking, as this increases the cooking time and hardens the pulse. Season only at the end of the cooking process. Cover pulses with plenty of fresh, cold water and bring them to the boil. Remove any scum and simmer for the required cooking time.

Pulses with toxins, such as kidney beans, need to be cooked faster and boiled longer, at least 15 minutes at full boil. The cooking liquid of toxic pulses should not be kept. However, the cooking liquid of non-toxic pulses may contain some valuable nutrients (vitamin B) and this stock could add valuable flavour to the dish. It will keep in the fridge for three to four days.

CANNED PULSES

There are now some excellent canned varieties of pulses available that cut out the soaking process. It is always best to read the label to see how much salt and sugar has been added and to purchase the pulses that have little or no salt and sugar added.

SPROUTING

Why sprout pulses and seeds?

Sprouted seeds and pulses are an excellent addition to the vegetarian diet, both with flavour and with the added benefit of increased nutritional properties in salads, pâtés, spreads and stir-fries.

Sprouting the pulses and seeds dramatically increases their nutritional value, i.e. the mineral and vitamin content doubles and can even triple. The digestibility increases; some of the complex carbohydrates are changed into simple sugar and proteins are then changed into free amino acids and peptones as the pulses germinate. Never sprout red kidney beans because they are toxic.

How to sprout and what to sprout?

Some of the better seeds to sprout are mung beans, aduki, pinto, alfalfa, radish, sunflower, mustard and fenugreek.

Either buy a propagator or simply take a glass jar (a bowl for larger beans) with a 1-litre capacity, then place 40–50ml of the smaller seeds into the jar (or 200g large beans or 400g sunflower seeds). Cover and soak the contents overnight in water at room temperature – small seeds for 8 hours, medium seeds for 10–15 hours, larger beans for 14–24 hours. Strain and return to the container, sealing the top with a muslin cloth and a tight rubber band. Rinse the pulses through the cloth, drain out excess liquid and leave in a warm environment. Repeat this process once to twice a day for approximately five days until the beans or seeds sprout or expand to the length required. Some devotees to sprouting of seeds and pulses drink the sprouting water as a beverage (tea).

It is best to keep them covered and out of direct sunlight for the first three days and then to put them into the sunlight. This will help with the development of a sweeter flavour and the increased green chlorophyll will increase its colour.

The sprouted seeds can be kept for up to 5–7 days in the fridge, then discarded.

TOXINS

A number of beans contain properties harmful to humans, for example, kidney beans contain **haemglutin** which, if eaten and digested, will cause nausea, vomiting, abdominal pain and diarrhoea depending on the amount of toxin ingested. Another harmful substance is *anti-trysin factor* contained in soya beans. It is not as immediate as **haemglutin** but can interfere with the digestion of protein and should be boiled for at least one hour before reducing to a simmer to kill off any toxins. Alternatively a pressure cooker will reach much higher temperatures much quicker and will kill off toxins within 15 minutes on full heat.

Canned kidney and soya beans have been exposed to very high temperatures during the canning process where the toxins have been killed.

TYPES OF PULSES

Pulse	Quality points	Soaking and cooking time	Culinary uses
ADUKI BEANS	Small dark red beans with an unusually sweetish nutty flavour. High in protein and potassium. Also contain other minerals and vitamins B1, 2 and 3.	Soak 3–5 hrs Cook 45–60 mins (15 mins pressure cooker)	Burgers, rice, stews, pies, breads and curries.
BLACK BEANS	Black, shiny and kidney shaped. High in protein, and a good source of minerals and vitamins B1, 2 and 3.	Soak 8–12 hrs Cook 90 mins (30 mins pressure cooker)	Stews, soups, salads and savoury dishes.
BLACKEYE BEANS	Grey to cream colour with black 'eye'. Smoky flavour. No need to soak. High in protein, natural sugar and potassium. Also contains other minerals, fibre, vitamins A, B1, 2, 3, 6 and C.	Soak n/a Cook 30–45 mins (10–12 mins pressure cooker)	Soups, rice, burgers, casseroles, salads and savoury dishes.
BORLOTTI BEANS (or Rose coco beans)	An Italian bean with brown, pink and red speckles. Contain protein, minerals and B vitamins.	Soak 8–12 hrs Cook 45–60 mins (10–12 mins pressure cooker)	Soups, rice, burgers, casseroles, salads and savoury dishes.
BROAD BEANS Fava beans Horse bean	Both fresh and dried, flat and bright green, the older they get the greyer they become. Best skinned. Contain protein, minerals, fibre, vitamins A, B1, 2, 3 , 6, C and E.	Soak 8–12 hrs Cook 60–90 mins (15–20 mins pressure cooker)	Stews, casseroles, pâté and salads.
BUTTER BEANS Lima beans	The smaller sweeter version is called the Lima bean. The larger flat bean is whitish in colour and similar in shape and size to the broad bean. Contain protein, fibre, minerals, vitamins B1, 2, 3, 6, and E.	Soak 8–12 hrs Cook 60–90 mins (15–20 mins pressure cooker)	Soups, pâté, stews, casseroles, salads and purées.

→

Pulse	Quality points	Soaking and cooking time	Culinary uses
→ CANNELLINI BEANS	A creamy-white coloured bean similar to haricots, with a light texture. Contain protein, minerals, B vitamins and fibre.	Soak 8–12 hrs Cook 50–60 mins (20–30 mins pressure cooker)	Soups, salads, stews, purées and casseroles.
CHICKPEAS (Garbanzo)	Large heart-shaped pea, beige in colour. Can be ground into flour. High in protein, natural sugars, magnesium, potassium and zinc. Also contains other minerals and vitamins A, B1, 2, 3, 6 and E.	Soak 8–12 hrs Cook 1–2 hrs (20 mins pressure cooker)	Soups, stews, pâté, falafel, hummus, salads, curries and meat substitutes.
FLAGEOLET BEANS	Pale green skin with a delicate and fine flavour. A kidney shape but a little longer. Contain protein, minerals, B vitamins and fibre.	Soak 8–12 hrs Cook 45–60 mins (10–15 mins pressure cooker)	Soups, salads, pâté, purées, curries and casseroles.
HARICOT BEANS	Haricot beans are better known as baked beans. Normally a greyish white pale colour. High in protein and contain a good source of minerals, vitamins A, B1, 2, 3, 6, E and fibre.	Soak 8–12 hrs Cook 45–60 mins (10–15 mins pressure cooker)	Baked beans, soups, salads, pâté, purées, curries and casseroles.
KIDNEY BEANS	Red plump and shiny bean shaped like a kidney with a white flowery texture. Goes well with spicy food. Boil for first 15 minutes of cooking. Do not sprout. High in protein, potassium, selenium, calcium and starch. Also contain other minerals, vitamins A, B1, 2, 3, 6, C, E and fibre.	Soak 8–12 hrs Cook 45–60 mins (boil for first 15 mins) (10–15 mins pressure cooker)	Stews, chilli, salads and casseroles.

→

Pulse	Quality points	Soaking and cooking time	Culinary uses
→ LENTILS: WHOLE	Vary in size, shape, texture and colour according to their variety. Green, brown or puy lentils. Retain shape when cooked, earthy flavour. Excellent source of protein, magnesium, potassium and calcium. Also contain other minerals, vitamins B1, 2, 3, 6, fibre and folate.	Soak n/a Cook 30–40 mins (5–10 mins pressure cooker)	Soups, salads, stews, lasagne, curries, moussaka, pasta and sauce.
MARROWFAT PEAS	Large green pea with a tough outer skin. Often called mushy peas. Contain protein, minerals, fibre, vitamin E and trypt.	Soak 8–12 hrs Cook 60–90 mins (20 mins pressure cooker)	Mushy peas, soups, pâté.
MUNG BEANS	Come in different colours from yellow to green, whole, split or sprouted (bean sprouts). High in protein and most minerals, also contain vitamins A, B1, 2, 3, 6 and fibre.	Soak n/a Cook 30–40 mins (10-12 mins pressure cooker)	Bean sprouts, stews, samosas, salads and curries.
PINTO BEANS	Kidney shaped with a mottled brown colour that alters to a pink skin when cooked. Good flavour with the addition of spices. Contain protein, minerals, B vitamins and fibre.	Soak 8–12 hrs Cook 60 mins (15 mins pressure cooker)	Refried beans, chilli, salads, stews and casseroles.
SOYA BEANS	Small oval and in different colours – black, red, green and yellow. *Boil for first hour of cooking.* Very high protein, natural sugar and mineral content. Also contain vitamins A, B1, 2, 3, 6, folate, biotin and pantothenate.	Soak 8–12 hrs Cook 2–4 hrs (boil for first hour) (30–40 mins pressure cooker)	Has many uses, e.g. tofu, miso, soya sauce, soya mil, soya flour, TVP and tempeh.
SPLIT PEAS	Come in yellow or green and have a mild flavour. Contain protein, minerals, fibre, vitamin E and trypt.	Soak n/a Cook 35–45 mins (12–15 mins pressure cooker)	Soups, rice, puree dishes and for thickening.

fruit and vegetables

The NACNE report suggests that people do not eat enough fresh fruit and vegetables and recommends that the intake should be increased to five portions per day. A portion, for example, would be a medium-sized portion of vegetables or salad, or one medium-sized piece of fruit, or one small glass of fruit juice. According to government reports, it is less well known that a poor diet is the second largest risk factor for cancer. Increasing fruit and vegetable consumption is the second most effective strategy to reduce the risk of cancer, after stopping smoking.

FRUIT

Fruitarian is a term used to describe someone who consumes only raw fruit, grains and nuts, and very few or no processed foods. Fruitarians eat only plant foods that can be harvested without harming or killing the plant.

Eating fruit has been proven to be beneficial to good health, although this benefit depends on the amount of fruit consumed. It is recommended that the average person should eat five portions (units) of fruit each day. Fruit is nutritionally packed with vitamins and minerals, so the more fruit that is consumed the greater the benefits. Fruit contains vitamins B, C and E which provide help to boost the body's defences against harmful diseases. Vitamin C, beta-carotene and vitamin E can help to prevent the by-product from cells in the body called free radicals, which can help initiate the growth of cancer, heart disease and arthritis. Fruit also provides a number of minerals – copper, folate, calcium, iron, potassium, magnesium and selenium – and many different fibres.

Many studies have shown that increasing the intake of fruit in the diet can decrease the chance of heart disease, strokes and breast, colon and stomach cancers.

Antioxidants (substances that prevent deterioration by oxidation) along with minerals, fibres and the natural plant extracts and chemicals play a large part in this. Bioflavonoids are another type of antioxidant. They help to boost immunity, blood capillaries and to help as an anti-inflammatory agent.

Fruit is the healthiest type of snack or take-away food and one of the cheapest. However, no one fruit is more beneficial than another; it is better to eat from a wide variety of fruits and berries giving a more beneficial spread of nutrients.

Fruit should always be washed before being eaten or cooked, as this will help remove any outer pesticides, waxes (which contain fungicide) or harmful bacteria from the surface area.

The following table is split into two categories: general fruits and berries, and tropical and exotic fruits.

General fruits

Fruits and Berries	Nutritional qualities	Availability and quality points
APPLES	Fibre, protein, minerals, vitamins E, C, B6, thiamin, riboflavin, niacin, trypt, biotin and folate.	Available all year, depending on variety. Best if firm and crisp. Many varieties but only two types, cooking and eating. Can be stored up to two weeks in a fridge.
APRICOTS	Vitamins A, B1, B6, C, protein, niacin, fibre, minerals, riboflavin, trypt, folate and pantothenate. Darker apricots have more carotenoid.	Pick plump unmarked apricots that give when slightly squeezed, not soft or green-looking apricots. Available all year through importation.
BANANAS	Protein, minerals, vitamins B6, C, E, carotene, thiamin, riboflavin, niacin, trypt, folate, pantothenate and biotin. Banana has a high natural sugar content, potassium.	Available all year. Pick yellow bananas with a little brown speckles. Do not store in the fridge as banana will go black.
BERRIES Bilberries	High in vitamin C, minerals and protein.	Available summer.
Blackberries	Vitamins E, B6, C, minerals and protein.	Available in late summer/autumn.
Blackcurrants	High in vitamins C and E, minerals, protein and fibre.	Sweet black summer fruit.
Blueberries	Vitamin C, minerals, protein and fibre.	Small dark summer fruit.

→

Fruits and Berries	Nutritional qualities	Availability and quality points
→ Cranberries Gooseberries Raspberries Strawberries	High in vitamin C and fibre. Vitamin C and fibre. Vitamin C. High in vitamin C, folate and iron.	Available in winter months. Available summer. Available summer. Available summer. Do not buy berries with mould or white patches on them. Buy only firm and plump berries. Wash them in cold water. Can be stored in fridge for up to two days.
CHERRIES	Protein, minerals, vitamins C, E and B6, carotene, thiamin, riboflavin, niacin, trypt, folate, pantothenate and biotin.	Available late June to August.
DAMSONS	Protein, minerals, vitamins C and E, fibre, beta-carotene, thiamin, riboflavin, niacin, trypt, folate, pantothenate and biotin.	Available September to October. Do not buy with mould on them. Buy only firm and plump damsons.
GRAPES	Protein, minerals, vitamins B6 and C, thiamin, riboflavin, niacin, folate, pantothenate and biotin.	Available summer. Do not buy with mould or white patches in them. Buy only firm and plump grapes.
PEACHES	Protein, minerals, vitamins B6 and C, thiamin, riboflavin, niacin, trypophen, folate, pantothenate and biotin.	Available summer. Do not buy with mould on them. Buy only firm and plump peaches.
PEARS	Protein, minerals, vitamins B6, C and E, thiamin, riboflavin, niacin, folate, pantothenate and biotin.	Available all year round due to importation.
PLUMS	Protein, minerals, vitamins A, B6, C and E, thiamin, riboflavin, niacin, trypt, folate and pantothenate.	Available August to October. Buy only firm plums with no bruises.
RHUBARB (not strictly a fruit, but its uses are mainly fruity in nature)	Protein, minerals, vitamins B6, C and E, thiamin, riboflavin, niacin, trypt, folate and pantothenate.	Available May to late October. Buy only firm stalks, never limp.

→

Fruits and Berries	Nutritional qualities	Availability and quality points
→ STRAWBERRIES	Protein, minerals, vitamins B6, C and E, thiamin, riboflavin, niacin, trypt, folate, pantothenate and biotin.	Available summer.

Tropical and exotic fruits

Fruits and Berries	Nutritional qualities	Quality points
CAPE GOOSEBERRY or PHYSALIS	Protein, minerals, vitamins B6, C and E, thiamin, riboflavin, niacin, trypt, folate, pantothenate, biotin and fibre.	Bitter sweet flavour, yellow or orange colour, best to avoid any coloured ones. Peel back paper covering to reveal the berry.
CARAMBOLA or STAR FRUIT	Vitamins A and C, potassium and fibre.	Yellow star-shaped fruit. Perfumed scent, savoury flavour. Avoid fruit with bruising to the edges.
CUSTARD APPLE or CHERIMOYA (other varieties are bullocks heart, sweet and sour sop)	Vitamin C, niacin and fibre.	Large pine cone shape, with a sweet pineapple flavour and texture.
DATES	Protein, minerals, vitamins B6 and C, thiamin, riboflavin, niacin, trypt, folate, pantothenate and fibre.	Deep dark glossy brown-black colour. Do not buy with mould or white patches on them. Buy only firm and plump dates.
DURIAN Turian	Vitamin C and minerals, and sugar content.	Large green-yellow spiky shell. Very strong 'rotting' odour and often banned from many hotels. Has a white sweet fluffy flesh with large seeds.
FEIJOA or PINEAPPLE GUAVAS	Vitamins C and B.	Dark green in colour with white flesh. Taste and flesh similar to pineapple.
GUAVAS	High in vitamin C and carotene. Also contains fibre, protein, minerals, vitamin B6, thiamin, riboflavin, niacin, trypt and pantothenate.	Pear shape, green skin and when ripe turns yellow. Skin and seeds contain high amounts of vitamin C. Taste like strawberry and pears.

→

Fruits and Berries	Nutritional qualities	Quality points
KIWI FRUIT or CHINESE GOOSEBERRY	Protein, minerals, vitamins B6 and C, thiamin, riboflavin, niacin and trypt. Contain a protein-splitting enzyme.	Oval fruit with thin hairy brown skin and green flesh and small black seeds. Choose firm plum fruits.
LYCHEES	Protein, minerals, vitamin C, thiamin, riboflavin, niacin and trypt.	Hard deep red shell with white highly perfumed flesh. Pick the heavy uncracked fruits.
MANGOS	High in vitamin C and carotene. Also contain protein, minerals, vitamins A, B6 and E, thiamin, fibre riboflavin, niacin, trypt and pantothenate.	Thin rubbery skin, colour varies from green, yellow and red. Flesh is yellow with a large stone in the centre. Perfumed smell. Choose firm plump fruits with no bruises.
MELONS	High in vitamin C and carotene. Also contain protein, minerals, vitamins B6 and E, thiamin, riboflavin, niacin, folate, pantothenate and fibre.	There are many different types and some are scented. Buy only firm, undamaged and ripe melons.
ORANGES	Protein, minerals, vitamins B, B6, C and E and fibre.	Many varieties, e.g. blood, Valencia.
CLEMENTINE	Protein, minerals, vitamins B, B6 and C and fibre.	Sharp citrus fruit with an edible skin.
KUMQUATS	Minerals, vitamins B and C.	Seedless mandarin.
MANDARIN	Protein, minerals, vitamins B, B6 and C and fibre.	Small orange with loose skin.
SATSUMA	Protein, minerals, vitamins B, B6 and C.	From Japan, with tight skin and no seeds.
TANGERINE	Protein, minerals, vitamins B, B6 and C.	Orange-red mandarin with unusual taste.
PASSION FRUIT or PURPLE GRANADILLA	Vitamins A, B and C, fibre, protein and minerals.	Purple or yellow dimpled skin, heavily scented and has a sweet pulp. Choose heavy fruit.
SHARON FRUIT or PERSIMMON	Vitamins A and C, fibre and potassium.	Yellowy orange skin, eaten only when ripe. Buy only firm and plump ones that give under pressure.

→

Fruits and Berries	Nutritional qualities	Quality points
→ PINEAPPLE	Vitamins C, E and B, high in natural sugar content, protein and minerals.	Choose only fresh looking and firm textured fruit with no bruising.
PRICKLY PEAR or CACTUS PEAR	Vitamin C, potassium and fibre.	Bright red or yellow flesh with black seeds. Smells of watermelon. Choose only firm pears.
POMEGRANATES	Vitamins B and C and iron.	Reddy brown colour and thick-skinned fruit with deep reddish pink centre full of edible seeds. Sweet and sour flavour. Choose heavy feeling fruit with no bruising.
QUINCE	Vitamin C and fibre.	Yellow skin when ripe. Eaten only when ripe. Buy only firm and plump fruit with no bruising.
RAMBUTAN or HAIRY LYCHEE	Vitamin C.	Looks like a lychee but has hairy spikes protruding from the skin. Choose heavy fruit.
TAMARILLO or TREE TOMATO	Vitamin C.	Deep red glossy and smooth skin. Flesh and flavour resembles that of tomato. Buy only firm and plump ones that give under pressure and also feel heavy.

Dried fruits

Drying is one of the oldest methods of preserving food. Fruits such as dates, grapes figs and tomatoes have been preserved in the Middle Eastern countries for well over 4000 years. Today it is still the preferred way for many to preserve fruit. Drying works because it removes the moisture before food-spoiling bacteria such as yeasts and moulds can begin to take hold and decomposition begins. It does not necessarily kill micro-organisms, but it inhibits or stops their growth.

Food can be dried in a number of ways, depending on the humidity (as it gets hotter the amount of water the air will hold increases), for example, by direct and indirect sunlight, freeze drying, in a low oven and also in airing cabinets and cupboards. Drying in the sunlight can change the flavour and colour, due to the increased effects of oxygen, but the ultra-violet sunrays can kill some surface bacteria and enable ripe fruit to accumulate its natural sugars. A light breeze is recommended as this will remove any stale air and reduce the drying time.

Drying food has become very important in commercial terms; it also reduces the size and weight of the food and prevents decomposition.

Before drying begins the larger and harder fruit such as apples, pears and pineapples need to be peeled, de-cored and sliced. The smaller, softer fruits can be left whole.

They are then placed on a string and hung in an oven or in direct sunlight to dry. If commercially dried the fruit will almost certainly have been dipped in a chemical to prevent it from turning brown.

Only the best fruit should ever be dried or preserved, so all its nutritional value is at its peak. Fruit is full of sugars that, when dried, become highly concentrated, so some dried fruit is very high in calories. Drying will reduce some of the water-soluble vitamins, mainly B and C.

The commercially dried products have almost certainly either been dipped in a potassium carbonate solution before the drying commences to assist in holding a little moisture, or sprayed with other chemicals that prevent sticking, or fumigated with a sulphur gas that acts as a preservative and kills insects that may be present. Fumigation also helps to keep fruit plump and colourful, but serious allergic reactions can occur from sulphur dioxide ranging from a rash and headaches to swelling tissue, and in asthmatics could lead to respiratory failure.

These chemicals and preservatives can be poisonous and are best washed off in water before eating. This is a major health concern for many people. It is best to read the label to check on the chemicals that are used or buy organic and naturally dried fruits.

It is easy to dry fruit by simply washing it and towel drying first. Then remove any pips or stones, lay the fruit on a muslin cloth tray and place in a cool oven with the door open a little. Keep on the lowest heat (in a fan-assisted oven if possible) and dry for 2–4 hours, or until the required level of dryness is achieved.

Storage

Once the fruit is dried or the packet is opened, store the fruit in an airtight container in a dry, cool place. Some fruits like apricot, prunes and figs may show a dry, white-coloured powder on the surface; this is probably sugar and not harmful. Dried fruits will last up to six months stored in this way.

Soaking and cooking

One of the good things about dried fruits is that they can be used raw or soaked. The main reason for soaking is to increase their size, making them softer textured and looking plump and fresh. If they are to be eaten raw they should still be washed to remove any chemicals and dust that they may have collected.

Dried fruit can be soaked in water, sugar syrups, juices and wines or in some countries they rehydrate in teas. The soaking liquid can be incorporated as a stock for further flavour.

Fruit	Information and description	Culinary uses
APPLES	Available in rings only. Contain pectin, fibre, sodium and carbohydrates and natural sugars.	Used in muesli, baking, preserves and confectionery.
APRICOTS	Normally available in whole or in halves. They contain copper, iron, sodium, fibre, beta carotene (vitamin A), protein and potassium. Used a lot in North African cookery, adding sweetness to dishes.	Salads, sauces, raw, baking (muffins), liquors, stuffings, confectionery, desserts and garnishing.
BANANAS	Either purchased whole, halved or sliced. Strong flavour with high sugar and fibre content, with protein, sodium, potassium and phosphate. Often mixed with other dried fruits.	Muesli, snacks, mixed with other dried fruits, baking, confectionery, desserts and garnishing.
BLUEBERRIES	These little whole berries contain mainly fibre, fatty acids and sodium. Provide a tangy flavour.	Sweets, baking and sauces.
CHERRIES	Either purchased whole or sliced. Cherries add tartness to baked goods and contain a high amount of calories, sodium and fibre.	Baking, mixes and confectionery.
CURRANTS	The dried fruit of the small Corinth grape, which take its name from the Greeks. They are a light blue to black in colour, with a sweet and slightly crisp texture. High in protein, natural sugars, sodium, potassium, calcium, B vitamins and vitamin A.	Muesli, snacks, mixed with other dried fruits, baking, confectionery, desserts and garnishing.
DATES	These come in a number of options, dry, semi-dry and soft. Mainly popular in the Middle Eastern countries. Contain protein, fibre, carbohydrates, natural sugars with an excellent source of minerals and vitamins including A and B types.	Raw, salads, baking, confectionery, and candied.

→

Fruits	Nutritional qualities	Culinary uses
→ FIGS	There are two types of figs: the Turkish fig (Smyrna) and the American fig (the mission). Both contain protein, carbohydrates, natural sugars, with high levels of sodium, potassium and calcium. They also have other minerals and contain vitamins A and B.	Muesli, snacks, fruits, baking, stuffings, compots, confectionery, desserts and garnishing.
KIWI	Usually comes in slices and has a good source of vitamin C, protein, sodium and fibre.	Muesli, snacks, baking, compots, desserts.
MANGOS	Mangos come in diced pieces and are a good source of vitamin A, potassium, protein, sodium and fibre.	Stir fries, muesli, baking, salads and confectionery.
NECTARINES	Usually available in slices and have a good source of potassium, vitamin A, some vitamin B and C. They also contain fibre and calcium.	Salads, sauces, raw, baking, stuffings, confectionery, purées, desserts and garnishing.
PAPAYA	Available either sliced or diced, and contains high amounts of vitamins A and C. Also contains protein, sodium and fibre. Papaine, taken from the stem and leaves, acts as a tenderiser and also contains enzymes that help digestion.	Baking, salads, fruit mixes and desserts.
PEACHES	Available either sliced or diced, and contains high amounts of fibre, iron, potassium, vitamin A and some of the B and C vitamins.	Salads, sauces, raw, baking, stuffings, confectionery, purées, desserts and garnishing.
PEARS	Purchased either as halves or in slices. They have a good source of iron and fibre as well as protein and sodium. The texture can be a little rough and chewy.	Used in muesli, baking, preserves, salads and confectionery.
PINEAPPLE	Available sliced usually in rings. Pineapple contains protein, fibre, potassium, calcium and a helpful enzyme called bromelin.	Muesli, snacks, mixed with other dried fruits, baking, confectionery, desserts and garnishing.

→

Fruits	Nutritional qualities	Culinary uses
→ PRUNES	Available with or with out the stone and either whole or halved. Excellent whether raw or cooked, do not need soaking. Good source of iron, vitamin A, protein, sodium and fibre. Prunes do have a laxative effect.	Raw, muesli, mixes well with other dried fruits, baking, confectionery, desserts and garnishing.
RAISINS	Traditionally made from the muscatel grape varieties. Rich in natural sugars, iron, sodium, potassium, fibre and protein. Also contain beta-carotene (vitamin A), B vitamins, copper and zinc.	Muesli, snacks, mixed with other dried fruits, baking, raw, confectionery, desserts, garnishing and rice dishes.
SULTANAS	Golden brown, sweet seedless grapes often covered with mineral oil to prevent them from sticking together. It is therefore advisable always to wash them first in hot water, otherwise it can interfere with the absorption of minerals and fat-soluble vitamins. High in natural sugars, potassium, calcium and iron. They also contain protein and vitamins B and E.	Muesli, snacks, mixed with other dried fruits, baking, confectionery, desserts, garnishing and rice dishes.
TOMATOES	Available whole or in halves with slightly sweet flavour. High in vitamins C and A. Also contain a range of minerals and fibre.	Bread, pizzas, pasta, sauces, dressings and salads.
STRAWBERRIES	Available either whole or slices with a sweet flavour to them. High in vitamin C, with smaller traces of vitamins B and E, minerals and fibre.	Muesli, snacks, mixed with other dried fruits, baking, confectionery, desserts, garnishing.

VEGETABLES

All vegetables are good to eat, whether cooked or raw. They are packed full of vitamins, minerals, fibres and water and are low in calories and fat.

It is always best to purchase vegetables fresh, from a reputable supplier, and to buy organic where possible. The soil, farming and vegetables are intrinsically linked. The Soil Association suggests many reasons for buying organic food. Many people suggest that it simply tastes extremely good and organic food has been shown to contain more vitamins, nutrients and cancer-fighting antioxidants than non-organic food. Organic systems aim to avoid the use of artificial chemicals, pesticides and fertilisers, produced without GMOs. There is great emphasis on animal welfare. Organic systems reduce dependence on non-renewable resources with production being more sustainable and friendlier to the environment and wildlife. There has not been a case of BSE in any herd that has been in full organic management since before 1985.

'Organic' is a term defined by law and all organic food produced and processing is governed by a strict set of guidelines. Producers, manufacturers and processors each pay an annual fee to be registered and are required to keep detailed records, ensuring a full trail of traceability from farm or production plant, to table. Any major infringement of this results in suspension of licence and withdrawal of products from the market. All organic farmers, food manufacturers and processors are annually inspected, as well as being subject to random inspections.

Organic food is produced from safe, sustainable farming systems producing healthy crops and livestock without damage to the environment. It avoids the use of artificial chemical fertilisers and pesticides on the land, relying instead on developing a healthy, fertile soil and growing a mixture of crops.

Preparation and cooking

All vegetables should be thoroughly washed under cold running water to remove any excess soil, insects, bacteria and pesticides. High amounts of fibre are contained in the skin and usually high amounts of nutrients are just under the skin of most of the vegetables, so where possible the skin should be left in place to increase the intake of these.

It is best to prepare the vegetables just before cooking and to consume immediately after serving, as they will begin to lose their nutritional value once they are cut, trimmed or peeled. Vegetables should never be left to soak in water because the water-soluble vitamins will slowly drain into the liquid. Vegetables will lose their nutritional value if they are reheated or left for long before being eaten. Bicarbonate of soda should never be added to any vegetables as this destroys the vitamin C content.

As a rule, cooked vegetables should still remain crisp. Vegetables that have been over-cooked will lose the vitamins and will look unappetising.

Most tinned vegetables are best avoided because of the added salt or sugar (always read the label). Most of the nutrients are contained in the liquid in which the vegetables are processed so it is best to incorporate the liquid into the dish or sauce.

For the purpose of this book the different plants will come under either general vegetables or exotic vegetables. The listing is not exhaustive but contains the vegetables most used and easily available to the chef and caterer.

General vegetables

Vegetables	Nutritional qualities	Availability and quality points
ASPARAGUS	Protein, minerals, vitamins A, E, B, B6 and C and high in carotene.	A very short season May to June, best to buy the fresh, green firm and straight tips.
BROAD BEANS	High in protein. Also contain minerals, vitamin A, B1, 2, 3, 6, C and E, folate, pantothenate and biotin.	Available May to July. Buy the heavy, bright green young pods. The bulky, large ones will be tough.
BEAN (RUNNER)	Protein, high in minerals and carotene, vitamins B, B6, C and E, biotin, fibre and folate.	Available July to October. Buy only really fresh young firm beans. The older beans that are dark green become stringy.
BEETROOT	Protein, high mineral and sugar content, vitamin B, B6 and C and folate.	Available all year, sizes and quality vary, best to buy young beet. Colour is a rich red to purple. Relative of the sugar beet and mangoldwurzle.
BROCCOLI	Protein, high in potassium, carotene and phosphorus, vitamins B, B6, C and E and folate. High in antioxidants.	Available all year round. Broccoli comes in different colours – green, white, purple. Do not buy limp or yellowing leaves.
BRUSSELS SPROUTS	Protein, high in vitamin C, potassium, carotene and phosphorus. Vitamins B, B6 and E, folate and biotin.	Available from early October until March. Only buy the ones that are small green and firm with tightly packed leaves.
CABBAGE Spring Pak choi Chinese White Savoy Red	Protein, sugar, high in carotene, vitamins B, B6, C and E, folate and biotin.	Available all year round depending on the varieties of cabbage. They come in an array of colours, shapes, sizes and flavours. Never buy wilting, yellowing or loose leaf cabbages.
CARROTS	Protein, high in carotene (A vitamin) and vitamin E. Also contain vitamins B, B6 and C, folate and biotin.	Available all year round. Buy the firm, crisp carrots with a good orange colour and no sign of infestation. If they still have their tops on buy the fresh green leaf ones not the wilted.

→

Vegetables	Nutritional qualities	Availability and quality points
→ CAULIFLOWER	Protein, minerals, vitamins A, B1, 2, 3, 6, C and E, folate pantothenate and biotin.	Available all year round. Buy the firm medium-sized cauliflowers with no wilting, yellowing leaves. The head (curd) should be white with no black spots.
CELERY	Protein, minerals, vitamins A, B1, 2, 3, 6, C and E, folate pantothenate and biotin.	Available all year round. Buy only the tight, crisp heads. Try to avoid the stringy and bigger celery or sticks that are looking a little brown with wilted leaves.
CHICORY	Protein, minerals, vitamins A, B1, 3, 6 and C and folate.	Available in summer but imported from Egypt in winter. Buy the firm, crisp heads that have no sign of wilting or browning leaves.
COURGETTES	High in potassium and vitamin A. Also contain protein, minerals, vitamins B1, 2, 3, 6 and C, folate and pantothenate.	Season June to October, but are available all year round. Buy the firm smaller ones with a fresh green colour that are heavy for their size and have no bruising or marks.
CUCUMBER	Protein, minerals, vitamins A, B1, 2, 3, 6, C and E, folate, pantothenate and biotin.	Season late March to October, but are available all year round. They come in all shapes and sizes. Buy the firm, green glossy looking ones with no bruising or marks. Always wash before use.
CURLY KALE	High in potassium, protein and vitamin A. Also contains minerals, vitamins A, B1, 2, 3, 6, C and E, folate, pantothenate and biotin.	Available late spring to late summer. Not widely used. Buy the dark green, tight, crisp and fresh looking ones.
CRESS (MUSTARD)	Protein, minerals, vitamins A, B1, 2, 3, 6, C and E and folate.	Available all year round. Buy the really fresh green cress that has a white firm stem. Never purchase limp, wilted cress.

→

Vegetables	Nutritional qualities	Availability and quality points
→ FENNEL	Protein, minerals, vitamins A, B1, 2, 3, 6 and C and folate.	Available all year round. Buy the crisp, tight bulbs with a scent of aniseed. If the leaves are wilted or the bulb has any marks or bruising do not purchase.
KOHLRABI	Protein, minerals and vitamins B and C.	A winter vegetable from the cabbage family with a flavour of a cross between a turnip and cabbage. A light green colour, with crisp green leaves. Buy only the young firm, heavy for their size ones with a thin-looking bark.
LEEKS	High in vitamin A and natural sugars. Also contain protein, minerals, vitamins B1, 2, 3, 6, C and E, folate, pantothenate and biotin.	Season August to May, but are available all year round. The leaves should be green and tight with a white base. The leek should be firm with good white roots. Late in the season they grow a hard centre core and start to turn to a woody texture.
LETTUCE Cos Endive Frezze Iceberg Lamb Lollo rosso Oak leaf Radicchio	The nutritional content may differ slightly with each variety. Contain protein, minerals, vitamins A, B1, 2, 3, C and E, folate, pantothenate and biotin.	Available all year round depending on the variety. There are hundreds of lettuces and they come in an array of colours, textures, flavours, shapes and sizes. Buy only fresh-looking, crisp, firm leaf lettuce, free from insects and pesticides. Buy organic if possible.
MARROW	Protein, minerals, natural sugar, vitamins A, B1, 3, 6 and C, folate, pantothenate and biotin.	Available late May to early October. Buy the smaller, young, firm and heavy for their size marrows with a good dark green colour. The larger ones tend to be woody and have less flavour.
MUSHROOMS General	The nutritional content may differ slightly with each variety. Contain protein, minerals, vitamins B1, 2, 3, C and E, folate, pantothenate and biotin.	Available all year round depending on the variety. Buy fresh firm and dry-looking mushrooms with little dirt or soil on them. Do not purchase wet, slimy or mouldy looking mushrooms. Always buy from a reputable supplier.

→

Vegetables	Nutritional qualities	Availability and quality points
→ ONIONS	High in natural sugars. Also contain protein, minerals, vitamins B1, 3, 6, C and E, folate, pantothenate and biotin.	Available all year round depending on the variety. There are many varieties of onion in all shapes, colour and sizes. Always buy firm well-shaped onions with no soft areas, and with a dry paper outer skin and no sign of sprouting.
PARSNIPS	High in natural sugars and potassium. Also contain protein, minerals, vitamins A, B1, 2, 3, 6, C and E, folate, pantothenate and biotin.	Available mid August to March. Try to purchase the younger ones, that are roughly the same shape and size. They need to be firm with a thin skin and no soft or bruised areas. Older parsnips tend to be woodier.
PEAS Garden Mange tout Petit pois Snow pea Sugar snap	High in protein and natural sugars. Also contain minerals, vitamins A, B1, 2, 3, 6, C and E, folate, pantothenate and biotin.	Season June to late September, but are available all year round depending on the variety. Pod peas should be firm and crisp with a bright green colour and no visible marks or spots. The younger ones are best and you should be able to snap them between your finger and thumb.
QUORN	High in protein and sodium. Also contains vitamins B1, 2, 3 and B12, folate, pantothenate and biotin.	Made by Rank Hovis McDougal from a fungus that is fermented and sold under the trade name of Quorn.
RADISH Mooli Daikon Salad radish	Protein, minerals, vitamins A, B1, 3, 6 and C, folate and pantothenate.	Available all year round. Radishes come in different sizes, shapes and colours: red, white, red and white, and black. The most common is the little red salad radish. Buy the firm, crisp well-shaped ones with a thin skin free from marks or holes.
SPINACH	High in protein, vitamin A and potassium. Also contains minerals, vitamins B1, 2, 3, 6, C and E, folate, pantothenate and biotin.	Season April to early November, but now available all year round. Buy the fresh-looking leaf that is firm, crisp and a good bright green colour. Never buy yellowing or wilting spinach.

→

Vegetables	Nutritional qualities	Availability and quality points
→ SWEDE	High in natural sugars. Also contains protein, minerals, vitamins A, B1, 3, 6 and C, folate, pantothenate and biotin.	Available early September to mid May. Buy the smaller, firm, heavy for their weight swedes that have a good purple and yellow skin, which is not bruised. Older ones tend to be to woody.
TOMATOES Plum Cherry (red, yellow) Vine	High in protein, vitamins A and C and low in fat. Also contain minerals, vitamins B1, 2, 3, 6 and E, folate, pantothenate and biotin.	Season late April to October, but available all year round depending on the variety. Buy firm, ripe-looking tomatoes. Buy organic vine plum tomatoes for the best flavour.
TURNIP	High in natural sugars. Also contains protein, minerals, vitamins A, B1, 2, 3, 6 and C, folate, pantothenate and biotin.	Available all year round. Buy the younger, firm, well shaped and crisp ones that are heavy in relation to their size with not to much of a bark. If you purchase the baby variety, the leaves should be bright and crisp.
WATERCRESS	High in protein and vitamins A and C. Also contains minerals, vitamins B1, 2, 3, 6 and E, pantothenate and biotin.	Available all year round. Buy only the fresh looking, crisp and dark green coloured bunches, that are free from grubs. Always wash before use. Never buy watercress that is yellowing or limp.

Exotic and imported vegetables

Vegetables	Nutritional qualities	Availability and quality points
AUBERGINE or EGG PLANT	Protein, minerals, vitamins E, B, B6 and C and folate.	Originally from Asia, now imported from Spain and Italy. Either a deep purple or white skin, buy only the plump and firm ones. Available all year.
AVOCADO	Protein, minerals, vitamins A, B, B6, C and E and folate. High in fat.	A tropical vegetable eaten by the Aztecs and introduced via the Spanish. Buy those that give a little when pressed. Colour varies from green to very dark green. Available all year.

→

Vegetables	Nutritional qualities	Availability and quality points
→ GARLIC	High in protein and potassium. Also contains minerals, vitamins B1, 2, 3, 6, C and E and folate.	Available all year round. There are many varieties of garlic in all shapes, colour and sizes. Always buy the firm, well-shaped bulbs with no soft areas, with a dry paper outer skin, and with no sign of sprouting.
OKRA	Good source of protein and vitamin A. Also contains minerals, vitamin B1, 2, 3, 6, C and E, folate and pantothenate.	Buy the firm fresh-looking ones with no visible signs of soft areas or bruising. When over-cooked it releases a slimy, sticky goo. Available all year.
PEPPERS Capsicum Pimentos Chillie	Protein, minerals, vitamins A, B1, 2, 3 and C and folate.	There are many varieties, shapes, colour and levels of fieriness. The most popular are the sweet peppers. Peppers change colour as they mature from green to red. This indicates the fieriness of the pepper. The conical shaped chilli peppers are the fieriest with a number of popular ones: Bullet, scotch bonnet, jalapeno and Serrano. Always buy the firm ones with no soft areas. Available all year.
PLANTAIN	High in natural sugars, potassium and vitamin A. Also contains protein, minerals, vitamin B1, 2, 3, 6, C and E, folate and pantothenate.	This is related to the banana. Buy only green and firm ones with no visible marks or bruising. Available all year.
PUMPKINS	High in vitamin A. Also contain protein, minerals, vitamins B1, 3, 6, C and E, folate, pantothenate and biotin.	There are a number of varieties and they come in all shapes, flavours, colours and sizes. Buy the firm and younger ones that are heavy for their size with no signs of bruising, holes or marks. Dependent on variety but all year imports.

→

Vegetables	Nutritional qualities	Availability and quality points
→ SQUASHES	Protein, minerals, vitamins A, B and C.	There are a number of varieties and they come in all shapes, colours, flavours and sizes for example: butternut, snake, custard, nugget and chayote. Buy the firm, small and young ones that are heavy for their size with no signs of bruising, holes or marks. The bigger ones tend to be woody and not very nice in flavour.
SWEET POTATOES	High in natural sugars, vitamin A and starch. Also contain protein, minerals, vitamin B1, 2, 3, 6 and C, folate and pantothenate.	From South and Central America, but not related to the common potato. Buy ones that are firm, without any soft areas. There are two types: dry yellow fleshed and white watery-fleshed ones. Treat just like a normal potato. Available summer to early autumn.
SWEETCORN Kernels Baby corn Corn on the cob	High in protein and sodium. Also contain protein, minerals, vitamins A, B1, 2, 3 and C.	Corn was a part of the staple diet of the North American Indians. Buy corn that is firm, plump and fresh looking, not dried and wilted. Free from insects. Available all year.
YAM	Protein, minerals, vitamins B1, 2, 3, 6 and C, folate and pantothenate.	A tropical vegetable from the tuber family. Used in Indian, West Indian and Oriental cookery. Buy only the firm, fresh looking ones free from marks and bruising with not too much skin or soft areas. Available all year.

Sea vegetables

Seaweeds are naturally found in our seas and oceans. They are a member of a primitive sea plant group called algae that dates back millions of years. Seaweeds are high in protein and a soluble fibre, low in cholesterol and unsaturated fat. They are also high in certain proteins and vitamins A, B1, B2, B6, E and C. There is still some debate over the type of vitamin B12 that seaweeds contain.

The seaweeds (sea vegetables) contain far more minerals and nutrients than land vegetables, which they absorb from the sea water. Sea vegetables included in a non-dairy vegetarian diet are very important for the calcium, iron and iodine properties they contain.

Seaweeds contain a wide range of minerals, iron, calcium and organic iodine. Sea vegetables used in the diet can help lower blood cholesterol and are essential for our own metabolism. They can also prevent the formation of goitres which are associated with an overactive thyroid gland. Pollution in the environment builds up as toxins in the body and seaweeds give protection from these toxins by binding with and removing them from the colon.

There are as many seaweeds as there are land vegetables. The many different climates and conditions all help to give a diverse and nutritious range of sea vegetables.

The seaweeds can be divided into three groups: green, red and brown. The best-known green seaweed in the UK is green Laver bread. It has been cultivated on the Welsh coast for hundreds of years, often just washed, boiled and spread onto Welsh bread. Some red seaweed is called true laver bread and is considered to have a better flavour. Also in the category are dulse and carrageen moss that are hand-raked off the Irish coast. They have a taste similar to spinach. The goo from the moss is called agar-agar, which is used as vegetarian gelatine. The brown seaweed as a general rule is called kelp. Because of its trace elements and minerals it is made into tablets and sold in health shops, such is its nutritional value. The coastal waters here in Britain are home to some 600 varieties of sea vegetables, for example dulse, bladderwrack, carrageen, dabberlocks, fingerware, sea lettuce and laver bread. Many are the same as those that are harvested in the Southern hemisphere.

Seaweeds have been cultivated all over the world, from Iceland to Chile, China, Japan and the Pacific Ocean cultures, such as the Maoris and the Hawaii Islanders. This food source is an important nutritious food for these communities.

The biggest eaters of seaweeds are the Japanese, and there are some excellent seaweeds that grow off the Pacific Coast such as arame, hijiki, wakame and nori that is used for wrapping Sushi dishes. Kombu is another famous seaweed that is used in a highly acclaimed Japanese stock called dashi. All of these can be obtained in the UK from good health food shops.

Traditionally the Japanese eat seaweed for healthy hair and skin, whereas sea vegetable nutrition goes much deeper. Its antibiotic properties are used in wound dressings and against penicillin-resistant bacteria. Its uses are very varied, from health foods, fertilisers, animal feeds and ice-cream to beer, toothpaste, paper textiles and paints!

Purchasing
Always buy fresh sea vegetables from a reputable supplier and ensure they are from unpolluted waters. However, it is more likely that they would be already cleaned and dried and just require soaking. Some dried seaweeds like arame or hijiki are good dried on salads or even left dry and deep fried as an alternative.

Storage
Packets of dried seaweed can be kept for long periods of time – check the best before date on the packet. Once opened keep in an airtight container in a dry place away from moisture. It is always advisable to use as quickly as possible after opening because seaweeds will absorb moisture easily from the atmosphere of a working kitchen.

Preparation
Most dried sea vegetables need to be

rehydrated before they can be used. Soak them in cold water until they are fully hydrated. Always follow the manufacturer's instructions as it is important not to over soak or waterlog the seaweed because this will cause flavour and texture to be lost. The seaweeds can expand up to three to four times the dried weight and size, so ensure an adequate container is used for hydration. Keep the water as it can be used as a stock. Rinse the seaweed to remove any sand or debris that could be still there. Give the seaweed a gentle squeeze to remove excess water. If there is any white residue, this is probably salt and can be wiped away only after soaking. If the seaweed needs to be cut or shaped use a very sharp knife or scissors.

How to use it?

Sea vegetables are very versatile, depending on the variety. They can be used dried or deep-fried in salads, they can be grilled, toasted, crumbled or even raw. They can also be used in casseroles, soups, stews and stir fries. They can be used as a protein enhancer when added to dishes, for example, nori seaweed is used to wrap around Japanese sushi.

Sea vegetables	Information and description
AGAR-AGAR OF KANTAN Red algae	Agar-agar comes from the red seaweed and is used as a gelling agent in sweet jellies and as a vegetarian alternative to animal-based gelatine. Available in various forms: flaked, granules, powdered or bars. Flakes and bars are made by cooking, pressing and freeze-drying to form bars which are then flaked. Powdered agar-agar is more likely to have been chemically processed. Agar-agar is a natural, transparent and neutral flavoured, firm jelly rich in trace elements and carbohydrates. Often used in laboratories to grow cultures.
ARAME Brown Algae	It is a naturally wide leaf seaweed when harvested. Usually purchased in a dried form, then cooked, dried and shredded. Soak in cold water for 8–10 minutes. When rehydrated it is a noodle like seaweed. It has an excellent mild, sweet flavour and a soft texture. It is naturally rich in minerals, potassium, calcium and iodine and protein. Excellent sautéed, goes well in stir-fries, soups stews and salads.
CARRAGEEN or IRISH MOSS CARRAGHEEN Red algae	This deep red and purple moss is the source from which agar-agar is obtained. It is usually hand-raked from the coastal waters off the west of Ireland and North America. It is high in iodine and vitamin A. During the sun-drying process it changes colour to a very pale yellow. When rehydrating it must be thoroughly washed and rinsed, before being cooked and eaten. It is used in salads and as a vegetable, but mainly for agar-agar.

→

Sea vegetables	Information and description
→ DULSE or DILLISK Red algae	This is reputed to be eaten raw, but is an acquired taste. The Irish used to chew this traditional Celtic sea vegetable. Up until the early part of this century it was called 'poor man's tobacco', in some coastal parts it still is. It is high in protein, iron, calcium, sodium, phosphorous and fibre. It grows mainly off the Atlantic coasts of Scotland and Ireland, North America and Iceland where they also chew another red dulse. Dulse has a rather chewy texture and mild flavour and is good with potato dishes, soups, pastas and vegetable dishes.
HIJIKI Brown algae	This Japanese seaweed grows to four times its original dried weight after rehydrating. It is often attributed to giving the Japanese their black hair. The seaweed is cooked, dried and coarsely shredded. (Soak in cold water for 8–10 minutes.) It has a delicate sweet taste and is high in calcium, protein, iron, fibre and low in fat. It is often mistaken for arame, but is thicker and has a more chewy texture. Excellent with tofu, vegetables and seeds.
KELP Brown algae	Kelp is a term that is used to describe any brown seaweeds (algae) such as bladderwrack, oarweed, tangle, sea girdle, henware and fingerware to name a few, which are common around the coasts of Britain. It usually comes in the form of a powder or in tablets. Kelp is high in calcium, organic iodine and trace elements. It is often used as a flavour enhancer or a tenderiser. Has a light sweet flavour. Good in dressings and stews.
KOMBU Green algae	Grown abundantly in cold oceans from the USA to Japan, Kombu grows in thick underwater forests of seaweed. It is commonly found in shops. Kombu is long black sheets of dried seaweed that are cut into strips to make Japanese stock called dashi and miso soup. It can also be made into tea and is used to wrap sushi. Ideal for making broths and soups. High in minerals, iodine, calcium and fibre. According to oriental medicine it is used to treat thyroid complaints.

→

Sea vegetables	Information and description
→ LAVER Green algae	Generally known as green Welsh laver bread, it is similar to Japanese nori seaweed. Red laver bread is considered to be stronger, fresher, sweeter and with a better flavour than the green laver. Best used in soups or purée and added to sauces and stocks. Another type is a silky vegetable called sea lettuce that is cooked and puréed.
MEKABU (root wakame) Brown algae	A prized seaweed which is the reproductive part at the base of the wakame plant. It is sold in curled dried strands. When it is cooked in any liquid it opens into the shape of a flower. Strong flavour of salt that is full of minerals. Only used in soups and salads.
WAKAME Brown algae	This is a sweet thin leaf that is rather mild in flavour and looks a little like kombu, but is a little softer in texture. It comes in curly strands. It is then soaked and the base is removed (mekabu) along with a tough centre rib. Contains calcium, glutamic acid, protein, sodium and fibre. Sold in the dried form, it requires soaking for a short period and needs only light cooking. Classic ingredient in miso soup, salads, pastas and vegetable dishes.

Soya products, seitan and mycoprotein

SOYA

The soya bean has been cultivated in Eastern Asia for several thousand years and has been a staple diet for many countries. The first recorded mention of the soya bean was by the Chinese Emperor Sheng-Nung in 2838 BC. The soya bean actually comes from the legume family and as a single seed can grow two to three pods.

Soya beans are small and oval in shape and come in several different colours: black, red, green and yellow. They are an excellent source of nutrients with a very high protein, natural sugar and mineral content. They also contain vitamins A, B1, 2, 3 and 6, folate, biotin and pantothenate. The soya bean is very versatile and has many uses – tofu, miso, soya sauce, soya milk, soya flour, TVP and tempeh. Soya can be used to enrich and enhance the nutritional content of dishes, simply by using the flour as a batter or as a roux in a sauce, by using the milk instead of cows' milk or just by adding soya sauce or miso to the dish.

The beans require lengthy soaking and cooking. They are naturally the richest nutritional vegetable and yet are one of the most tasteless, so it requires imagination to enhance the flavour. Having a neutral flavour can be an advantage – soya products like tofu can take on flavours from other sources such as marinades, smoking, cooking in rich sauces or batters and coatings.

The soya bean contains a chemical substance called anti-trypsins. These can interfere in the body's digestion of protein within the small intestine. If the beans are sprouted, fermented, cooked or even dehulled, then this will destroy the anti-trypsins. Most soya products today are normally free from this inhibitor.

It is said that just one acre of land can produce enough soya to feed one person for well over 2000 days, yet if that person were to eat beef from the same acre of land he/she would live for only 72 days. Even with this wealth of nutrition, soya beans and their products only started to become popular in the West in the late 1950s, but in the UK they have really taken hold since the mid-1970s and are growing in popularity all the time.

SOYA PRODUCTS

Soya milk

The soya beans can be made into milk that can be used as an alternative to dairy milk, which vegans can use. The beans are soaked and ground to a fine paste, then brought to the boil with water and filtered to make milk.

It can also be used to feed infants with specially formulated soya based formulae. Infants should not be given soya milk as a drink until a year old. Soya milk can also be used to make yoghurts and cheeses for vegetarians.

How to use soya milk?
Soya milk can be used as a straight replacement for cows' milk, but it may be necessary to try a few brands as the taste and quality varies a little. Check also that the soya contains added calcium.

The skin from heated soya bean milk is called yubia. This can be used to wrap food or as a thin lasagne in dishes.

How to use it?
To use yubia, simply place a damp cloth on top of it for a few minutes, then it becomes pliable. It can also be used straight from the packet.

Tofu

Tofu or bean curd is made from the soya bean and is an excellent form of protein with very little fat. It has been used in eastern parts of Asia as long as the soya bean.

To make tofu, take 1kg soya bean powder and soak it in water for approximately 6–8 hours, then boil and simmer for 5 minutes. Add 20–30ml of lemon juice or an alternative and stir until it has curdled. Place it into a muslin cloth and drain like cheese. The finished tofu should be a white, firm block with very little taste. Keep under water in a fridge for up to five days.

Some brands make tofu from soya milk and use nigari or calcium sulphate to curdle the milk. The curds are transferred to a lined setting box and pressed to drain off the whey, then transferred to water. It will keep for a week if the water is changed regularly. Tofu can be purchased frozen, vac packed, smoked, diced or marinated.

There are two main types: firm tofu (fresh) or silken tofu. Fresh tofu is normally sold in block form underwater; it is firm, rubbery and sweet tasting with a bean smell and very little flavour. Fresh tofu will absorb the flavours of other ingredients such as stocks, marinades, herbs, spices and sauces, a major advantage when cooking. Tofu can be used in savoury and sweet dishes just as easily.

The silken tofu is mainly long life and comes in terapacks either soft, firm and extra firm packs. It has a much softer texture than fresh tofu, so careful handling is required. Once it has been opened it needs to be used within two to three days. Read the manufacturer's instructions for best before date.

If silken tofu is used in desserts it gives an added nutritional value, as it is high in protein. It is more suited to blending, i.e. dressings, sauces, desserts and flan fillings, adding texture and bulk to recipes.

How to use tofu?
Tofu can be deep-fried, shallow-fried, stir-fried, grilled, baked, steamed and lightly poached.

Freezing tofu will change the texture completely. When the tofu has thawed, it will require a gentle squeeze to remove any liquid. It will look more like a sponge and this will aid the absorption of other liquids and flavours, so it will lend itself more to savoury recipes and dishes.

Tempeh

Tempeh is a live product and is a main staple food in Indonesia. It is made from dehulled, part cooked, pressed and fermented soya beans, grain and rice mould culture. It is a complete protein and contains all the essential amino acids and is possibly the vegetarian's best source of vitamin B12. It is also high in iron, fibre and has no cholesterol.

The flavour can best be described as a cross between cheese, yeast and mushrooms – it is very different. You either like it or you don't!

Tempeh is made like Stilton cheese and yoghurts, by culturing the soya beans, which forms a mould called rhizopus oligosporus. The spores from the mould cause a fermentation of the beans, which in turn causes a white mycelium that binds the beans together and makes the tempeh more edible and digestible. This fermentation process together with the mould stops the anti-trypsins from working.

How to use tempeh?
Tempeh can be used as an alternative for sweet meat and it can be grilled, sautéed, steamed and even deep-fried. It is best used for savoury dishes due to its strong flavour. Tempeh lends itself to marinades or being mashed, crumbled or sliced because of its semi-firm texture. Tempeh comes fresh, frozen or in jars covered in water. As tempeh is a live product, it will continue to ferment unless frozen. This will strengthen its flavour and is not harmful. It is not advisable to eat tempeh raw.

SEITAN (pronounced SAY-tan)

Seitan is not a soya bean product but is a rich protein food that is made entirely from wheat gluten. It is often called wheat-meat; this is due to its firm chewy texture which, like tofu, can absorb other flavours easily.

Seitan can replace meat in many recipes. Mock chicken, pork or beef in vegetarian or Oriental restaurants is highly likely to have been seitan. Some vegetarians avoid seitan, because it resembles meat too much.

Seitan has been an important part of the staple diet in parts of China and the Far

East for some 2000 years, eaten by vegetarian monks in China and by Mormons and wheat farmers in Russia for centuries. It is made from high gluten white flour that is mixed with water into dough, then kneaded for approximately 20 minutes and washed under running water continually, which takes away the carbohydrates leaving the high protein dough. Then it is ready to be boiled in a flavoured liquid such as stock or broth for around 60–90 minutes, then cooled and used as required.

It is possible to purchase seitan as a pre-made 250g block that is either foil or vac-packed or as a ready-mixed powder that forms straight into seitan by adding water. It is also available in tins and jars.

Seitan may be stored for up to a week covered in the fridge, but if pre-packed read the manufacturer's instructions. A growing number of seitan products, such as wheat burgers, vegi sausages and wheat-style chicken, are slowly entering the market. Seitan can be purchased from health food shops and in some Asian shops, and can also be found under the name of Mi-Tan.

How to use seitan?
It is already cooked and can be sliced, dressed and served in sandwiches or salads. Seitan can also be shallow- or stir-fried, deep-fried in batter or cut up and added to soups, stews, casseroles or threaded on kebabs. If you have never used seitan, it will open up a whole new world of creative cookery. There are a number of basic seitan dough recipes to try.

TEXTURED VEGETABLE PROTEIN

Textured vegetable protein (TVP) is made from defatted soya bean that is run into threads to look like meat fibres, then pressed into shape under high pressure and cut into small pieces to look like minced beef. TVP, like tofu and seitan, is lacking in flavour and will absorb other flavours well.

It was originally intended as an extender or enhancer of processed meat products and savoury baked goods. The early versions of TVP were chewy and hard to digest, which gained it a bad press. The TVP available today is better quality, but there are variations in quality and price. It is better to purchase the better quality brands. TVP has since gained considerable popularity as a meat replacement, for example, in veggie mince, veggie burgers and pies.

TVP is often fortified with iron, thiamin, riboflavin and vitamin B12. Available plain or flavoured, it is also an excellent form of low-fat protein.

How to use it?
TVP is best used in stews, casseroles or any wet dishes. It should be soaked in a good strong vegetable stock prior to use as it trebles in size when wet. This allows the TVP to absorb more flavour.

MYCOPROTEIN

Better known as Quorn and developed by Rank Hovis McDougal, this is made from a fungus called *Fusarium gramineurum*.

Quorn is an excellent nutritional product with a high content of protein, vitamin B1, biotin and some B2, B3 and B12. It is also low in carbohydrates and fatty acids. However, Quorn is not really suitable for vegetarians, Lacto vegetarians or vegans because egg albumen is used from battery-farmed eggs to bind it.

When making Quorn the fungus is continually fermented in large tanks that have oxygen, glucose, nitrogen, vitamins and minerals added continually. After the fungus has been harvested, heat-treated, filtered and drained the fungus is mixed with the albumen to bind it; the Quorn is textured before slicing, dicing or shredding ready for packing.

Quorn itself is rather flavourless and needs to be treated like tofu, TVP and seitan, which will aid its flavour through marinating, etc. It is understood that alternatives to the egg albumen are being researched.

nuts and seeds

Generally speaking nuts can be defined as single seeds that have a hard outer shell that contains the kernel (the edible part). Some form the fruit of the plant, for example, pumpkin and almonds, while others are the seeds, such as pine nuts. This is the plant's way of ensuring that the seeds are distributed. Early man collected and ate nuts, which provided them with a vital source of nutrition.

There are hundreds of different nuts and seeds that vary in size, colour, taste, texture and nutritional content. They are an excellent provider of protein, minerals, vitamins and fibre. Nuts such as almonds, Brazil nuts, cashew nuts, hazelnuts, peanuts, pecan nuts and walnuts all contain a rich source of natural oil, which can be extracted through pounding and used in the making of peanut butter, for example. Both nuts and seeds make excellent oils for cooking and dressings in foods. Examples are peanut and walnut oil, sesame and sunflower oils. Peanuts

are not really nuts as such, because they are grown inside a case below the ground, but they are generally known and used as nuts.

Ground almonds and cashew nuts can also be made into cream and milk substitutes if blended with soya milk or water. Use 200g ground nuts to 300ml liquid and increase or decrease the amount of nuts or liquid depending on the level of consistency required. This can be used in dairy-free (egg, milk, cream) sauces or dips or baked goods such as pies and flans.

The shells protect the kernels from oxygen and from micro-organisms. Many nuts can go rancid once exposed to the air and have to be vacuum packed or have preservatives added to them. Nuts that are rancid should never be used or eaten as they can be dangerous to health and could cause food poisoning.

From a nutritional point, both nuts and

seeds can combine well (protein combining) in recipes and dishes, fortifying the nutritional content of a meal. Seeds such as pumpkin and sesame are excellent either dry roasted or pan toasted and served with salads, or with a touch of maple syrup and eaten as a snack.

How to use them?

Nuts and seeds come in varying forms: whole, flaked, nibbed, broken or even ground. Their use is endless: whole nuts can be used to decorate desserts; chopped nuts can be used to make nut loaves or nut burgers; flaked nuts can be roasted or toasted and used in salads, breakfast cereals and stir fries; nibbed nuts can be used in desserts and fillings or toasted and used on salads; ground nuts can be used to coat, dip or dust, in pâtés and dips, and added for texture in bread and stuffings.

It it vital to remember that some people are allergic to nuts and seeds. For more information see page 105.

Purchasing and storage

It is possible to buy nuts in many different varieties, forms, sizes, weights and mixes. Always buy nuts and seeds from a reputable supplier then there should not be a problem whether they are shelled or unshelled. If purchasing in the shell ensure that the shells are not open or damaged in any way; if so, do not buy them. Nuts that have been commercially removed from their shells and packed may have been exposed to antioxidants, dyes and preservatives.

Once you have purchased your goods, the length of time that they will keep will depend on the variety, condition, light, air, temperature and the moisture of storage conditions. It is best to store them in a sealed container with a tight-fitting lid, in a dark cool place out of direct sunlight. Nuts and seeds can be frozen, but they must be really fresh.

Removing the skins from nuts

Nuts such as pistachios and almonds need to have their skins removed before use. Blanch the nuts in a pan of boiling water (no salt) for 2–3 minutes, remove from the water and place on a tea towel. Place another towel on top and rub them together. This process should release the skin and make picking out the kernels much easier.

NUT BUTTERS

It is relatively easy to make nut butters. The better nuts such as peanuts, almonds, hazelnuts and pecans make the better nut butters.

To start, simply toast and then grind the nuts in a food processor, grinder or a chopping bowl until they reach the required texture, then blend with vegetable oil and season to taste. It may be necessary to add a little water to let down the consistency. Variations on this theme can be to add herbs and spices to taste. If stored in the fridge the butter will keep for up to four days.

ROAST SEEDS AND NUTS

To roast nuts and seeds, place the ingredients into a dry pan and gently heat and toss the ingredients until a golden brown colour is achieved. This process should take no longer than 10 minutes. Alternatively, place the ingredients onto a baking tray and put them in a pre-heated oven (180°C). Shake the tray continually to achieve a good even golden colour. This should take no longer than 10 minutes.

TAHINI

Tahini has become increasingly popular in recent years. It is a smooth oily paste made from puréed sesame seeds that have usually been toasted first.

There are two varieties, dark and light. Light tahini has a softer flavour than dark; this is because the seeds have been de-hulled. In dark tahini, the seeds have not been hulled but have also been roasted. This intensifies the flavour and gives it such a deep colour. Dark tahini is more nutritious than light tahini.

Adding lemon juice to tahini will make it crumbly and sticky, but adding more water will make it a silky smooth paste. Tahini can be used as a replacement for egg as a binding agent in a number of dishes.

Nuts	Quality points	Culinary uses
ALMOND	One of the most popular and versatile nuts, they can be purchased in many forms: whole, flaked, ground, etc. Still popular in the Middle East. Two varieties, bitter and sweet. It is this sweet nut that is edible. High in protein, fatty acids, folate and biotin. Also contain minerals, vitamins B1, 2, 3, 6 and E.	Sauces, stir-fries, milk, oil, baking and desserts.
BRAZIL NUT	Brazil nuts can be eaten raw. They have firm white kernels and a creamy flavour, and tend to go rancid very quickly. Harvested in May each year from the Amazon basin rain forests of Brazil, Bolivia, Ecuador and Peru. Each pod holds up to 32 segments, similar to an orange. High in fat (68%), with a good source of minerals, protein, folate, biotin, vitamin B1, 2, 3, B6 and E.	Raw, stuffings, nut roast, nut burgers, baking and desserts.
CASHEW NUT	Pale white in colour with a sweet taste and texture. Widely used in Chinese, Thai and Indian cuisine. High in protein, fat and calcium. Also contain minerals, protein, vitamins B1, 2, 3, 6 and E, folate, biotin and pantothenate.	Szechuan dishes, curries, stir-fries, baking and oil.

→

Nuts	Quality points	Culinary uses
→ CHESTNUT	Chestnuts were brought to Britain by the Romans and are more like a vegetable as they contain more starch than other nuts. Available fresh, dried, canned, whole and puréed. Season is October – November. Best ones are the *marrons* from France. High in starch, but also contain protein, minerals, vitamins B1, 2, 3, 6 and E, biotin and pantothenate.	Soups, cereals, stews, casseroles, puddings, pâtés, purée and stuffings.
COCONUT	Only the liquid and the white meat are eaten. The juice is from the unhusked green coconut. Palm sugar is made by boiling down the juices. Desiccated coconut is made by shredding the coconut and drying it. Coconut milk and cream are different from juice; boiling water is poured over the desiccated coconut and then left to cool down. Then it is squeezed out through a cloth. High in fat and natural sugar. Also contain vitamins B1, 2, 3 and E, folate, fibre and pantothenate.	Indian, West Indian, Thai, and Malaysian cuisine, curries, beverages, baking, confectionery and oil.
GINKGO NUTS	From the ginkgo tree, which is often called the maidenhair tree because it looks like the maidenhair fern tree. The fruit looks like a greenish yellow plum and has a vile smell, but the kernels within are sweet and have a flowery scent. Contains protein, minerals and B vitamins.	Used in Japanese cookery, eaten raw, roasted, etc.
HAZELNUT Filbert or cob nut	Cob nuts and filbert nuts are both classed as hazelnuts. Hazel is the Anglo-Saxon name for helmet and the nut is shaped like the helmet of a Roman Warrior. The filbert nut is from the same plant, which blooms on St Filberts day. It has a woody taste and gives a better flavour when roasted. Also give an excellent fragrant oil and are good as a flour. High in fat, mainly unsaturated. Good source of protein, minerals, vitamins B1, 2, 3, 6 and E, folate, fibre, biotin and pantothenate.	Baking, desserts, nut roasts, nut butter, oil in dressings and salads.

→

Nuts	Quality points	Culinary uses
→ MACADAMIA Queensland nut	From Australia and now grown in the USA, this nut has a sweet buttery flavour and texture, similar to that of the candlenut used in Malay and Thai cookery. Available shelled and roasted. High in fat, mainly unsaturated. Good source of protein, minerals, vitamins B1, 2, 3, 6 and E, fibre, biotin and pantothenate.	Raw, desserts, baking, used as snacks. Can be used as a substitute for candlenuts.
PEANUT Monkey nut Ground nut	The peanut is widely used in Middle Eastern, African and Oriental cookery. In Indonesia a spicy peanut sauce is served with 'sate', giving the dish sweetness. Grown in underground pods it is high in unsaturated fats, and packed with protein, minerals, vitamins B1, 2, 3, 6 and E, fibre, biotin and pantothenate.	Soups, salads, sauces, butters, dips, desserts and baking.
PECAN NUT	One of the hickory nuts that is native to America. It has a thin, elongated, smooth shell. It is a little like the walnut but much oilier and goes rancid quickly when shelled. High fat content (70%), mainly unsaturated. Also contain protein, natural sugar, minerals, fibre, vitamins A, B1, 2, 3, 6 and E and folate.	Pecan pie, candied, sauces, cakes, cookies, butters, stuffings and oil.
PINE NUT Pine kernel Indian nut	Small, creamy nut with distinctive flavour. Goes rancid very easily. Favoured by the Romans. Primarily grown in Asia, above 5000 ft. High protein content. Expensive, used whole or chopped. Increased flavour when toasted. High fat content (68%), mainly unsaturated. Also contain protein, minerals, fibre, vitamins A, B1, 2, 3 and E.	Sauces, soups, pesto sauce, salads, rice dishes, stuffings.
PISTACHIO	Gathered from the mountainsides in Turkey, Iran, Afghanistan and now grown in California in orchards. This pale green nut has a very distinct flavour, but skins must be removed. Contain protein, minerals, fibre, vitamins A, B1, 2, 3 and E and folate.	Salads, stuffings, rice dishes, desserts, baked goods, ice cream, garnishes, sesame halva, cocktail nut and pistachio oil.

→

Nuts	Quality points	Culinary uses
→ TIGER NUT Chufa nut Yellow nut Earth almond nut Rush nut Pig nut	This plant is related to the ancient Egyptian papyrus. The chufa nut has been eaten for thousands of years and is sweet in flavour. High in fibre and carbohydrate. Also contain minerals, vitamins and protein.	Raw, snacks, ice cream, and a drink called 'horchata de chufa'.
WALNUT English walnut Persian walnut Black or American walnuts	The black walnut is grown wild in the USA and has a distinctly pungent taste. Available fresh, dried and pickled but most often used dried. Blanch to reduce bitterness. Yield delicious oil. Black walnuts are low in calories compared to the English variety, yet lower in protein. The walnut tree is revered not just for its nut but also for its timber. The fruit is highly nutritious. When picked green or immature the nut can be pickled or preserved in syrup. Ripe walnuts should be dry and have a good brown colour and look like a brain. High fat content (68%), mainly unsaturated. Also contain protein, minerals, fibre, vitamins A, B1, 2, 3, 6 and E, folate and biotin.	Raw, desserts, pastries, salads, sauces, baking, garnishing, bread, oil and used for pickling.

Seeds	Quality points	Culinary uses
LINSEED	Linseeds are the seeds from the flax plant. They are rich in the essential fatty acids, fibre and have good oil content.	Baking, confectionery, cereals and oil.
MUSTARD	There are three types of mustard seeds: black, white and brown. Black seeds are very pungent and are native to Europe, but are rarely seen today. They now grow in North America and are the true mustard. The white seeds grow mustard cress. The seeds are a pale, light yellow and have a mild flavour. Brown mustard seeds look a little like the black seeds, but are a lighter brown colour, and are used in Indian cookery where they are fried in oil. They taste nutty. Contain protein and some minerals.	Condiments, sauces, dips, coatings and toppings.

→

Seeds	Quality points	Culinary uses
→ PUMPKIN	Pumpkin seeds are from the squash family. Mainly imported from China. The seeds are washed, dried and then salted. The flavour is further increased if toasted. Rich in minerals like zinc and iron; also a good source of protein.	Salads, garnishing, nut roast, cereals, baking and stuffings and fillings.
RAPE Colza Cole Coleseed	Mainly used for oil but pressed further for rape seed cake as cattle feed. Also sold as spring green vegetables when grown from seeds. Even sold in punts to grow your own as rape and cress seeds. High in unsaturated fats and vitamin E.	Salads, cress, vegetables and oil.
SESAME	The seeds can be toasted and used in salads and in baking. Highly prized oil, used in Oriental cookery giving it a spicy nutty flavour. High fat content, most unsaturated, with a good source of protein, B vitamins and minerals. Tahini made from the seeds is high in fat content (58%) most unsaturated. A good source of protein, minerals, vitamins B1, 2, 3, 6 and E, folate, biotin and pantothenate.	Salads, baking, hummus, crumbles, tahini, sesame halva, stir-fries. Flavour enhancer, thickener, dips, soups and sauces.
SUNFLOWER	Seeds are good toasted and used as garnish adding and fortifying dishes with extra nutrients. The oil is a pale yellow colour and a little tasteless. High fat content (46%) most unsaturated, with a good source of protein and vitamin E. Also contain fibre, vitamin B1, 2 and 3.	Salads, garnishing, bread, oil, fillings and stuffings

fungi

There are thousands of mushrooms, toadstools and fungi and many are edible. However, many are not and are therefore harmful not only to humans but also to animals and crops.

Fungi have great value for us – they serve as a cheap flavouring for our food, and can also have great medicinal value. Fungi, only slightly related to the toadstool and mushroom, play a great part in our daily diet.

Mushrooms give a nutritional benefit only when cooked.

They are relatively high in protein – on average they give 20 per cent of their dried mass – low in fat and contain essential amino acids, fibre and also several vitamins such as thiamin, riboflavin, biotin, niacin and ascorbic acid. The ability to release and produce carbon dioxide as a by-product with oxygen and alcohol has been used in the making of bread and beer for centuries. Yeasts are a source of vitamin B and also contain amino acids and protein.

Fungi are also used to flavour blue cheese. Penicillin is a fungi and is used as a drug to help fight off infections. Mushrooms contain more protein per 100 grams than most other vegetables. Many are extremely dangerous, like the death cap, for obvious reasons, and some are used as hallucinogenic drugs (LSD).

The king of the fungi is the truffle, valued for its flavour, perfume and colour, and highly prized by French chefs for centuries.

Listed below are some of the more popular and best-known edible mushrooms, which can be purchased fresh and dried. If purchased dried follow the manufacturer's instructions. Mushrooms are best stored in the fridge inside a paper bag to keep out moisture.

Fungi	Information, description and availability	Culinary uses
BOLETES SPECIES CEP 'PENNY BUN'	Stems are generally fat with dark veins and exceptionally good flavour. Found on woodland floors. Olive brown or chestnut in colour. Available August to October.	Soups, salads and omelettes.
BAY-CAPPED BOLETE	Smooth cap and domed. Coloured chestnut brown with yellowish spores and a pale brown stem. Commonly found in green and coniferous woodland. Available September to November.	
BRACKET FUNGI CHANTERELLE	Trumpet shaped, has a distinctive smell of apricots with a deep egg-yellow colour and a light orange colour on top. Found mainly in deep woodland. Available September to November.	Soups, salads and omelettes.
HORN OF PLENTY	Funnel or horn shaped but very irregular in size. Thin and leathery texture. Has a pleasant smell and taste. Found in green woodland. Available September to November.	Soups, salads and omelettes.
CAP FUNGI MORELS	Oval head with honeycomb ridges and deep crevices. Brown in colour with the texture of a sponge. The stem and head are often hollow. Deep full bodied flavour of fresh cut wood. Prized mushroom. Found in grassy woodland, fields, verges and hedgerows. Available March to May.	Soups, salads and omelettes, good with pasta.
TRUFFLE	Red truffle, buried in soil in oak woodland, irregular shape. Reddish orange in colour. Has a nice nutty flavour. Old ones have an unpleasant smell.	Soups, salads, omelettes.
	White truffle, round, with a black outer skin and white inside. Good flavour, but not the best or most prized. Widespread in southern England. Found in chalky soil in beech woods.	Soups, salads and omelettes, good with pasta.
	Perigord truffle, round in shape, with a black outer skin and dark brown marbled flesh inside. Excellent flavour, best and most prized of the truffles by French chefs who consider them worth their weight in gold. Available September to November.	Soups, salads and omelettes, good with pasta.

→

Fungi	Information, description and availability	Culinary uses
→ GILL FUNGI FIELD MUSHROOM	The well-known wild field mushroom. Wide domed cap and pale brown or offwhite in colour with pinkish gill and flaky flesh. Gives a mushroom smell. Good flavour and widely used. Found in meadows and pastures, but can be found widely. Available July to November.	Soups, salads and omelettes, good with pasta.
HORSE MUSHROOMS	Thick and stout mushroom. Wide domed cap, off-white in colour which yellows with age, has a brown gill and white flesh. Very good flavour and widely used. Found in meadows and pastures, but can be found widely. Available July to November.	Soups, salads and omelettes, good with pasta.
SCALY WOOD MUSHROOM	Domed cap covered with brown fibres. The gills are tight-knit and pink and darken with age to a brown colour. Flesh will turn reddish when cut. Good flavour. Found in woodland with conifers. Available September to November.	Soups, salads and omelettes, good with pasta.
FUNNEL CAP (yellow) Ciltocybe geotropa	Starts with a domed cap and turns and folds into a funnel cap with age. Light yellow in colour with the gills a lighter colour than the cap. The flesh is white and smells of hay. Found in green woodland. Available September to November.	Soups and omelettes, good with pasta.
MEADOW WAX-CAP	Starts conical then flattens out as it grows older. The top of the cap is tan colour and sticky. Has white flesh and a heady mushroom smell. Found in grassy areas and in pastures and meadows. Available September to November.	Soups and omelettes, good with pasta
CULTIVATED BUTTON MUSHROOMS	Creamy white in colour. Size varies from very small to as large (mature ones) as 15 cm. Caps are very tight and closed. Flavour is mild to woody. All purpose mushroom. Keep for up to seven days.	Soups, hors d'oeuvres salads and omelettes, good with pasta.

→

Fungi	Information, description and availability	Culinary uses
→ CHESTNUT MUSHROOM	Often called Paris mushroom. Naturally light tanned on the cap, very firm. Earthier flavour than Button (white) mushrooms. Keep for up to seven days. Mature Chestnut mushroom has open cap up to 15 cm in diameter. This gives a deep meat-like texture to the flesh. Keeps up to 10 days in fridge.	Soups, salads and omelettes, good with pasta and vegetable dishes. Good alternative to meat in vegetarian dishes, soups, salads and omelettes, good with pasta and vegetable dishes.
OYSTER MUSHROOM	Usually found on dead logs, but the majority are now are cultivated in a variety of colours. Fluted with long stems and a mild flavour, with a velvety texture. Keep for 5 to 7 days in fridge.	Soups, salads and omelettes, good with pasta and vegetable dishes.
IMPORTED ENOKI	Originally from Japan, fragile and flower-like with long stems. Grown in small clusters. Very slight mild flavour. Require very little cooking and keep up to 14 days in the fridge.	Oriental soups, salads and stir-fries.
MAITAKE	Cluster of dark fronds and a firm texture at the base. Become brittle and crumbly around the edges. Distinctive aroma with a rich woody taste. Keep 7 to 10 days.	Soups, salads and good with vegetable dishes.
SHIITAKE	Oriental mushroom, increasingly cultivated. Brown to tan in colour with umbrella-shaped caps, excellent strong mushroom flavour and meaty texture. Caps are soft and spongy. Do not use the stems as they are tough. Keep up to 14 days in the fridge.	Oriental soups, stir-fries and good vegetable dishes.

How to use them?

Mushrooms are very versatile and can lend themselves to almost all methods of cookery; they are best shallow-fried in a pan with very hot olive oil. If adding mushrooms to a wet dish, remember they are very high in water content and are best added last.

herbs and edible flowers

HERBS

Herbs have been used by ancient civilisations for thousands of years. They were used just as much for their healing properties as for their cooking flavours.

It was not until the medieval monasteries evolved that the use of herbs became extremely popular and they were cultivated and harvested. Many have retained their original names, for example, St Johnswort and worm wood. Many herbs have medicinal properties and are used today, in alternative medicine as well as contemporary medicine.

The use of herbs has become part of the culinary heritage of regions as well as nations, for example, in Britain we eat roast lamb accompanied by mint sauce, pork with sage and onion stuffing. In France one would eat chicken with tar-

ragon (chasseur), *court bouillon* and stocks with thyme, bay leaf and parsley (bouquet garni), and lamb with rosemary. Italy uses a mix of basil, cheese and olives, and then there is the famous mix of salt, dill and black pepper used to cure salmon in Norway and Sweden. The list is endless.

Because only small amounts of herbs are used in cooking, their nutrional value is low. However, the scent, colour and flavours that they impart into the food is critically important, making the food a pleasant and enjoyable experience, not just for the customer but the creator of the dish.

Vegetarian cuisine has suffered the indignity of being labelled bland and unappetising to eat and this is far from the truth! Herbs play a major part in helping to enhance and flavour a huge range of vegetarian dishes.

Whether herbs are dried or fresh their flavours can be utilised. Fresh herbs add greater colour and need little cooking compared to dried herbs, although it is necessary only to use half the amount of the dried herbs, due to the stronger flavour. Fresh herbs lose their flavour, colour and scent quickly when picked, so buy or pick only the amount that is required. Wrap some damp kitchen paper around the herbs and put them in a plastic bag and keep in the fridge. If it is large bunch, put it in a jug of cold water with a damp kitchen towel over the top and store in the fridge until required.

Herbs should only ever be chopped or cut with very sharp knives or scissors. The plants store essential oils in their leaves, stems and flowers which are released if cut or crushed, or when the cooking process begins.

FLOWERS

Through pollination flowers provide the next generation of plants, and they contain vitamins and oils in small amounts. As such they do not add much nutritional value to a meal, but they do add flavour and colour to the most mundane dish.

For centuries Egyptians, Roman and Persians all used flowers such as rose petals to flavour wine, and lavender to flavour honey. The Chinese and Japanese have used chrysanthemums and jasmines for making tea, because of the 'cool' fragrance that the flowers give.

In the Middle Ages flowers were widely used for medical remedies by monks or to dye cloth and in Elizabethan times people would dry flowers and hang them in their wardrobes or lay them between their clothes in dressers to keep them fresh. Here we will look at only a few edible flowers, for example, violets, nasturtiums and roses, which should be readily available. Herbs and flowers are still widely used in alternative and Chinese medicine today.

Flowers should always be washed before use. Always purchase from a reputable supplier and ensure that no harmful sprays have been used.

Names and varieties	Areas used	Culinary uses
→ ANISE Sweet cumin	Seeds Leaves	The seeds were cultivated as far back as the Pharaohs. Used in drinks like the Greek ouzo. Also used in Indian and Chinese cookery. Leaves – in salads, for garnish.
ANGELICA	Stems (young) Leaves	The stems are used for its sweet flavour. Can be candied and used in sweets and desserts. The leaves can be used in salads.

→

Names and varieties	Areas used	Culinary uses
→ BALM Lemon balm	Leaves Stem	Introduced by the Romans, it has a lemony flavour and can be used in place of fresh lemon zest and lemongrass. Nice in salads, stuffing, and desserts.
BASIL	Leaves	There are many varieties of basil, sweet and purple to name two. One of the most aromatic herbs grown in Spain, Greece and southern Italy, it is used in Mediterranean cookery. It is an important ingredient in pesto/pistou, pasta, egg dishes and salads. Long cooking of basil must be avoided as this will cause loss of colour and turn the flavour bitter.
BAY	Leaves (fresh and dried)	Used as a victor's crown by the Greeks and the Romans, it has become an essential part of the European kitchen for bouquet garni, stocks, *bouillons*, stews and many other dishes. It can also be used in dessert syrups. Dried leaves require longer cooking to give added flavour. Some varieties of laurel leaf are poisonous.
BORAGE	Flowers Leaves (use small and tender leaves)	A wild blue flower with a light fresh cucumber flavour that can be used in salads, fruit punches and in ice-cubes for decoration, or cooked like spinach and used with pasta.
BOUQUET GARNI	Combination	A faggot of herbs used in European cookery. Classically it includes bay, parsley and thyme. Use in stocks, *bouillons*, stews, soups and casseroles There are many variations on this theme; some may use cinnamon, tarragon, basil, etc.
CELERY	Seeds Leaves	Celery is rather bitter and grown as a herb and a vegetable. The seeds are very pungent, so a small amount only is required. Used in soups, stews and sauces. The leaves give a nice addition to salads and garnishes.

→

Names and varieties	Areas used	Culinary uses
→ CHERVIL	Leaves	A feathery herb reminiscent in flavour to parsley. Used in salads, omelettes, cheese dishes, herb butters and is an ingredient in *fines herbs*. It is universally used today for garnishing dishes.
CHIVES	Leaves Flowers	Cultivated from the time in the Middle Ages. Chives are from the onion family, and look like grass, but are tubular with lilac flowers. Chives have a subtle onion flavour and are native to northern Europe. Used in salads, herb butters, cheese, soups and egg dishes. The flowers can be used in salads and in ice-cubes in drinks for a garnish.
CHRYSANTHEMUM	Leaves Flowers	Both are used in salads in their raw state, leaves in stews and in making tea. Better to use the young, tender ones.
COMFREY	Flowers Large leaves	This was prized by herbalists and was prescribed for a number of conditions. It contains vitamins B, B12, C and E, allantoin, iron, magnesium, phosphorus and calcium. Comfrey can be used in the same way as borage. The flowers can be used in salads and for decoration. Leaves can be cooked as spinach or dried and used to make tea.
CORIANDER Cilantro or Chinese parsley	Leaves Roots Seeds	Possibly the most used herb in the world and the oldest known to man. It is indispensable in Indian and Thai cookery with its musty scent. It is chopped and used as parsley in Japanese and Chinese cookery. The root is ground down and used to spice up dishes. The leaves can be used to flavour casseroles and stews and stir-fries. The seeds are used in curries, chutneys and vegetable dishes.

→

Names and varieties	Areas used	Culinary uses
→ CURRY LEAF	Leaves	An important part of the flavouring of dishes in Indian vegetarian cookery and Malaysian cuisine. The plant grows in southern Asia. There is no substitute for this herb. The leaf is used to make many different powders and pastes, all with their unique flavour.
DILL	Leaves Seeds	Dill is grown all over the world and is mainly associated with fish and pickles. Its feathery leaves have a flavour similar to caraway and aniseed. It is good in soups, egg dishes, cream-based sauces, cucumber, potato dishes and mayonnaise. The seeds are used in light cooking as a spice.
ELDER	Flowers Leaves Berries	Flowers and leaves are used to make wine and flowers can be deep-fried in batter or used in syrups by infusing its fragrance for desserts. Berries can be used for desserts.
FENNEL	Leaves Seeds	Fennel looks like a bigger version of dill. It has a stronger flavour of aniseed than dill. It has a natural freshness when used raw in salads and is even used in drinks.
FENUGREEK Methi	Leaves Seeds	Not widely used in western cookery, but used extensively in Indian cuisine. Very rich in iron. The flavour varies from very bitter to lightly bitter and the young leaves can be used in salads. The seeds are normally gently roasted and ground to a fine power. Seeds can be sprouted.
FINES HERBES	Leaves	A mixture of freshly chopped tarragon, chervil and parsley. The mixture can sometimes differ to include chives for example. Used in omelettes, sauces and salads.
HYSSOP	Leaves	Not commonly used in cooking, it has a warm, pungent aromatic smell. It is used to flavour chartreuse and the liquor Benedictine. The leaves are a little similar to those of rosemary and lavender.

→

Names and varieties	Areas used	Culinary uses
→ KAFFIR LIME	Leaves	Kaffir lime leaves are light to dark green in colour. Widely used in Indonesian, Malay and Thai cooking. It has a pleasant lime scent when gently rubbed with the fingers. It is normally very finely shredded and added to dishes during the cooking process or as a garnish.
LAVENDER	Leaves Flowers	This is one of the oldest and most pleasant English garden herbs. Not really used in cookery, but more cultivated for its oil used in aromatherapy. The leaves can be used to make fragrant sauces and mixed with other herbs can be added to salads. Flowers can be used in salads and making cakes.
LOVAGE	Stem Leaves Seeds	This herb has a musky fragrance and a lemony flavour with a hint of celery. It has a large leaf similar in shape to that of flat parsley. It is totally underused and neglected as a herb. Because of its strong flavour it must be used sparingly in soups, stews, stuffings, stocks, sauces, salads and potato dishes.
MARIGOLD	Flowers	The young flowers can be used in salads, soups, stews, cakes and puddings. Can be used as a replacement for saffron to colour dishes.
MARJORAM	Leaves	From the family of oregano, marjoram is a sweet smelling herb and has been cultivated since medieval times. Grown in bundles of knots, it is good either fresh or dried. When fresh it loses its flavour during long cooking so it is best to add this herb towards the end of cooking. Used in pastas, salads, soups, stews and egg dishes.

→

Names and varieties	Areas used	Culinary uses
→ MINT	Leaves Flowers	There are many varieties of mint, spearmint and peppermint just to name two. Used mainly in desserts and to make condiments such as mint sauce, mint jelly, etc. Mint is an excellent addition to vegetables, such as new potatoes and peas, and is also used in salads, fruit salads, stuffings, summer drinks, ice creams and teas. Contains protein, calcium, folate, vitamin E, thiamin, riboflavin, niacin, sodium and potassium.
NASTURTIUM	Flower Leaves	Leaves are peppery hot in flavour. Excellent in salads or soups. The flowers are an excellent colourful addition to dishes.
NETTLE	Leaves	Pick with gloves. Cook and use as spinach, after cooking the nettles lose their sting. Serve on their own, puréed or in soups.
OREGANO	Leaves	Oregano is probably best known for its use in Italian and Mediterranean cookery. It is excellent with tomato, cheese, egg and pizzas and is often mistaken for marjoram.
PANSIES	Flowers	Excellent in salads, also nice mixed with a soft goat's cheese, and in cakes and puddings.
PARSLEY	Leaves Stalks	The most used herb in Europe and second to coriander as the most used herb in the world. There are four varieties of parsley; we only use two in the UK. The curly or moss curled parsley and the flat or Italian parsley. Its leaves are rich in vitamin C, iron and carotene. Some gourmets have said that flat parsley has a more superior flavour; I have yet to be convinced of this. Parsley contains vitamins A, C and E, sulphur, calcium, iron, thiamin, riboflavin, niacin, trypt, folate, potassium and minerals.

→

Names and varieties	Areas used	Culinary uses
→ ROSEMARY	Leaves Flowers	This popular hardy herb from the Middle Ages grows wild all over Europe, and has spike-shaped leaves, a very aromatic scent and strong flavour. Care must be given to the amount used in dishes due to the intense flavour; use in moderation in sweet dishes. The flowers can be used in salads and for decoration. Universally used.
RUE	Leaves	This herb is from the orange and lemon family and is common in southern Europe. It is not used to any great degree, due to its strong un-appealing scent. It can be used with discretion in salads, with eggs and cheese, in vegetable juice cocktails and some savoury dishes.
SAGE	Leaves	There are a number of different varieties of sage. Sage is a pungent and hardy plant. The leaves vary in colour and strength of flavour. It is a versatile herb that works well with fresh vegetables, potatoes, cheeses and pastas. The flowers can be used in salads. Sage is high in carbohydrates, protein, riboflavin, niacin and many minerals.
SAVOURY	Leaves	There are two different types of savoury, summer and winter savoury. Winter savoury is considered to be the most bitter and coarse of the two. Both have a strong peppery flavour and require some discretion when being used. Savoury has the same property as thyme and is good with cheese, peas, beans and pasta.
SORREL	Leaves	This herb belongs to the dock leaf plants, of which there are several different varieties. The older leaves are rather acidic, coarse and tough; it is therefore advisable to use only younger and tender sorrel and in small quantities in salads. Also can be used in omelettes, as purées and sauces.

→

Names and varieties	Areas used	Culinary uses
→ SWEET CICELY	Leaves	Not often used in the modern kitchen and not widely available. The flavour is sweet and aromatic and likened to anise. The stems can be boiled and served as a vegetable or chopped and used as an addition to salads or soups and stews. Good with fruit compotes and purées.
TANSY	Leaves	Tansy was an important herb in the early sixteenth and seventeenth centuries as it was believed to have medicinal and flavouring properties. Tansy has an unpleasant odour and a rather bitter taste. It can be used chopped, cooked and added to baked goods, stuffings and pies. Is not often used in the modern kitchen and not widely available. Use sparingly as excess can be dangerous.
TARRAGON	Leaves	There are two different varieties of Tarragon: one is French tarragon and the other is Russian tarragon, which is often called 'false tarragon'. It is very inferior to the French tarragon, with none of its subtle flavour or the delicate, slender leaves. French tarragon is held in high esteem by gourmets as one of the finest culinary herbs. Used in *fines herbes*, stocks, salads, egg dishes, sauces, stews, casseroles, pastas, flavoured vinegars and butters.
THYME (many varieties)	Leaves	One of the greatest and noble herbs from the kitchens of Europe. The ancient Greeks revered thyme. There are a number of varieties: lemon thyme, silver thyme and caraway thyme to name just a few. It has a rich pungent and aromatic scent it is high in protein, carbohydrates, riboflavin, trypt, niacin and full of minerals. Used in bouquet garni, stocks, stews, casseroles, eggs, salads, pasta dishes, stuffings and for adding extra flavour to vegetables.

→

Names and varieties	Areas used	Culinary uses
→ VIOLET	Leaves Flowers	Leaves are used in soups, sauces and salads. The flowers can be used in salads or are crystallised for cake decorating.

fats and oils

The major source of fat for anyone on a vegetarian diet comes from nuts, dairy foods, vegetables and oils such as olive oil.

These nutrients are called lipids, a term that refers to fats and oils used in cooking. Oils at room temperature remain a liquid whereas fats remain solid. But what use are fats to the body?

Fats protect vital organs, aid cell structure, maintain body temperature and are a source of energy. A number of substances can be made in the body from the fat in our food. The one most commonly known is called cholesterol. If the body overproduces cholesterol for a long period this can increase the risk of obesity, hardening of the arteries and high blood pressure, leading to the possibility of heart attacks, strokes or heart disease.

COMA published a report in 1994 on Nutritional Aspects of Cardiovascular Disease. It recommended that only 10 per cent of energy should come from sat-urated fatty acids. It also suggested that percentages of energy provided from other fatty acids should be as follows: monounsaturated 12 per cent, polyunsaturated 6–10 per cent of which linoleic acid 1 per cent and linolenic acid 0.2 per cent, trans fatty acids 2 per cent, saturated fatty acids 10 per cent with a total of 35 per cent. The figures are intended as population averages not individual targets.

There are some fatty acids the body cannot make; these are called essential fatty acids.

Other substances that make up fats are called triglycerides. These consist of glycerol and fatty acids, which give fats and oils their flavours.

There are two categories of fats, animal- and vegetable-based sources. They differ in their make up: the cells contain carbon atoms that in turn hold hydrogen atoms. Saturated fatty acids contain as much hydrogen atoms as it is possible to hold, thereby 'saturating' the carbon cells. If there are hydrogen atoms missing, the carbon will form a single double bond and this is called monosaturated. If there is more than one hydrogen atom missing, the carbon will form more double bonds and these are called polyunsaturated fatty acids.

Saturated fats These are normally animal-based fats that over long periods of time can be harmful to health: they harden the arteries, causing increased cholesterol in the blood, leading to strokes and heart disease. In this category we can include palm and coconut oil.

Unsaturated fats In this category we can include monounsaturated and polyunsaturated fats. These fats can reduce blood cholesterol and polyunsaturated fatty acids. When heat is applied they can pro-duce free radicals, which can help reduce the risk of heart disease and some cancers.

RANGE OF AVAILABLE OILS

There is a huge range of oils that are available to today's caterer and chef, from seed oils such as rapeseed to powerful nut oils such as walnut and coconut. Each oil has its own characteristics of flavour, texture and aroma. Each of these characteristics can alter the taste of the dish or recipe. However, the flavour of oils can be altered by the chef by adding herbs, vegetables, fruit or spices. For example, adding whole chillies, coriander and garlic to vegetable oil, then allowing it to infuse, will give a strong flavour for hot stir-fries or dressings.

Oil	Brief description of flavours and characteristics	Culinary uses
ALMOND	Distinctive flavour, pale in colour but this limits the use of this oil. Made from the sweet almond which has some 50 per cent oil content.	Confectionery, baking, mayonnaises and salad dressings.
COCONUT	From the white meat of the coconut, called copra. The oil contains natural lethicin and is used in Southern India, Malaysia and Indonesia giving the food a coconut taste. It is high in saturated fats (85 per cent) and has a small amount of vitamin E.	Used in Asian and Indian cooking.
CORN (MAIZE)	Good flavour, but a little to heavy for salads and dressings. Has a golden yellow colour. High in fatty acids, mainly unsaturated, with a good source of vitamin E.	Baking, popular in the USA and a good frying oil.

→

Oil	Brief description of flavours and characteristics	Culinary uses
→ COTTON	Mostly used for making margarine, commercial salad creams and dressings. Made from the cotton seed. Contains around 69 per cent unsaturated fatty acids and high in vitamin E.	Good in salads, mayonnaise and frying.
GRAPESEED	Not that widely used with a weak flavour and pale in colour. Best used as a compliment with other oils.	Salads, margarine, frying, mayonnaise.
GROUNDNUT Peanut Arachide	High in fatty acids of which 47 per cent are monounsaturated, but has a good source of vitamin E. This oil has a light scent and no flavour as such and is best used in dressings and for frying foods with good flavours. Used in mainly Oriental cookery.	Oriental cookery and frying, salads, baking dressings and mayonnaise.
HAZELNUT	A brown colour and strong nutty flavour adding depth and body to dressing and frying foods. This oil is one of the most expensive. Mainly contains monounsaturated fats and a small amount of vitamin E.	Dressings, baking and frying.
OLIVE	Olive oil is made from the pressings from the green olive and has a strong flavour. Oil is graded by its acidity, with extra virgin olive oil 1 per cent and a deep green colour and the lower grade olive oil 3–4 per cent and a much lighter green. There are great differences in olive oil from country to country. The Mediterranean countries produce large amounts of this oil. Contains a large amount of monounsaturated fats (69 per cent), with a small amount of iron and vitamin E.	Salads, bread, baking, frying and dressings.
PALM	Mainly used in the production of margarine. It has a distinctive flavour, a high fat content with 45 per cent saturated and 41 per cent monosaturated and a good source of vitamin E.	West African, Brazilian, Thai and Caribbean cooking.

→

Oil	Brief description of flavours and characteristics	Culinary uses
→ RAPESEED (Colza, Canola)	High in unsaturated fats and vitamin E. Produced from a number of these different seeds. Used commercially from chocolate to bread making. A rather bland flavour and the only oil produced in the UK.	Chocolate making, frying, baking and desserts.
SAFFLOWER	From India, it comes from a red and orange flower also used as a dye and sometimes called false saffron. The seeds are used to make the oil, giving it an orange/gold colour. High in polyunsaturated fats and also contains linoleic acid and vitamin E.	Frying, dressings, substitute for saffron.
SESAME	Has a high fat content, most is polyunsaturated, with a good source of protein, B vitamins and calcium, potassium and sodium. Highly prized oil, used in Oriental cookery giving it a spicy nutty flavour. There are light and dark oils. Light sesame oil has a light brown colour. It has a high smoking point, which makes it a good frying oil, especially in Oriental cookery. The darker version gets its colour from toasting the sesame seeds. It is not as good for frying as the lighter oil, because of its low burning point.	Salads, Baking, dressings, Oriental cookery, frying. Oriental cookery, Salads and dressings.
SOYA	Not as good a flavour as many of the other oils, but a good all-round cooking oil. Mixes well with other oils in dressings. High in polyunsaturated fatty acids (56 per cent) and vitamin E. Mainly used commercially to make margarines and spreads.	Salads, dressings, frying and baking.
SUNFLOWER	It has a light yellow colour and texture, which is matched by a very bland flavour. This makes it ideal to mix with other oils in dressings, dips, salads and a good all-round cooking oil. High in polyunsaturated fatty acids (63%), with a good source of vitamin E and linoleic acid.	Salads, dressings frying, baking and desserts.

→

Oil	Brief description of flavours and characteristics	Culinary uses
→ WALNUT	A deep rich golden colour with a nutty flavour to match. It is a little expensive, more than virgin olive oil, and goes rancid rather quickly once opened. It is also high in polyunsaturated fatty acids and iodine.	Salad, dressings, frying, confectionery and baking.

savoury flavouring agents

In this chapter it is hoped that the myth that vegetarian food is bland and uninteresting can be dispelled.

The caterer must be able to serve food that looks good but tastes even better. It is the taste of the food that will leave the lasting impression on the customer. This chapter suggests a few flavourings that can be added to the dishes or recipes to help enhance the food, rather than take over the flavours in the dish.

SOYA, MISO AND SOYA SAUCES

The soya bean is the richest legume that is known to the human race, packed with some 35 per cent oil and protein. Soya bean lacks flavour when compared to other beans, but it is only in the last 50 years that it has been take seriously in the West as a valuable food source. Yet it has been evolving for centuries in the Orient, with a whole range of soy products coming from the fermentation of the bean – miso and soy sauce to name just two in this chapter.

Miso

Miso originated in Japan and is made by fermenting cereal grains and soya beans with salt and water for up to two years in wooden kegs. The residue from the surface of the fermentation is removed and used to make tamari, which is then used to make an excellent soya sauce that is gluten free. The miso paste is used in soups, stews and sauces to add flavour. It dissolves quickly in liquid, but it is better to dissolve it first in water, then add a little at a time. Miso is highly concentrated and rich in protein, vitamins and minerals. Excessive heat will destroy vitamins and enzymes in the paste so it should be added towards the end of the cooking process.

There are a number of different types of miso, but recipes will normally state which to use. Miso comes either pasteurised or unpasteurised. Pasteurised miso has a smoother texture, both will be puréed. There are four basic types of miso available:

- Genmai or Kome – made from soy, rice and sea salt, this is rich and light and is best used generally in dishes.
- Hatcho – made from soya and sea salt, this is quite strong in flavour and best used for savoury dishes. It is made with no grains.
- Mugi – made from soya, barley and sea salt, this is strong and rich and like Genmai is suitable for general use in dishes.
- Sweet white – made from soy, yeasted wheat grain and sea salt, this is a lighter colour and flavour and is better suited for sauces with a light flavour and colour.

Soya sauce

Soya sauce is made in more or less the same way as tamari is made from miso, i.e. cooking the beans, fermenting, ageing and pressing. There are many different types, brands, colours and flavours of soy sauce but three are worth serious consideration. The first is Tamari which is gluten free and has a strong taste. It is a by-product of miso. The second is Kecap Manis, which is a thick soy sauce used in Malaysian and Indonesian cookery. It is much sweeter than tamari and shoyu.

The third is a Japanese sauce called Shoshoyu or Shoyu for short. This is much lighter and sweeter than tamari and is naturally brewed with wheat. It is better to add the soy at the end of the cooking process to keep the nutritional value. Soya sauces should be stored in a cool dark place out of sunlight.

Soy marinade

This Japanese marinade, called teriyaki, is a soy-based tamari sauce, with the addition of mirin, sake and sugar. There are a number of variations on these ingredients, such as rice vinegar, plum juice, garlic and honey, for example. It is ideal for marinating tofu and pineapple, among others.

YEAST

Yeast is a rich source of vitamin B and is therefore an important fortifying nutrient. Yeast extracts such as Marmite are often fortified with added vitamins, such as B12. Yeast is also used as a fermenting agent and when added to sugar converts it into alcohol.

STOCKS

A fresh stock correctly made will give a good base for a dish. The main purpose of a stock is to extract as much flavour from the stock ingredients as possible and to use that strained liquid to flavour the dish. It is vitally important in vegetarian cookery that the stock is a vegetable stock and contains absolutely no meat or meat by-products.

Stock should never be boiled rapidly for a long period of time, as this will cloud it. It should always be brought up to a simmer, and any debris skimmed from the surface from time to time. It is possible to freeze stock for up to three months.

CONVENIENCE STOCKS

There are many brands of stocks varying in taste, colour, strength, consistency, ingredients and price. It is very important to check the labels of these products, because they may say vegetable stock, but could still contain meat or animal by-products that are unsuitable such as lactose, whey or casein. It may also contain gluten, making it unsuitable for coeliac's so check before using. A large number of these convenience stocks, *bouillons*, pastes and powders contain high levels of salt. There are a number of very good vegan and vegetarian products that are available from whole food suppliers (see section on useful addresses) and stores.

VINEGARS

Sour wine was originally used in European cooking before being replaced by lemon juice. Vinegars contain around 5 per cent acetic acid.

Variations on the basic vinegars can often be made by adding herbs, spices, fruits and even vegetables and will add character to the dish. To make these you must infuse the added ingredient in the vinegar for three to four days. Vinegar is known as a preservative as well as a flavour enhancer, because of its high acidic properties, for example, pickled onions,

cabbage, gherkins, etc.

Listed below is a selection of vinegars that are readily available:

Balsamic vinegar

One of the best vinegars, this comes from the town of Modena in Northern Italy where it is called *aceto balsamico*. It is dark, with a sweetish yet sour flavour. It is said that the wine vinegar grows in flavour the longer it is aged, which could be as long as 10 to 20 years. There is an increasing number of inferior imitations of this vinegar; if the label does not have the words made in or from Modena it is best not to purchase it.

Wine vinegars

There are many speciality vinegars, not just red and white wine, that are made from differing wines, for example, sherry vinegar, rice wine vinegar, malt vinegar (beer vinegar). Always check the ingredients on the label as not all may be suitable for vegetarians.

Herb and fruit vinegars

These are all easily made from any fruit (the harder fruit are the best) or herbs, or a combination, for example, apple and sage with shallots and peppercorns. The possibilities are endless. Simply choose a vinegar or wine vinegar and add the herbs or fruit and steep for three to four days. Then remove the ingredients by straining them or leave them to infuse more flavour and add as a garnish to the vinegar.

Cider vinegar

This vinegar is more popular in North America than in the UK, but its popularity is increasing. It is made by fermenting apples and has a strong flavour.

Rice vinegar

A mild, sweet and delicately flavoured vinegar from Japan. However, there are more sour and sharper varieties that are used in Chinese cookery.

Other vinegars

Vinegar essence, distilled vinegar and spirit vinegar are all used to preserve vegetables, especially vegetables with a high water content.

special dietary considerations

The information in this chapter is not intended as a substitute for medical advice. While it is believed to be correct, it should not be used to diagnose or treat a health problem or disease. A doctor or health carer should always be consulted to answer any questions or concerns. The publishers and author can take no responsibility for actions taken on the basis of this information or how it is used. Please note that medical information is changing rapidly.

The majority of people can eat any food without thinking or worrying about it but an increasing number will react very badly to a single food or a combination of foods. The effects of these reactions vary from feeling uncomfortable to the possibility, in some severe and rare cases, of death. The types of reaction can be broken down into two categories, food intolerance and food allergy.

- **Food intolerance** is when the consumption of a particular food, for example, eggs, milk, cheese, fish and shellfish, wheat, barley, rye and oats or even additives can bring on a reaction within minutes or a few hours. Intolerances are more common in children, but they are more likely to grow out of them as their body develops. Symptoms are vomiting, diarrhoea, stomach pains, skin rash, itching, tingling of lips or throat, swelling of the mouth, headaches, and the onset of other conditions such as asthma.

- **Food allergy** is when the body's immune system reacts against a particular particle or substance that has been consumed. Some people are allergic to shellfish, milk or some proteins that are contained within wheat. Allergies to peanuts are becoming common in children. Symptoms of allergic reactions to food can be the same as for intolerance, but in some cases can be severe and even result in death.

Customer and caterer responsibility
It is the responsibility of the consumer to make the caterer, chef or management aware that they have a particular dietary requirement. It must also be noted that younger customers may be embarrassed by their requirement and not wish to draw attention to themselves. Putting a sign or a note stating '**This dish may contain…**' is simply not enough. The caterer should know whether the dish contains nuts, milk, shellfish, etc. The customer or guest may or may not take a chance on eating the dish. It is the responsibility of the purveyor of food to label, display and explain clearly to the customer what the food contains. This should not be seen as a chore, but as a good customer service and plus point for the business. A proactive approach is far better than a reactive one. It is also important that the strictest hygiene is observed in the kitchen, when preparing food for anyone suffering from intolerance or an allergy. Special attention should be paid to the possibility of cross contamination.

LACTOSE INTOLERANCE

This intolerance is more common in ethnic groups where milk or dairy products are not traditionally consumed. It is caused by the lack of an enzyme called lactase. This enzyme breaks down the sugar (lactose) in milk. The undigested lactose builds up in the large intestine where it can cause diarrhoea and stomach pains.

Chef's notes
Avoid all milk and dairy products and dishes that include them.

LOW FAT DIET

A person on a low fat diet could be trying to reach their ideal weight or they could have health problems such as heart disease, high cholesterol or high blood pressure. By reducing and eliminating most harmful fats, for example, animal-based saturated fats and replacing them with poly/monounsaturated fats and beneficial fibre-rich whole fruits, vegetables, cereals and grains like brown rice that give protein, beneficial carbohydrates and polyunsaturated oils, their condition should improve.

Chef's notes
When cooking use the healthier cooking processes like steaming, poaching, boiling, stir-fry and microwave rather than deep and shallow frying and use olive oil, sunflower oil and margarines.

HIGH PROTEIN DIET

This type of diet is used only on rare occasions for people with extremely poor appetites, for example, the very elderly and frail. The diet is full of calories and high nutrient dense and people are encouraged to eat in such a way for short periods.

Chef's notes
This sort of diet must be given only under specialist advice and guidance, such as a GP or dietician.

COELIAC DISEASE

Coeliac disease is both a genetic and digestive disorder that affects approximately one in 250 people. Coeliacs are intolerant to gluten, the proteins found in wheat, rye and barley (although oats have traditionally been thought to be toxic to coeliacs, there has been much debate, controversy and research into this area and it is much too early to speculate). This intolerance leads to the destruction or stunting of the villi in the small intestine resulting in the malabsorption of the nutrients, causing a range of symptoms and effects such as bloating of the stomach, weight loss, diarrhoea, osteoporosis, tooth decay, central and peripheral nervous disease, pancreatic disease, internal haemorrhaging, organ disorders, gynaecological disorders and fertility disorders. Then, in addition to these, *dermatitis herpetiformis* can appear, a disease in which a rash can appear on the back, buttocks, knees, elbows and head. Untreated coeliacs can also suffer from temporary lactose intolerance.

The disease is considered to have been underdiagnosed for some 15 to 20 years. It mainly affects people of white European descent, rarely affecting Black or Asian people or communities that do not include wheat in their diet.

This condition is permanent and may present itself at any age. In children it can show with symptoms of diarrhoea and general irritability; as they grow signs of rickets, anaemia and stunted growth may be seen.

What's safe and what is not?

Products that are made from wheat, rye, barley and oats should not be used when cooking or making foods for coeliacs. Some of these products go by other names such as durum, semolina, spelt, kamut, spelta, small spelt, polish wheat, einkorn, corn maize or trital (a cross between rye and wheat).

Safe foods such as chickpeas, lentils, peas, ragi, soy, tapioca, wild rice and rice can all be made into flours and used by coeliacs. Please see Appendix 1 (p.312) for a more detailed list of suitable and unsuitable foods.

Other foods that can be consumed by most coeliacs, although some may find they are sensitive to them, are: millet, buckwheat, quinoa, amaranth, alcohol, grain vinegars and vanilla extracts that may contain alcohol. Alcohols made from grains are not safe but rum, wine, tequila and sake are considered safe.

Chef's notes
Research any product that you purchase to reduce the risk of a reaction. Always read the label and **'if in doubt do without'**. Coeliac UK produces a food and drink directory containing 10,000 gluten-free products. It is important for the strictest hygiene to be observed in the kitchen when preparing food for a coeliac. Cross-contamination by stirring a dish with a spoon that has been used to make a flour-based dish and not washed correctly could cause a reaction – it takes just 0.1 gram, less than $\frac{1}{50}$th of a slice of bread.

ANOREXIA NERVOSA

This is a disorder where a person loses and maintains a much lower weight than is normally expected. A person suffering from this disorder is usually preoccupied with losing weight. Food containing fats are typically avoided and very often the people with anorexia do not believe that they have the disorder and often feel and become frustrated. They can become angry with family and friends who show or express concern.

The disorder of anorexia has been recognised for hundreds of years, but has been on the increase in the last 20 years, especially in the West where thinness is desirable and considered as an attractive attribute. This is one of the reasons why this disorder shows little signs of going away.

Very serious medical problems can often occur and people can die from this disorder. Signs are fainting, chest pains, irregular heartbeat, profound weakness, stomach pains and mental confusion. It is very important that sufferers get regular treatment from a medical practitioner.

BULIMIA NERVOSA

This is a disorder in which people binge-eat considerable amounts of food (while they feel out of control), which they then counteract by self-induced vomiting, use of laxatives or extreme dieting or exercise. This disorder is attributed to people who are dissatisfied with their physical appearance or weight and are very sensitive to changes in their weight. Often the sufferer can be ashamed of their condition and

it can lead to more emotional stress.

This disorder can lead to gastrointestinal problems such as diarrhoea and constipation though irregular eating patterns. By induced vomiting the stomach acids can damage the mouth, teeth and the oesophagus. The induced physical force of vomiting can also cause internal tears and bleeding. This will also expel vital body vitamins, minerals and salts.

The results can be stomach and muscle cramps, heart pain, irregular heartbeats, poor concentration and possible brain seizures. It is very important that sufferers get regular treatment from a medical practitioner.

OBESITY

The term obesity refers to the accumulation of body fat by overeating. The body needs energy for its normal daily body processes, i.e. moving and using muscles and beating of the heart etc. So this will burn off most of the food and drink that is converted into energy.

The body stores any excess food and drink that is not used as energy as fat, resulting in extra weight. If this continues it will lead to being overweight and then into obesity.

The process of measuring body weight is called, the "Body Mass Index Calculator" in short BMI. This is when the weight is measured by the height.

The causes of obesity are wide and varied, for example: genetic, socio-economic, psychological, lack of physical activity, developmental, physical damage or medication and drugs.

Obesity is becoming increasingly common in the West, and has been linked to lifestyle and eating habits. Some one that is considered obese will require the expert advice from a medical practitioner and dietician who will advise on the safest way to lose weight and maintain a balanced diet.

NUT ALLERGY

Nut allergies occur when the body's immune system reacts against a nut substance that has been consumed. Allergies to peanuts are becoming more common in children. Allergic reactions to nuts in some cases can result in severe consequences and even death.

There has been a great deal of publicity surrounding the labelling of products in recent years and it is now recognised that putting a sign out or a note stating 'This dish may contain nuts…' is simply not enough. The caterer should know whether the food offered contain nuts. It is the responsibility of the purveyor of food to label, display and explain clearly what the food contains.

Check with manufacturers for information about nut-free products. Supermarkets will provide or produce a nut-free list if requested. In-store bakeries and bakers' shops may make products without nuts, but there is a risk of cross contamination.

Chef's notes
Always check the labels and **avoid all nuts**, nut pastes, marzipan, frangipane, praline, peanuts that are often called ground nuts, monkey nuts, Chinese nuts, goober, goober peas, ground peas, pindas

and earth nuts. Also avoid nut oils, and vegetable oils unless the composition is nut free.

Please note that although products may be listed as nut-free by the manufacturers and supermarkets, some could contain small traces of nuts within the ingredients, so always double-check the ingredients list.

When cooking for a person with a nut allergy, strict attention must be paid to hygiene to avoid cross contamination.

LOW-CHOLESTEROL DIET

Cholesterol is a fat that is found naturally within the blood, but it is normally supplied from animal fats in food. Cholesterol is found in every cell in the body and is important in a number of functions. The body makes all the cholesterol that is needed, but if it makes too much the levels in our blood increase, clogging up the blood vessels. These fatty particles then stick to the walls of the blood vessels and arteries, making them narrower, thus making it harder for the blood to flow and straining the heart. The blood also becomes thicker. This increases the risk of developing heart disease and conditions such as angina, high blood pressure, heart attacks, strokes and arteriosclerosis. It has been proven that lowering the bad cholesterol in the diet can decrease the risk of angina, strokes and heart attacks.

There are several types of fats in the blood: the 'bad' type or low-density cholesterol (LDL-C), the 'good' type (HDL-C) and triglycerides, which are a buttery type substance. There is a mass of evidence to show that if the cholesterol is high in the bad fats, such as lard, butter, and other animal-based fat products, i.e. saturated fats, there is a much greater risk of damage to the blood vessels.

Changing the diet can lower the bad cholesterol and improve health. Suggestion on how to accomplish this are:

- Eat moderately to maintain a healthy weight.
- Eat less fat (only 30 per cent of total calories).
- Eat less saturated fat (these are mainly animal and dairy fats).
- Eat more high-fibre foods such as fruit, vegetables and whole foods. Increasing the type of fibre such as oat bran, pectin and psyllium may help to lower blood cholesterol, in some cases by 10 per cent.
- Eat small amounts of polyunsaturated fats.
- Do not cook in fats. It is much healthier to poach, steam, boil, grill and microwave food.
- Cut down on sugar or replace it with low calorie sweeteners and sugar free drinks.
- Stop smoking as this causes a slight increase in cholesterol and significantly decreases the good cholesterol, leading to damage of the blood vessels in the heart and legs, doubling the risk of heart attack.

Chef's notes
People suffering from high cholesterol should eat the following foods:

- polyunsaturated fat margarine or low-fat spreads
- oils such as corn, soya, vegetable ghee and sunflower

- skimmed or semi-skimmed milk
- low-fat yoghurts
- pulses, beans, peas, pasta and lentils
- low-fat cheese such as cottage cheese
- fresh fruits and vegetables and salad foods
- eggs (reduce to three to five a week)
- wholemeal bread and flour, high-fibre cereals and rice to help increase fibre intake.

A medical practitioner or dietician will advise the sufferer on the safest way to reduce cholesterol and maintain a balanced diet. If possible, always speak to the sufferer and discuss their requirements in detail.

DIABETES

A person with diabetes (*Diabetes mellitus*) is unable to process the carbohydrate that they have eaten properly. Most of what we eat is digested and turned into glucose, which is the sugar found in blood. The glucose is carried around the body by blood to the organs and then transferred to individual cells and used as energy. The majority of the body's organs need the hormone insulin to get the glucose into the individual cells. With diabetes the insulin is either not present, not enough is present or it is ineffective. This can result in a build-up of glucose in the bloodstream, called hyperglycaemia and can result in short-term effects, for example, blurred vision, weakness, thirst, constant urination, inability to concentrate, loss of coordination and possible loss of consciousness.

The complications of diabetes are far-reaching with the possibilities of increased risk of strokes, heart attack, vision problems and foot ulcers, infections, gangrene and trauma. The number of people being diagnosed with this condition is on the increase and it is expected to double at least over the next ten years.

There are two types of diabetes. The first, type 1, is Insulin Dependent Diabetes, and although diet and exercise can help, there is no cure. Type 2 is Non-Insulin Dependent Diabetes. Obesity is considered to be the main risk for this type of diabetes, but there is a small percentage of sufferers who may use insulin. Typically people suffering from type 2 produce sufficient or excess insulin, but the cells are resistant to the insulin. In many cases losing weight may help to get blood glucose levels down to normal levels.

The diabetic diet is based on three areas:

1. *Lowering saturated fat by eating a low-fat diet.* Food that is high in fat is also high in calories and this has a major effect on obesity. High-saturated fatty diets are often associated with the condition arteriosclerosis and should therefore be avoided. Sugar intake should also be reduced at the same time.

2. *Increasing carbohydrate, i.e. starch.* Increasing the intake of starchy foods, for example, breakfast cereals, potatoes, bread, rice and pastas will help to control the blood glucose levels.

3. *Increasing the intake of water-soluble fibre* will help to slowly release the natural sugars into the blood, and the fibre will help to reduce the blood cholesterol levels. However, remember that fibre is found only in plant food. Good source of fibre are pulses, fresh peas, vegetables, fruits oats, bran and barley.

Eat regular meals (3 per day with snacks in between depending on the individual).

Chef's notes
To increase fibre intake and lower fat intake, give high-fibre cereals in place of fried breakfasts, replace white bread with wholemeal bread, cook potatoes in their skins and encourage eating of the skin, replace white flour with wholemeal in baking and serve at least two fresh vegetables and one portion of fruit a day. Also use low-fat alternatives and encourage the diabetic to drink as much fluid as required. Sugar replacements can also be used, but be aware that excessive amounts could have a laxative effect.

It is also important to cut out salt, as this will help to lower the blood pressure and decrease the possibility of complications. It is advisable to check with the person or medical adviser before using a salt alternative.

basic stocks and sauces

Béchamel (white sauce) 1 litre

- 100g Margarine
- 100g Plain white flour
- 1l Soya milk
- 1 Onion studded with cloves and a bay leaf

1 Place the margarine in a thick-bottomed pan and melt over a gentle heat.

2 Add the flour and cook out without any colour for a few minutes, making a roux.

3 Remove from the heat and cool slightly.

4 In a separate pan bring the milk and the studded onion almost to the boil then simmer, infusing the flavour of the onion, for 10 minutes. Strain off the milk through a fine strainer.

5 Gradually add the milk to the roux, stirring until a smooth sauce is achieved. Simmer for 15–20 minutes and pass through a strainer to remove any debris.

6 Cover with greaseproof paper brushed with margarine to prevent a skin forming.

NOTES

There are many different soya milks; it may be necessary to try several. The soya milk may be substituted with other milks if preferred. ❑

Brown Vegetable Stock — 1 litre

- *100g*   *Celery*
- *100g*   *Carrots*
- *100g*   *Leeks*
- *100g*   *Onions*
- *60g*   *Tomatoes*
- *1 clove Garlic*
- *1*   *Bay leaf*
- *50g*   *Mushroom purée*
-   *Parsley stalks and thyme sprigs*
-   *Salt*
- *8*   *Black peppercorns*
- *70ml*   *Vegetable or sunflower oil*
- *10g*   *Miso (do not use barley miso for gluten-free recipes)*
- *1½l*   *Water*

1 Wash, peel and cut the celery, carrot and leeks, then cut onions, tomatoes and garlic into small dice.

2 Place all the ingredients (except water and miso) in a suitable thick-bottomed pan and fry until golden brown.

3 Drain off any excess oil and add the water, bring to the boil and incorporate the miso, then simmer for 1½–2 hours, skimming off any debris that may rise to the surface.

4 Allow to cool, then pour gently through a fine conical strainer lined with a muslin cloth. Discard the vegetables and seasoning.

NOTES

For extra flavour the stock can be reduced by boiling down by three quarters to 200ml, giving a flavoursome Jus. If reduced down further to 50ml it can be used as an essence, adding flavour to salads and other dishes. It must be reduced slowly otherwise it could turn bitter. ❏

Red Pepper Sauce — 4 covers

- *4*   *Red peppers*
- *75g*   *Onions*
- *75g*   *Shallots*
- *50g*   *Leeks*
- *2 cloves Garlic*
- *40g*   *Celery*
- *60ml*   *Olive oil*
- *10g*   *Thyme*
- *1*   *Bay leaf*
- *10g*   *Caster sugar*
- *5ml*   *Worcester sauce*
- *550ml Tomato juice*
-   *Salt and pepper*

1 Wash, skin and deseed the peppers and then peel and cut the onion, shallots, leeks, garlic and celery into small dice.

2 Put the oil in a suitable pan and sauté off all the vegetables for 3–4 minutes.

3 Add the herbs, sugar, Worcester sauce and tomato juice and simmer gently for 10–15 minutes.

4 Liquidise, then pass through a fine sieve. Discard the vegetables.

5 Correct seasoning.

NOTES

This is an excellent sauce and is suitable for vegans. Omit the sugar for low-cholesterol and diabetic diets. ❏

Satay Sauce

- 125ml Boiling water
- 40g Tamarind
- 250g Roasted peanuts
- 2 Lemongrass
- 2.5cm Galangal
- 2.5cm Ginger
- 2 Shallots
- 5–10g Ground chilli powder
- 150g Caster sugar
- Salt

1 Pour the boiling water on to the tamarind and let stand for 15 minutes. Then squeeze out the juice and throw away the pulp.

2 Grind the roasted peanuts in a blender and leave to one side.

3 Cut the lemongrass in half, remove the stalk and dry outer leaves and shred. Peel and cut the galangal and ginger into rough dice then blend into a fine paste.

4 Peel and slice the shallots then stir-fry until soft. Next add the ground chilli, cooking for approximately one minute.

5 Add the galangal, ginger and lemongrass and fry off for two minutes and then add the tamarind water and the peanuts, sugar and salt.

6 Simmer until the sauce thickens.

NOTES

Keep stirring once the peanuts been added to prevent sticking and burning.

This sauce is excellent with compressed rice and tofu. ❑

Sauce Supreme
1litre

- 100g Margarine
- 100g Plain white flour
- ½l Soya milk
- 1 Onion studded with cloves and a bay leaf
- ½l Vegetable stock (white)
- 50g Button mushrooms, puréed
- 120ml Double cream
- 10ml Lemon juice

1 Place the margarine in a thick-bottomed pan and melt over a gentle heat.

2 Add the flour and cook out until a sandy texture has been achieved, making a roux.

3 Remove from the heat and cool slightly.

4 Bring the milk and the studded onion almost to the boil then simmer, infusing the flavour of the onion, for 10 minutes. Strain off the milk through a fine strainer.

5 Gradually add the milk and stock to the roux, stirring until a smooth sauce is achieved.

→

6 Add the mushroom purée and simmer for 45–60 minutes then pass through a strainer to remove any debris.

7 Return the sauce to a gentle heat and add the cream and lemon juice, and seasoning to taste.

8 Cover with greaseproof paper brushed with margarine to prevent a skin forming.

NOTES

The soya milk may be substituted with other milks if preferred.

For a richer sauce, mix two egg yolks with the cream, add a little of the boiling sauce and stir until it is incorporated, then return it to the sauce. Do not re-boil at this stage or the sauce may split.

Many other sauces can be made from this, for example, wild mushroom, vegetable and herb, simply by adding a fine purée. ❑

Spicy tomato sauce   4 covers

- 75g   Margarine
- 40g   Onions
- 10g   Leeks
- 40g   Carrots
- 40g   Celery
- 1   Bay leaf
- 5g   Thyme
- 1 clove Garlic
- 1l   Vegetable stock
- 120g   Plain flour
- 85g   Tomato puree
- 70ml   Passata
- 5–10g Pesto (vegetarian)
- 40g   Sugar
- ▪   Salt and pepper

1 Peel the onions, leeks, celery, garlic and carrots and then cut into 1cm dice.

2 Melt the margarine in a suitable pan, add the vegetables and herbs and fry until golden brown.

3 Simmer the stock slowly until required.

4 Add the flour to the fried vegetables and make a roux, then add the tomato purée, passata and the pesto. Mix in well, then gradually add the stock and mix in.

5 Season with salt, pepper and sugar, simmering gently for 45–60 minutes. Skim any debris from the surface.

6 Pass through a fine strainer, check the seasoning and serve.

NOTES

Use vegan margarine for vegan diets and omit the flour and decrease the stock by one-third, adding an extra 250ml passata for coeliac diets. ❑

Vegetable Stock (white) 1 — 1 litre

- 150g Shallots
- 1 stick Celery
- 1 Carrot, medium
- 1 Baby fennel
- 1 clove Garlic
- 1 Bay leaf
- 1¼l Water
- Parsley stalks, tarragon and chervil sprigs
- Salt and pepper

1 Wash, peel and cut the shallots, celery, carrot, fennel and garlic into small dice.

2 Place all the ingredients in a suitable thick-bottomed pan and bring to the boil, then simmer for one hour, skimming off any debris that may rise to the surface.

3 Allow to cool, then pour gently through a fine conical strainer lined with a muslin cloth. Discard the vegetables and seasoning.

NOTES

This is a good stock for flavouring clear soups and broths. ❏

Vegetable Stock (white) 2 — 1 litre

- 100g Onions
- 100g Celery
- 100g Carrots
- 1 clove Garlic
- 1 Bay leaf
- 1¼l Water
- Parsley stalks and thyme
- Salt and white pepper

1 Wash, peel and cut the onion, celery, carrot, leeks and garlic in to small dice, called mirepoix.

2 Place all the ingredients in a suitable thick-bottomed pan and bring to the boil, then simmer for one hour, skimming off any debris that may rise to the surface.

3 Allow to cool, then pour gently through a fine conical strainer lined with a muslin cloth. Discard the vegetables and seasoning. ❏

Vegetarian Gravy — 4 covers

- 100g Onions
- 100g Celery
- 1 large sprig Thyme
- 1 small sprig Rosemary
- 50g Margarine
- 1 Bay leaf

1 Peel and finely dice the onions and celery. Crush the thyme and rosemary to help release more flavour.

2 Melt the margarine in a suitable thick-bottomed pan, then sweat off the onions and celery until golden brown. Add the herbs and the red wine and reduce by half.

→

➜

- *50ml* *Red wine (vegetarian)*
- *5g* *Grain mustard*
- *650ml* *Vegetable stock*
- *10g* *Miso (soya bean)*
- *30g* *Tapioca or rice flour*
- *Salt and black pepper*

3 Stir in the mustard and then the stock, bring to the boil and simmer, skimming any debris from the surface. Add miso. Cook for 15 minutes.

4 Mix a little cold water with the flour and slowly add this to the gravy until it begins to thicken.

5 Simmer for a further 5 minutes and adjust the seasoning as required.

6 Pass through a strainer and serve.

NOTES

Suitable for vegan, diabetic, coeliac and low-cholesterol diets.

If more flavour is needed add a little tamari or shoyu. ❑

Velouté   1 litre

- *100g* *Margarine*
- *100g* *Plain white flour*
- *1l* *Vegetable stock (white)*

1 Place the margarine in a thick-bottomed pan and melt over a gentle heat.

2 Add the flour and cook out until a light sandy texture has been achieved, making a roux.

3 Remove from the heat and cool slightly.

4 Bring the stock almost to the boil and simmer.

5 Gradually add the stock to the roux, stirring until a smooth sauce is achieved. Simmer for 45–60 minutes then pass through a strainer to remove any debris.

6 Cover with greaseproof paper brushed with margarine to prevent a skin forming.

NOTES

There are many different stocks, flavoured with herbs and spices, that can make a difference to the dish. ❑

A Summer Salad with a Crunch   4 covers

- 60g   EBLY®
- 5g   Garam masala

Salad
- 400g   Mixed salad leaves
- ½ bunch Watercress (less stalks)
- 200g   Fresh baby spinach (optional)
- 4   Hard-boiled eggs
- 6   Spring onions
- 15g   Fresh chives, chopped into 1cm lengths
- 15g   Fresh dill

Dressing
- 25ml   Olive oil
- 5–10ml Red wine vinegar
- 2–3g   Garlic purée
         Salt and pepper

1 Cook the EBLY® in simmering salted water for 12 minutes, refresh under cold water and drain on a paper towel.

2 Deep-fry the cooked EBLY® (180°C) for approximately 3–4 minutes, until it begins to crisp. Remove and drain on kitchen paper, and ensure that all the grains are separate.

3 Coat with garam masala and salt, then put on one side.

4 Carefully tear the salad leaves into small pieces, add the watercress and spinach and mix carefully.

5 Cut the boiled eggs into quarters.

6 Add the spring onions and herbs to the leaves, season with a little salt.

7 To make the dressing, mix all the ingredients together, lightly season the dressing, pour over the salad, and mix the dressing in gently. Put the egg on the salad and sprinkle with the fried EBLY®. ❑

Aramé pancakes 4 covers

- 80g Aramé (soaked)
- 60ml Vegetable oil

Batter
- 100g Plain flour
- 125ml Milk
- 1 Free-range egg
- 125g Water
- Nutmeg
- Salt and pepper

1 Sift the flour, nutmeg, salt and pepper into a suitable bowl and whisk in the milk, egg and water until fully incorporated.

2 Squeeze out the excess water from the aramé, chop and add to the pancake batter.

3 Heat an 18–20cm pan, add a touch of oil, then add the batter and tilt the pan until the batter has covered the base of the pan evenly.

4 Return the pan to the heat and cook the batter until it looks dry and the underneath looks golden brown.

5 Loosen the edge of the pancake and flip over with a pallet knife, then cook for 20–35 seconds.

6 Turn the pancake out onto a greaseproof or silicon paper; fill with the aramé, fold in half and serve when required.

NOTES

This recipe can be used with wakame and hijiki in replace of aramé.

The pancakes can be used with a spicy vegetable salsa, a bean filling or a broccoli and cheese filling.

Broccoli filling
- 30g Margarine
- 100g Sliced onion
- 150g Cooked chopped broccoli
- 250ml Béchamel
- 75g Low-fat vegan Cheddar cheese

1 Heat the margarine in a saucepan, sweat off the onion until transparent, then add the broccoli and béchamel and stir in until all the vegetables are covered.

2 Season and grate half the cheese into the sauce. Spoon evenly into the pancakes, grate the remaining cheese on top of the pancakes and grill for 1–2 minutes until the cheese has melted and is golden brown.

3 Serve and garnish with fresh crisp salad. ❏

Basil Scented Millet Salad 4 covers

- 225g Millet
- 550ml Water

1 Put the millet in a large frying pan and dry roast, stirring until it turns golden.

→

→

- 3 Shallots
- 1½ cloves Garlic
- ½ Lime (juice only)
- 40ml Balsamic vinegar
- 30ml Virgin olive oil
- 100g Cucumber
- 100g Vine cherry tomatoes
- 3 sprigs Basil
- Coarse ground sea salt
- Ground white pepper

2 Now add the water, bring to the boil and simmer for 20 minutes until water has been absorbed.

3 Peel and slice the shallots. Then chop the basil and keep to one side.

4 Peel and purée the garlic and place in a suitable bowl and add the lime juice, vinegar, olive oil, salt and pepper. Mix well with a fork.

5 Wash and dice the cucumber and cut the tomatoes into quarters, then grind some salt over both and leave for 8–10 minutes. Drain off any water.

6 Add the tomatoes, shallots, cucumber and half of the basil to the marinade and add the warmed cooked millet. Mix gently.

7 Garnish the salad with the remaining chopped basil and serve. ❑

Bean salad 4 covers

- 200g Onion
- 2 Celery stalks
- 4 Spring onions
- 40g Cauliflower florets
- 1 Green pepper
- 1 Red pepper
- 20g Parsley, freshly chopped
- 2 cloves Garlic
- 100g Red kidney beans (cooked)
- 100g Cannellini beans (cooked)

Dressing
- 2.5g Salt
- 5g Demerara sugar
- 20ml Malt vinegar
- 60ml Water

1 Peel and thinly slice the onions and the celery. Peel back the outer leaves of the spring onions, top and tail and very finely dice.

2 Skin, deseed and thinly slice the peppers. Peel and purée the garlic.

3 Drain the beans in a colander then put in a suitable saucepan with cold water and bring to the boil for 10 minutes. Skim off any debris that comes to the surface.

4 Simmer the beans for 1½ hours until tender. Drain, refresh under cold running water and allow to cool.

5 Mix all the vegetables and the beans together.

6 To make the dressing, place the salt, sugar, vinegar and water in a suitable pan, bring to the boil then remove from heat and allow to cool.

7 Pour the dressing over the bean and vegetable mixture, stir well to coat all ingredients, garnish with a sprinkling of chopped parsley and serve. ❑

Black Olive and Chilli Salad

- 4 — Plum tomatoes
- 1 — Red onion
- 10 — Sorrel leaves
- 250g — Seedless black olives
- 150g — Watercress
- 1 bunch Rocket
- 40g — Red chillies (can use bottled chillies)
- 5g — Grain mustard
- — Coriander

Dressing
- 20ml — Olive oil
- 10ml — Lemon juice
- 5g — Sugar
- 2 sprigs Rosemary
- 5g — Cumin seeds
- 1 clove Garlic

1. Wash the tomatoes and then cut into wedges. Peel and slice the onion. Wash and shred the sorrel leaves and then cut the black olives lengthways.

2. Wash and pick the watercress and rocket leaves.

3. Top and tail the chillies, then de-seed and very finely slice into strips. Peel and purée the garlic. Wash the rosemary and finely chop the leaves.

4. In a bowl mix the oil, lemon juice, sugar, cumin seeds, garlic and rosemary and whisk until well incorporated.

5. Place the tomatoes, onion, sorrel, olives, watercress, rocket, chillies and grain mustard in a bowl. Mix well, then drizzle with the dressing; top with coriander. ❏

Bow Pasta Salad with Hazel and Pine Nuts
4 covers

- 4 — Spring onions
- 30g — Hazelnuts
- 20g — Pine nuts, crushed
- 55g — Red chard (baby red spinach)
- 110g — Pasta bows
- 40ml — Virgin olive oil
- 10ml — Cider vinegar
- 10g — Chives, chopped
- — Salt and freshly ground black pepper

1. Peel and slice the spring onions, roughly chop the hazelnuts and wash and shred the spinach. Chop the chives into 2cm lengths.

2. Cook the pasta in boiling salted water with a dash of oil. Refresh under cold running water, drain and reserve.

3. Mix the oil, vinegar and seasoning and whisk well.

4. Place the pasta, spinach, spring onions, nuts and dressing in a suitable bowl and gently mix together.

5. Serve garnished with chopped chives. ❏

- *300g   Shallots*
- *½   Yellow pepper*
- *½   Green pepper*
- *150g   Carrots*
- *150g   Parsnips*
- *8 cloves Garlic*
- *1   Baby aubergine*
- *150g   Courgettes*
- *300g   Vine cherry tomatoes*
- *142g   Bulgar wheat*
- *1   Lemon (juice only)*
- *Salt and ground black pepper*

1 Peel the shallots, peppers, carrots and parsnips and cut into large dice. Peel the garlic and leave whole. Wash and cut the aubergines and courgettes into large dice. Wash, de-stalk and cut tomatoes in half.

2 Place all vegetables on a pre-heated griddle brushed with oil. Turn vegetables on all sides and remove when cooked. Keep warm.

3 Place the olive oil, herbs, salt and pepper and lemon juice in a bowl and whisk to make the dressing.

4 To cook the bulgar wheat, pour boiling stock over the wheat and cover with a lid, and let it stand off the heat for 15–20 minutes to absorb the stock.

→

❑ Bulgar Wheat and Griddled Vegetable Salad ❑

Dressing
- *100ml Olive oil*
- *5 leaves Fresh basil*
- *5g   Fresh marjoram*

→ 5 Drain any liquid not absorbed from the wheat and add the cooked vegetables and a little of the dressing to taste. Serve with fresh crisp lettuce.

NOTES

This is an excellent dish for vegetarians. Be careful with the dressing, it is quite sharp. ❏

Bulgar Wheat and Tomato Salad   4 covers

- *200g   Bulgar wheat*
- *360ml Vegetable stock*
- *60ml   Olive oil*
- *1   Lemon (zest and juice)*
- *5 sprigs Mint*
- *5 sprigs Parsley*
- *3 cloves Garlic*
- *450g   Tomatoes*
- *½   Cucumber*
- *   Salt and ground black pepper*

1 Wash and chop the parsley and the mint separately. Remove the zest from the lemon, blanch and refresh it, then cut into a very fine dice. Extract the lemon juice and reserve until required.

2 Peel and chop the garlic. Blanch, refresh, skin and then deseed the tomato and cut into concasse (small dice).

3 Wash the cucumbers and cut into dice the same size as the concasse.

4 Bring the stock to the boil, then place the wheat and salt in the same pan, cover with a lid and leave to stand off the heat for 15 minutes.

5 Put the olive oil, lemon juice, zest, mint, parsley and garlic into a suitable bowl and whisk until incorporated.

6 Add this mixture to the wheat and leave for 3–4 hours if possible.

7 When the salad is cold add the tomatoes and cucumber.

8 Check the seasoning.

NOTES

This dish is suitable for vegan, low-cholesterol and diabetic diets.

It can be used as a base for other salads, by adding nuts, herbs, spices, marinated diced tofu, for example. ❏

- *100g   Onions*
- *450g   Carrots*
- *25ml   Walnut oil*
- *900ml White stock*
- *10g   Fresh oregano*
- *1   Orange (zest and juice)*
- *55g   Brazil nuts*
-         *Salt and white pepper*

1 Peel and slice the onions and carrots. Chop the nuts.

2 Zest the orange and extract the juice. Roughly chop the oregano.

3 Sweat off the onions and carrots in the oil without any colour.

4 Add the stock, seasoning and half the oregano and bring to the boil. Simmer for 40 minutes.

5 Pour the ingredients into a food processor with the zest and orange juice. Liquidise and pass through a sieve.

6 Bring back to a simmer, check the seasoning and serve garnished with the remaining chopped oregano. Garnish with chopped nuts. ❑

❑ Top left: Enoki and Watercress Broth   Top right: Carrot, Orange and Nut Soup
Bottom: Nettle Soup ❑

Cashew Nut and Carrot Salad
4 covers

- *100g*   *Banana shallots*
- *100g*   *Carrots*
- *1 clove Garlic*
- *2 stalks Celery*
- *100g*   *White cabbage*
- *5g*   *Sesame seeds*
- *40ml*   *Sesame oil*
- *75g*   *Cashew nuts*
- *5g*   *Poppy seeds*
- *25ml*   *Cider vinegar*
- *10g*   *Fresh parsley,*
  chopped
-    *Salt and ground*
  black pepper

1 Peel the carrots, shallots and garlic and cut into fine julienne (fine strips).

2 Wash and remove the stalks from the cabbage and then cut into julienne. Toast the nuts under the grill until golden brown.

3 Mix all the vegetables and sesame seeds together in a suitable bowl and season.

4 Pour the sesame oil into a suitable pan and place over a medium heat. Add the poppy seeds and a lid. Allow the seeds to pop, remove the pan from the heat and allow to cool down.

5 Add the vinegar to the oil and seeds, then add to the vegetable mixture and toss, ensuring an even covering. Add cashew nuts.

6 Serve in a suitable dish or bowl, garnished with sprigs of herbs and chopped parsley.

NOTES

This recipe is suitable for vegan, diabetic, gluten-free and low-cholesterol diets. ❑

Chilli Bean and Mushroom Soup
4 covers

- *30ml*   *Vegetable oil*
- *400g*   *Red kidney beans,*
  tinned
- *150g*   *Whole baby*
  corncobs
- *50g*   *Spring onions*
- *50g*   *Shallots*
- *50g*   *Carrots*
- *2*   *Red bird's eye*
  chillies

1 Wash and drain the kidney beans. Clean the mushrooms, chilli and baby corncobs and cut into slices.

2 Peel the carrots, spring onion and shallots and cut into 1cm dice.

3 Fry the shallots, garlic and carrots in the oil for 2–3 minutes then add the mushrooms and cook for a further 3 minutes.

4 Pour in the tomatoes, baby corn and kidney beans, cooking out for 8–10 minutes.

→

- 400g Chopped Italian plum tomatoes, tinned
- 500ml Vegetable stock
- 230g Button mushrooms
- 10g Garlic purée
- 10g Marjoram
- Salt and pepper

➜ 5 Add the chillies and the marjoram and seasoning. Bring to the boil, skimming any debris from the surface.

NOTES

Suitable for vegan, diabetic and low-cholesterol diets, although a little palm sugar may be needed to be added to sweeten the tomatoes, depending on their quality and acidity. ❏

Ciabatta and Goat's Cheese   4 covers

- 5g Pesto (vegetarian)
- 30ml Olive oil
- 100g Red onion
- 1 Red pepper
- 115g Button mushrooms
- 1 Ciabatta bread
- 150g Goat's cheese (vegetarian)
- 8 leaves Fresh basil
- Salt and freshly ground black pepper

1 Skin and deseed the pepper and cut into 1cm strips. Peel the onion and cut into 1cm strips.

2 Slice the bread diagonally into four large slices or eight smaller slices. Thinly slice the goat's cheese and reserve.

3 Mix the pesto, olive oil and seasoning together in a bowl. Then brush each side of the bread with the pesto oil, allowing it to sink into the bread.

4 Put the onion, pepper and mushrooms into the pesto mixture and coat well.

5 Place the vegetables on a preheated griddle or under the grill and cook until golden brown on each side.

6 Toast the bread until golden brown on each side, then put the goat's cheese on top of the bread and return to the heat to glaze the cheese.

7 Serve with the griddled vegetables and garnished with basil leaves. ❏

❏ Top: Warm Mixed Salad with Toasted Sunflower Seeds and Orange
Bottom: Ciabatta and Goat's Cheese ❏

Coffee, Hazelnut and Rice Salad 4 covers

- ■ 340g Cooked rice (long grain)
- ■ 56g Coffee essence
- ■ 70g Sultanas
- ■ 56g Whole hazelnuts
- ■ Salt and ground white pepper

1 Wash the sultanas and soak in warm water for 20 minutes.

2 Mix the well-drained cooked rice with the coffee essence and salt and pepper.

3 Drain the sultanas and mix with the rice, adding the hazelnuts.

4 Serve in a salad bowl. ❑

EBLY® and Wild Rice Salad 4 covers

- ■ 100g EBLY®
- ■ 150g Wild rice
- ■ 50g Margarine
- ■ 120g Red onion
- ■ 10g Garlic purée
- ■ 100g Green pepper
- ■ 100g Yellow pepper
- ■ 100g Chickpeas, tinned
- ■ 50g Sultanas
- ■ 25g Sunflower seeds, toasted
- ■ 4 Spring onions
- ■ 100g Russet apple
- ■ 20g Fresh parsley, chopped
- ■ Salt

Dressing
- ■ 80ml Sunflower oil
- ■ 20ml Extra virgin olive oil
- ■ 30ml White wine vinegar
- ■ 15ml Balsamic vinegar
- ■ 5g Lemon balm, chopped

1 Cook the EBLY® in plenty of boiling salted water for 15–20 minutes depending on the consistency required. Drain and leave to one side.

2 Skin and deseed the peppers and cut into 5mm dice. Peel and dice the onion, shred the spring onions. Wash and soak the sultanas, de-core the apples and cut into 5mm dice. Wash and drain the chickpeas.

3 Place the wild rice in a suitable saucepan, cover with water and simmer for 25 minutes or until cooked. Drain, season and cool.

4 Heat the margarine in a pan and add the onion, garlic, peppers and the chickpeas. Stir and cook for 2 minutes.

5 Add the sultanas, toasted sunflower seeds, wild rice and the EBLY® to the pan. Combine all the ingredients for the dressing and put in the pan with the spring onions and apple.

6 Season and serve immediately garnished with chopped parsley. ❑

EBLY® Vegetable Broth 4 covers

- 200g EBLY®
- 70g Margarine
- 50g Onions
- 50g Leeks
- 50g Celery
- 50g Carrots
- 1075ml Vegetable stock
- Bouquet garni
- 50g French beans
- 50g Savoy cabbage
- 20g Fresh parsley, chopped
- 20g Fresh tarragon, chopped
- Salt and pepper

1 Cook EBLY® in plenty of boiling salted water for 15–20 minutes depending on the consistency required. Drain and leave to one side.

2 Peel the onions, leeks and carrots and cut into 1cm dice. Wash and shred the cabbage into 2.5 cm lengths. Peel the celery and slice into half moon shapes. Top and tail the beans and cut into 1 cm lengths.

3 Melt the margarine in a saucepan and add the onions, leeks, celery and carrot rounds. Cook slowly with a lid on until tender (do not colour).

4 Add hot stock to the bouquet garni, add a little seasoning and simmer for approximately 15 minutes.

5 Meanwhile blanch and refresh the green beans.

6 After 15 minutes add the washed cabbage, EBLY® and green beans to the stock, simmer for 5 minutes, remove the bouquet garni, add the parsley and tarragon, correct the seasoning and serve. ❏

Egg-free Scrambled Egg 4 covers

- 452g Fresh and firm tofu
- 20ml Vegetable oil
- 50g Shallots
- 1 Red pepper
- 80g Button mushrooms
- 5ml Turmeric
- 10g Fresh parsley
- 5ml Shoyu soya sauce
- 10ml Ground white pepper

1 Peel and dice the shallots, skin, deseed and dice the peppers and slice the mushrooms. Reserve four sprigs of parsley and chop the rest.

2 Remove the tofu from the water and drain, then whisk it gently until it resembles scrambled egg.

3 Sauté the vegetables in the vegetable oil until soft, then add the turmeric and fry for a further one-minute. Add the chopped parsley.

4 Add the whisked tofu, season with shoyu and pepper to taste. Garnish with sprigs of parsley.

NOTES

This is a good substitute for vegan and coeliacs, but use tamari soya sauce for a gluten-free diet. ❏

Enoki and Watercress Broth (p.120) 4 covers

600ml	Clear vegetable stock
■ 250g	Enoki mushrooms
■ 1 clove	Garlic
■ 1	Banana shallot
■ 320g	Watercress
■ 120g	Basmati rice, cooked
■ 5g	Fresh chives, chopped
■	Salt and ground white pepper

1 Wash and trim the watercress. Peel and thinly slice the garlic and the shallots. Clean and cut the mushrooms into edible sizes and discard the lower stalk.

2 Bring the stock to a simmer and add the mushrooms, garlic, shallots and watercress and simmer for 3–4 minutes.

3 Skim the surface for debris, then add the rice and chives. Simmer for 1–2 minutes then season, stir and serve.

NOTES

Suitable for vegan, diabetic and low-cholesterol diets. ❏

Falafel with a Mint and Chilli Sauce 4 covers

■ 300g	Chickpeas, tinned
■ 100g	Shallot
■ 20g	Parsley, fresh
■ 20g	Mint, fresh
■ 30g	Garlic purée
■ 15g	Ground coriander
■ 15g	Ground cumin
■ 1	Medium size free-range egg
■ ½	Lemon (juice and zest)
■ 50g	Cornflour

1 Peel and finely chop the shallot. Peel and purée the garlic.

2 Wash and roughly chop the mint and parsley.

3 Drain the chickpeas and place in a grinder. Purée until very fine. Add the parsley, mint, garlic, spices and a beaten egg. Add onions.

4 Mix well and season to taste with lemon zest and juice, salt and pepper.

5 Check the consistency and then roll and shape into balls about 20–30mm, Coat in the cornflour.

6 Heat the oil in a suitable frying pan and fry until golden brown, drain on kitchen paper.

Sauce

■ 200ml	Natural yoghurt
■ 15g	Mint (fresh)
■ ½	Lemon (juice and zest)
■ 5g	Chilli powder
	Salt and black pepper

1 Mix together the natural yoghurt, finely chopped fresh mint, lemon juice and salt and black pepper. Garnish with a little chopped mint and lemon zest.

→

→ | NOTES

For a vegan diet, omit the egg and use gram flour (35g) and water (60ml) and seasoning. Also replace the yoghurt with soy yoghurt in the sauce.

Falafels are an excellent snack or starter; they keep will in the freezer.

If the falafel mix is too wet add a little flour or breadcrumbs. ❑

Garlic Croûtons with a Garden Salad (p.128)   4 covers

- *110ml* *Extra virgin olive oil*
- *10g* *Garlic purée*
- *4 slices* *Thick bread*
- *½* *Small cos lettuce*
- *30g* *Rocket lettuce*
- *20g* *Flat parsley*
- *10g* *Coriander*
- *½* *Small curly endive lettuce*
- *½* *Small oak leaf lettuce*
- *8* *Nasturtium flowers and leaves*
- *8* *Pansies*
- *8* *Marigolds*
- *10g* *Sesame seeds, toasted*
- *Sea salt and fresh ground black pepper*

Dressing
- *50ml* *Olive oil*
- *20ml* *Cider or white wine vinegar*
- *20ml* *Hazelnut oil*
- *200g* *Puréed sorrel*
- *Salt and pepper*

1 Cut the bread into 2cm dice. Heat a suitable pan and put the olive oil in the pan with the garlic and the bread cubes. Toss until golden brown, drain on kitchen paper and reserve.

2 Wash, drain and break the lettuce into suitable sizes, put them in a salad bowl and reserve in a fridge.

3 Combine all the dressing ingredients until emulsified, then check the seasoning.

4 Place the salad, warm garlic cubes, dressing and flowers in a bowl together and toss them gently.

5 Divide equally into four portions, garnish with toasted sesame seeds and serve. ❑

❑ Top: Garlic Croûtons with a Garden Salad
Bottom: Genoa Garden Salad ❑

Garlic, Pasta and Mushroom Salad

4 covers

- 250g   Conchiglie shells
- 150g   Button mushrooms
- 100g   Red onions
- 150g   Celery
- 50g   Artichoke bottoms
- 2   Beef tomatoes
- 170g   Red pepper
- 15   Tarragon leaves

Dressing

- 50ml   White wine vinegar
- 50ml   Olive oil
- 100g   Vegetable oil (or sunflower oil)
- 5g   Dijon mustard
- 10g   Black peppers, pitted
-         Salt and pepper

1 Cook the pasta in boiling salt water with a little oil for approximately 15–20 minutes until 'al dente', then refresh under cold running water, drain and reserve.

2 Clean and slice the mushrooms. Peel the onion and celery and cut into 2cm dice. Clean the artichoke bottoms and cut into quarters.

3 Skin and deseed the tomatoes and peppers, then into 2–3cm dice. Cut the tarragon into large rough pieces.

4 Place all the dressing ingredients into a blender or food processor and process until they make a thick creamy dressing. This would be best done on pulse speed. Do not over blend.

5 Place all the ingredients into a suitable bowl, mix well and fold in the dressing. Check the seasoning and serve. ❑

Genoa Garden Salad

4 covers

- 200g   Purple broccoli
- 150g   Cucumber or courgettes
- 100g   Shallots
- 1   Red pepper, large
- 250g   Button mushrooms
- 150g   Vine cherry tomatoes

Dressing

- 50ml   White wine vinegar
- 50ml   Olive oil
- 100g   Vegetable oil (or sunflower oil)
- 2.5g   Dijon mustard

1 Wash the broccoli and cut into florets, then peel and cut the shallots and pepper, cucumbers and courgettes into large dice. Clean the mushrooms and cut into quarters and cut the tomatoes in half.

2 Place all the dressing ingredients into a blender or food processor and process until they make a thick creamy dressing. This would be best done on pulse speed. Do not over blend.

3 Combine all the dry ingredients in a suitable container and pour over and fold in the dressing.

4 Marinate the ingredients for 3–4 hours.

5 Drain a little then serve.

→

→ | NOTES

- *100ml Clear honey*
- *100ml Balsamic vinegar*
- *8 leaves Sweet basil*
- *2 cloves Garlic*
- *Salt and pepper*

Serve with crisp lettuce and ciabatta bread. ❑

Grapefruit and Avocado Salad (p.133)   4 covers

- *65g Rocket leaves*
- *2 Grapefruit*
- *3 Pink grapefruit*
- *2 Avocado*

Dressing
- *5g Caster sugar*
- *5g Dijon mustard*
- *20g Garlic purée*
- *57ml Olive oil*
- *Squeezed juice from the grapefruit*
- *Salt and ground white pepper*

1 Peel the grapefruit and avocado, then separate the grapefruit into segments and cut the avocado in half lengthways. Remove the stone from the avocado and then slice.

2 To make the dressing mix the sugar, mustard and garlic purée together in a suitable bowl.

3 Add the juice and seasoning. Gradually whip the oil into the mixture.

4 Place the rocket on a suitable plate and arrange the fruit and avocado over it. Trickle the dressing over the salad.

NOTES

Suitable for vegan and coeliac diets. ❑

Greek Style Tomato and Feta Salad   4 covers

- *5 Beef tomatoes*
- *500g Feta cheese*
- *1 bunch Spring onions*
- *1 Cos lettuce*
- *18g Sesame seeds*
- *20g Walnuts, roughly chopped*
- *5g Cumin seeds*
- *5g Coriander seeds*

1 Blanch the beef tomatoes then refresh, peel, deseed and cut into 2 cm dice. Drain the cheese and then cut into 2 cm dice.

2 Peel and top and tail the spring onions, then cut into large diamond shapes. Wash and pick over the cos lettuce.

3 Toast the sesame seeds under the grill. In a blender finely chop the walnuts, cumin seeds, coriander seeds and toasted sesame seeds and keep as garnish.

Dressing

- 80ml   Olive oil
- 1 clove Garlic
- 60ml   Lemon juice
- 2   Banana shallots
- 2 sprigs Mint

→

4 To make the dressing peel the garlic and shallots and cut into fine dice. Then whisk the olive oil, garlic and lemon juice in a small bowl. Add the shallots and mint, mixing well.

5 Split the dressing in two: pour one half on the chopped mint and cheese. Pour the other half on the tomatoes, spring onions and shallots and gently stir.

6 Cover both bowls and place in the fridge for 30–40 minutes. Place the lettuce on a suitable dish and cover with the cheese mixture and spread some of the garnish on top. Then place the tomato mixture on top followed by the remaining garnish. ❏

Grilled Polenta with Niçoise Style Salad   4 covers

- 200g   Polenta
- 4 tbsp Parmesan
         (vegetarian)
- 1oz   Butter
- 40ml   Olive Oil
- 2   medium sized
         Free-range eggs
- 120g   Small new potatoes
- 120g   Green beans
- 1   Red onion
- 2-3   Plum tomatoes
- 1tbsp Chives
- 12   Black pitted olives
- 100g   Mixed lettuce
-        Salt and pepper

Dressing

-        Olive oil
- 4tbsp Balsamic vinegar

1 Mix the olive oil and balsamic vinegar together for a dressing, and season.

2 Peel and thinly slice the red onion. Finely chop the chives

3 Line a baking tray with silicone paper.

4 Cook the polenta according to packet instructions, adding a little water if required. Stir in the Parmesan, butter, salt and pepper and pour into the tin and cool.

5 Fry the polenta in hot oil until browned on both sides.

6 Hard boil the eggs, shell and cut into quarters.

7 Wash the potatoes and cook in salted water, then slice into a bowl.

8 Top and tail the beans, cook in boiling salted water, then refresh in iced water.

9 Mix the potatoes, beans, onion, tomato, olive oil and chives in a bowl.

10 Pour the dressing over the vegetables, using just enough to moisten them.

11 Divide the vegetables between plates, arrange the eggs on top and garnish with mixed lettuce. ❏

Haricot and Leek Salad   4 covers

- 180g   Young leeks
- 50g   Kenya beans
- 100g   Haricot beans, cooked
- 60g   Flageolet beans, cooked

Dressing
- 60ml   Sunflower oil
- 20g   Poppy seeds, toasted
- 40ml   Olive oil
- 35ml   Red wine vinegar
- 1.25ml Salt
- 2.5g   Ground coriander
- 2.5g   Ground cumin
- 2 cloves Garlic, crushed
- 20g   Fresh parsley, chopped

1 Peel and slice the leeks and blanch and refresh in cold water. Drain in a colander. Top and tail the Kenya beans, blanch and refresh then cut into 2½cm lengths.

2 Make the dressing by whisking all the ingredients together.

3 Combine the beans and the steamed leeks in a bowl and pour the marinade over.

NOTES

Suitable for vegan, diabetic and coeliac diets. ❑

Mango and Rambutan Lime Salsa   4 covers

- 250g   Yellow mango (must be ripe)
- 100g   Rambutan
- 85g   Banana shallots
- 20g   Red chilli
- 1   Lime
- 10g   Fresh coriander, chopped

1 Peel the mango, rambutan and shallots. Dice the mango, cut the rambutan in half and slice the shallots into rings.

2 Deseed and very finely slice the chilli.

3 Zest the lime and extract the juice. Blanch and refresh the zest.

4 Combine all the ingredients and chill for 45 minutes before serving.

NOTES

This recipe is suitable for vegan, low-cholesterol, diabetic, coeliac and nut-free diets. ❑

❏ Top: Mango and Rambutan Lime Salsa   Bottom: Grapefruit and Avocado Salad ❏

- *200g   EBLY®*
- *8–10   Sundried tomatoes*
- *2   Red peppers*
- *2   Green peppers*
- *2   Lemons (juice of)*
- *120ml Olive oil*
- *12–16 Black olives*
- *10g   Fresh parsley, chopped*
- *10g   Chives, chopped*
- *8 leaves Mint, chopped*

1 Cook the EBLY® in plenty of boiling salted water for 15–20 minutes depending on the consistency required. Drain and leave to one side.

2 Cut the sundried tomatoes, red and green peppers into cubes.

3 Squeeze the lemons and mix the juice with the olive oil.

4 Mix all the ingredients together and serve cold.

NOTES

For extra flavour, braise the EBLY® in vegetable stock. ❏

❏ Mediterranean EBLY® Salad ❏

- *30g*   *Stuffed olives*
- *100g*   *Red vine cherry tomatoes*
- *100g*   *Yellow vine cherry tomatoes*
- *10g*   *Pine kernels*
- *200g*   *Cucumber*
- *400g*   *Button mushrooms*
- *150g*   *Red onions*
- *4 sprigs Purple basil (holy basil)*
- *130g*   *Pesto (vegetarian)*
- *40ml*   *Red wine vinegar*
- *250g*   *Fresh crisp mixed lettuce*

1 Cut the olives and tomatoes in half. Dry roast the pine kernels in a pan until golden brown.

2 Wash, peel and dice the cucumber. Clean and quarter the mushrooms. Peel and slice the onions.

3 Mix together the pesto, vinegar and seasoning and pour into a bowl.

4 Add all of the other ingredients except the basil and mix well. Leave to marinate for 15–20 minutes.

5 Serve with crisp lettuce and flowers, garnished with basil sprigs.

→

❏ Mediterranean Mushroom Salad ❏

→ NOTES

- *Edible nasturtium, pansy and marigold flowers*
- *Salt and freshly ground black pepper*

Suitable for vegan, diabetic and low-cholesterol diets. ❑

Mexican-style Stuffed Mushrooms 4 covers

- *1*   Red pepper
- *120g*   Spring onions
- *4*   Field mushrooms, medium
- *300g*   Button mushrooms
- *40ml*   Vegetable oil
- *2.5g*   Chilli powder
- *1*   Red chilli
- *70g*   Cucumber
- *120g*   Tortilla chips, crushed
- *120g*   Cheddar cheese, grated (vegeterian)
- *120g*   Cherry tomatoes

1 Remove and finely chop the stalks from the field mushrooms and also chop the button mushrooms. Peel and slice the spring onions. Dice the tomatoes and cucumber, then deseed the red pepper and chilli and cut into small dice.

2 Sweat off the peppers, onions, and chopped mushroom in the oil for 2–3 minutes until soft, then add the chilli powder. Cook for a further minute and add the diced chilli.

3 Stir in the cucumber, tortilla chips and half of the tomato and cheese.

4 Oil the bottom of a baking dish and lay the field mushrooms cap side down. Fill each cup with the prepared mixture.

5 Top with the remaining cheese and slices of tomato.

6 Bake in a preheated oven at 180°C/Gas Mark 4 for 10–15 minutes until tender.

NOTES

Serve with a crisp salad. Suitable for diabetic and low-cholesterol diets. ❑

Millet Salad (p.138) 4 covers

- *225g*   Millet
- *550ml*   Light vegetable stock

1 Peel and finely dice the garlic and shallots. Squeeze the juice from the lemon and reserve.

→

→

- 1½ cloves Garlic
- 1   Banana shallot
- ½   Lemon (juice only)
- 40ml   Balsamic vinegar
- 22ml   Olive oil
- 100g   Cherry tomatoes
- 100g   Cucumber
- 6 leaves Basil
-          Salt and white
           pepper

2 Wash and quarter the tomatoes and dice the cucumber. Finely shred the basil leaves.

3 Put the millet in a suitable pan and dry roast, stirring until it turns golden.

4 Add the stock, bring to the boil and simmer for 20 minutes until stock has been absorbed.

5 Put the garlic and shallots in a bowl and add the lemon juice, vinegar, olive oil and salt and pepper, stirring well.

6 Add the tomatoes, cucumber and half of the basil to the marinade and add the cooked millet. Mix gently together.

7 Garnish the salad with the other half of the chopped basil and serve.

NOTES

This is a nice salad that can be used for vegans and people on a variety of diets. It is best served warm. ❑

Miso Soup   4 covers

- 15g   Wakame
- 1200ml Light vegetable
          stock
- 100g   Banana shallots
- 100g   Carrots
- 30g   Miso
-          White ground
           pepper

1 Soak the wakame and cut into julienne (thin slices).

2 Peel the shallots and carrots and cut into a fine brunoise (small dice).

3 Add a little to water to the miso to dilute.

4 Bring the stock up to a simmer, add the vegetables and cook uncovered for 2–3 minutes.

5 Add the wakame and simmer gently for 10 minutes, then add the miso and simmer for a further 3–4 minutes.

6 Skim the surface to remove any debris. Season with pepper.

NOTES

Do not over-boil. Add rice noodles and tofu cubes to make the dish more substantial. ❑

❏ Top: Triple Bean and Fungi Salad   Bottom: Millet Salad ❏

Mushroom and Hazelnut Pâté
4 covers

- 120g   Field mushrooms
- 40g   Margarine
- 5g   Garlic purée
- 10g   Parsley, chopped
- 10g   Marjoram leaves
- 20g   Pine nuts
- 40g   Hazelnuts
- 30ml   Dry sherry (vegetarian)
- 60g   Cream cheese (vegetarian)
-   Salt and black pepper

1 Clean and finely dice the mushrooms and sweat off in the margarine and garlic for 3–4 minutes, then add the herbs and seasoning.

2 Pour the mixture into a food processor, add all other ingredients and process into a smooth paste.

3 Spoon into a suitably lined container or terrine and chill for 1½ hours until it has set.

NOTES

The field mushrooms can be replaced with more flavoursome mushrooms and the nuts can be replaced with other oily nuts. ❑

Mushroom and Wild Rice Soup
4 covers

- 500g   Button mushrooms
- 100g   Onions
- 100g   Spring onion
- 100g   Celery
- 113g   Margarine
- 113g   Plain flour
- 500ml   Vegetable stock
- 100g   Cooked wild rice
- 10g   Thyme leaves
- 10g   Oregano leaves
- 125ml   Double cream (optional)
- 4 sprigs Chervil
-   Salt and ground white pepper

1 Clean the mushrooms and cut into quarters. Peel and dice the celery and onions.

2 Sweat off the vegetables in the margarine with no colour and then add the flour to make a roux. Cook the flour out for 2–3 minutes then add the stock gradually to make a smooth sauce. Bring to the boil and simmer gently.

3 Add the cooked rice, seasoning and herbs. Add the cream if desired and cook for a further 3–4 minutes.

4 Garnish with chervil.

NOTES

Serve with fresh crusty bread. This soup is suitable for vegan and low-cholesterol diets if the cream is omitted. It is also suitable for diabetic diets. ❑

Nettle Soup (p.120)   4 covers

- 450g Nettles, washed and clean
- 1 clove Garlic
- 500g Potatoes
- 150g Onions
- 30ml Olive oil
- 60ml Vegetable stock
- 113g Double cream (optional)
- Salt and ground black pepper

1 Peel and dice the onion, garlic and potatoes. Roughly chop the nettles.

2 Fry off the onions and garlic in the oil for 2–3 minutes over a medium heat. Add the potatoes, cook and stir for a minute

3 Add the stock to the onions, nettles, potatoes and garlic, bring to the boil and simmer for 20 minutes.

4 Once the potatoes are completely cooked remove the pan from the heat and liquidise all the ingredients.

5 Return to the heat and check the seasoning.

6 Stir in the cream and serve.

NOTES

Wear plastic gloves when collecting and washing the nettles. Serve with garlic croûtons.

Suitable for vegan (omit the cream), low-cholesterol, nut allergy, coeliac and diabetic diets. ❏

Noodle and Bean Salad   4 covers

- 228g Egg noodles, cooked
- 45ml Tamari
- 70g   Sultanas and currants
- 40g   Green beans, cooked
- 220g Spring onions
- 40g   Cashew nuts
- 40g   Beansprouts

1 Cut the cooked noodles into 6cm lengths and mix with the tamari.

2 Wash the sultanas and currants in warm water and soak for 20 minutes in fresh warm water.

3 Cut the beans and spring onions into 3–4cm diamonds.

4 Mix the fruit, nuts, beans, beansprouts and noodles together, folding gently to coat all the ingredients evenly with tamari.

5 Dress neatly into a salad bowl, check seasoning and garnish. ❏

Nutty Rice Salad

- 230g Long grained rice, cooked
- 120g Cooked Kenya beans
- 230g Spring onions
- 120g Walnuts, peanuts and almonds
- 50ml Vinaigrette (see below)

Vinaigrette

- 70ml Olive oil
- 50ml Vegetable oil
- 5–10g Dijon mustard
- 30–40ml White wine vinegar
- Salt and pepper

1 Season the cooked rice.

2 Chop the beans and spring onions into 3cm diamonds.

3 Add the nuts and mix together.

4 To make the vinaigrette combine all the ingredients and whisk until it emulsifies.

5 Combine all the ingredients and mix together well.

6 Correct the seasoning and dress neatly into a suitable salad bowl. ❑

Orange and Couscous Salad

- 170g Couscous
- 100g Spring onions
- 1 Green pepper
- 155g Chickpeas, canned
- 30g Sultanas
- 30g Raisins
- 20ml Groundnut oil
- 10g Fresh mint, chopped
- 8 Cherry tomatoes
- 65g Pitted dates
- 2 Oranges
- Salt and fresh ground black pepper
- Crisp salad leaves

1 Wash and cut the tomatoes in half and reserve. Chop the dates into 1cm dice.

2 Deseed the pepper and cut into 1cm dice. Peel and cut into the spring onion 1cm dice.

3 Wash and soak the sultanas and raisins in warm water until required.

4 Put the couscous in a suitable container, cover with boiling water, place a tight lid on top and leave for 12–15 minutes until the grains have absorbed the liquid and are light when stirred with a fork.

5 Lightly sweat the spring onions, pepper, chickpeas, sultanas and raisins off in the oil with no colour then add the couscous. Season and add the chopped mint, keeping four sprigs back for garnish.

→

Dressing

- *170ml Natural yoghurt*
- *15ml   Orange juice*
- *2.5g   Ground coriander*
- *15g   Fresh mint, chopped*
- *15g   Orange rind, finely grated*

→

6 To make the dressing, combine all the ingredients and mix well. Add tomatoes.

7 For the garnish remove the skin and white pith from the oranges and separate into segments.

8 Serve the couscous on suitable dishes or plates and garnish with the dressing, orange segments, mint and salad leaves. ❑

Orange and Mango Salad 4 covers

- *4   Oranges*
- *2   Mangoes, ripe*
- *4   Belgian endive*
- *50g   Rocket leaves*
- *20g   Peanuts, finely chopped*

Dressing

- *20ml Dijon mustard*
- *5g   Caster sugar*
- *4 cloves Garlic*
- *20g   Chives, chopped*
- *20g   Orange zest*
- *20g   Lime juice and zest*
- *   Olive oil*
- *   Salt and black pepper*

1 Peel and cut the oranges into segments, then cut the orange and lime peel into a fine zest, blanch and refresh under cold running water.

2 Peel, remove the stone and slice the mangoes.

3 Wash and slice the endive and place in acidulated water to prevent discolouring.

4 To make the dressing mix the mustard, sugar, garlic and chives together in a suitable bowl. Stir in the blanched orange zest, orange juices and lime juice and zest and gradually whisk in the oil. Season to taste with salt and freshly ground black pepper.

5 Arrange the oranges, mangoes and rocket on a plate. Pour over the dressing, sprinkle with the nuts and chives and serve immediately. ❑

Orange, Pink Grapefruit and Fennel Salad   4 covers

- *1   Large orange*
- *1   Pink grapefruit*
- *1 head Baby fennel*
- *340g Mixed lettuce (rocket, oak leaf, radicchio)*
- *4   Chive flowers*

1 Zest the orange and then remove the peel and segments from both the orange and the grapefruit.

2 Wash and finely dice the baby fennel. Wash and break the lettuce into bite-sized pieces.

3 Combine all the dressing ingredients and whisk.

→

→
- *20ml Balsamic vinegar (optional)*

Dressing
- *60ml Sunflower oil*
- *40ml Olive oil*
- *10g   Dijon mustard*
- *35ml White wine vinegar*
- *1.25ml Salt*
- *2.5g Fresh ground black pepper*
- *20g   Fresh parsley, chopped*
- *Salt*

4 Place the orange, grapefruit, fennel and mixed lettuce in a suitable bowl, pour the dressing over and carefully fold in.

5 Divide the salad into four portions and then drizzle a little balsamic vinegar over.

6 Garnish with chive flower leaves and serve immediately.

NOTES

This recipe is suitable for vegan, low-cholesterol, diabetic and coeliac diets if you leave out the balsamic vinegar. ❑

Oriental Enoki and Snow Peas Salad (p.144)   4 covers

- *50g   Beansprouts*
- *200g Mouli (Chinese white radish)*
- *100g Spring onions*
- *200g Mange tout (snow peas)*
- *100g Button mushrooms*
- *200g Cucumber*
- *150g Fresh Enoki salad*
- *5g   Purple basil (Holy basil)*
- *10g   Cashew nuts, toasted*

Dressing
- *50ml Rice wine vinegar*
- *20ml Sunflower oil*
- *3cm   Fresh ginger*
- *5g   Garlic, minced*
- *30ml Shoyu*

1 Wash the beansprouts. Peel and slice the ginger, mouli and spring onions. Top and tail the mange tout and then blanch and refresh in ice cold water to retain the colour. Drain and reserve.

2 Clean and quarter the mushrooms and discard the stalks. Wash and slice the cucumber.

3 Place all the mushrooms and vegetables in a suitable bowl.

4 To make the dressing whisk the oil, shoyu, ginger, garlic and rice wine vinegar. Then pour it over the vegetables and stir.

5 Serve with a garnish of broken toasted cashew nuts.

NOTES

Suitable for vegan, diabetic and low-cholesterol diets. If tamari is used instead of shoyu, the salad will also be suitable for coeliac diets. ❑

❑ Oriental Enoki and Snow Pea Salad ❑

Oriental Noodle Soup   4 covers

- 700ml Vegetable stock
- 30ml Shoyu
- 20g Garlic purée
- 20g Ginger, chopped
- 280g Carrots
- 113g Diced tofu
- 100g Chinese mushrooms, dried
- 150g Angel hair (noodles)
- 5g Fresh coriander, chopped
- 4 Spring onions
- Salt and white pepper

1 Rehydrate the mushrooms in warm water, remove the stalks and thinly slice. Peel the spring onions and cut into diamonds.

2 Break the noodles into smaller pieces. Drain and cut the tofu into 1–2cm dice.

3 Peel and cut the carrots into a fine Julienne (very fine slices).

4 Bring to the boil the stock, shoyu, garlic and ginger, then simmer for 10 minutes.

5 Remove any debris from the surface. Add the carrots and tofu and gently simmer for a further 5 minutes. Add spring onions, mushrooms and noodles.

6 Serve with a sprinkling of chopped coriander. ❑

Oriental Soup

- 600ml *Strong vegetable stock*
- 100g *Carrots*
- 50g *Mouli (Chinese white radish)*
- 100g *Celery*
- 200g *Straw mushrooms*
- 30ml *Shoyu*
- 100g *Shallots*
- 250g *Chinese cabbage*
- *Salt and pepper*

1 Clean the mushrooms and slice in half. Peel and cut the carrots, celery, mouli and shallots into julienne (fine strips).

2 Wash and shred the cabbage.

3 Bring the stock to the boil and add the carrots, mouli and celery. Bring to the boil and simmer for 3–4 minutes then add all the other ingredients and skim the surface continually for any debris. Cook for 5 minutes.

4 Serve immediately.

NOTES

Suitable for vegan, diabetic and low-cholesterol diets. If tamari is used instead of shoyu this recipe is also suitable for coeliac diets. ❏

Pasta Bean Salad

4 covers

- 8 sheets *Filo pastry*
- 20ml *Olive oil*
- 190g *Riccini or Gnocchetti pasta*
- 100g *Carrots*
- 4 *Spring onions*
- 200g *Red kidney beans (cooked or tinned)*
- 200g *Borlotto beans (cooked or tinned)*
- 200g *Butter beans (cooked or tinned)*
- 40ml *Lemon juice*
- 2.5g *Garlic salt*
- 2.5g *Ground black pepper*
- 2.5g *Cayenne pepper*

1 Place two sheets of filo pastry into each of four suitable round moulds to make the pastry resemble a cup. Brush with oil and bake in a preheated oven at 180°C for 8–10 minutes until golden brown. Remove and reserve.

2 Cook the pasta in boiling salted water with a dash of oil for 10–15 minutes until cooked. Cool under cold running water, drain and reserve.

3 Peel the carrots and spring onions and cut into julienne (fine slices). Fold the beans into the vegetables. Add the lemon juice and pasta.

4 Season with black pepper and garlic salt.

5 Serve in the cups and garnish with crisp lettuce, cucumber and tomato. Add Cayenne pepper.

→

→

NOTES

Suitable for vegans, if vegan filo pastry is used. Suitable for diabetic and low-cholesterol diets.

This will serve four main portions or six to eight starter portions. If riccini or gnocchetti pasta is not available substitute with farfallini or conchiglie piccole rigate pasta. ❏

Peanut, Cucumber and Pine Salad — 4 covers

- 1 — Lime (zest only)
- 1 — Cucumber
- 1 — Green pepper
- 20g — Desiccated coconut
- 10g — Millet seeds
- 50g — Pine nuts
- 100g — Peanuts
- 20g — Fresh mint, chopped
- 5g — Cumin seeds
- 5g — Fresh parsley, chopped
  Salt and ground white pepper

Dressing
- 20ml — Palm sugar or honey
- 1 — Lime (juice only)
- 40ml — Sunflower oil

1 Remove the zest and extract the juice from the lime.

2 Wash, décor and cut the cucumber into 1cm dice. Deseed the pepper and cut into 1cm dice.

3 Toast the coconut, millet seeds, pine nuts and peanuts in a dry pan under the grill until they are golden brown.

4 To make the dressing mix together the palm sugar, lime juice and oil with salt and pepper.

5 Place all the ingredients in a suitable bowl and mix in the dressing.

6 Place in a fridge for 10–15 minutes, stir and serve.

NOTES

Garnish with crisp lettuce and a pinch of paprika or cayenne pepper. Suitable for vegan and coeliac diets. ❏

Pepper Flavoured Rice Salad — 4 covers

- 150g — Long grain rice
- 50g — Red kidney beans (tinned)
- 30g — Wild rice
- 100g — Tomatoes
- 50g — Red peppers
- 100g — Onions
- 100g — Spring onions
- 50g — Celery

1 Cook the rice in boiling salted water with a little oil for 15–20 minutes until just cooked, then refresh under cold running water, drain and reserve. Wash and drain the beans

2 Place the wild rice in a suitable saucepan, cover with water and simmer for 25 minutes until cooked. Drain, season and cool.

→

→

- 20g Garlic purée
- 10g Thyme leaves
- Pinch Cayenne pepper
- Crisp mixed lettuce
- Salt and freshly ground pepper
- Fresh parsley, chopped

Dressing

- 60ml Sunflower oil
- 40ml Olive oil
- 35ml Cider vinegar
- 1.25ml Salt
- 2.5g Fresh ground black pepper
- 2 cloves Garlic, crushed
- 20g Fresh parsley, chopped
- Pinch Chilli powder

3 Skin and deseed the tomatoes and peppers, then cut into small dice.

4 Peel the onions and spring onions and cut into small dice.

5 To make the dressing whisk all the ingredients together.

6 Place all the ingredients in a suitable bowl and mix together, seasoning with salt and lots of ground black pepper. Add the dressing and stir well.

7 Check the seasoning and serve with fresh chopped parsley. ❑

Pineapple, Macadamia and Smoked Tofu Salad (p.148)

4 covers

- 1 Baby pineapple
- 50g Banana shallots
- 50g Celery
- 250g Smoked tofu
- 200g Macadamia nuts
- 5g Dijon mustard
- 20ml Pineapple juice
- 15ml White wine vinegar
- 150g Vegetarian mayonnaise
- 4 sprigs Coriander
- 4 Edible nasturtium flowers
- Salt and pepper

1 Peel and de-core the pineapple then cut into 1–1½cm dice. Peel the shallots and cut into rings. Peel and slice the celery.

2 Drain the tofu and cut into dice. Toast the nuts under the grill in a dry pan until golden brown, the roughly chop them.

3 Place all the ingredients except the coriander and nasturtiums in a suitable bowl and gently fold in until fully coated.

4 Garnish with flowers and coriander sprigs.

NOTES

Suitable for vegan, low-cholesterol, diabetic and coeliac diets. ❑

❏ Pineapple, Macadamia and Smoked Tofu Salad ❏

Potato and Parsley Soup 4 covers

- 120g   Potato
- 100g   Fresh parsley
- 100g   Onions
- 1 clove Garlic
- 500ml Vegetable stock
         (strong)
- 30g   Arrowroot
- 250ml Milk (semi-
         skimmed or soya)
- 80ml   Double cream or
         yoghurt (optional)
-         Salt
-         Ground white
         pepper

1 Wash and peel the potato and then cut into dice.

2 Wash and chop the parsley.

3 Peel and finely chop the onion and garlic.

4 Put the onion, parsley, garlic and potato in a suitable pan with the stock, bring to the boil and then simmer for 35 minutes.

5 When the potatoes have begun to break up place the mixture in a liquidiser and purée it. Season to taste. Return to a clean pan and simmer.

6 At this stage, depending on how waxy the potatoes are, the soup may need to be either thickened or let down slightly. To thicken, add a little milk to the arrowroot and mix until it forms a paste, then add this a little to the

→

→ soup at a time, stirring until the required consistency is achieved. To let the soup down simply add the milk until the required consistency is achieved.

7 Check the seasoning, whip up the cream until it stiffens, then serve a small spoonful of cream or yoghurt in the centre of the soup bowl.

8 Serve with freshly baked, crispy bread rolls. ❑

Potato, Oregano and Marjoram Salad   4 covers

- 750g New or mid potatoes
- 2–3 Baby fennel bulbs
- 60ml Vegan mayonnaise
- 4 Spring onions
- 2 sprigs Fresh oregano
- 2 sprigs Fresh marjoram
- Salt and freshly ground black pepper

1 Wash and cook the potatoes in boiling salted water for 12 minutes until cooked. Cool under cold running water, then cut into quarters.

2 Trim and roughly chop the fennel. Reserve the leaves for the garnish. Lightly blanch the fennel and refresh in ice-cold water.

3 Fold in the potatoes and fennel with the mayonnaise and season.

4 Fold in the herbs and spring onions and check the seasoning. Garnish with chopped fennel leaves.

NOTES

Suitable for vegan, diabetic, low-cholesterol and wheat- and gluten-free diets. ❑

Pumpkin Soup (p.151)   4 covers

- 75g Onions
- 75g Carrots
- 20g Celery
- 20g Leeks
- 475g Pumpkin
- 25g Dried pumpkin seeds
- 30g Margarine
- 500g Milk (semi-skimmed or soya)

1 Peel the onions, carrots, celery and leeks and cut into rough dice.

2 Peel and deseed the pumpkin and cut into rough dice.

3 Toast the pumpkin seeds.

4 Sauté the vegetables and the pumpkin in the margarine for 2–3 minutes, then add the milk.

5 Bring to the boil and simmer for 35 minutes.

→

- 250g Vegetable stock
- 20g Fresh parsley
- 150g Yoghurt
- ■ Salt and ground white pepper

→

6 Take all the ingredients except the parsley, yogurt and toasted seeds and liquidise until the soup is completely smooth.

7 Put back on the heat and add half the parsley. Season to taste, then garnish the top of the soup with the remaining parsley, adding a spoonful of yoghurt and the toasted seeds.

NOTES

Suitable for vegan diets if soya milk is used instead of dairy milk, and soya yoghurt instead of dairy yoghurt. Serve with crusty bread. ❏

Radish and Pea Salad with Blue Cheese Dressing 4 covers

- 250g Peas (frozen are acceptable)
- 120g Radish (baby red radishes or salad radish)
- 100g Green beans, cooked
- 100g Shitake mushrooms
- 100g Oyster mushrooms
- 100g Spring onions
- 20g Chives, chopped
- 5g Marjoram leaves
- ■ Salt and pepper

Dressing
- 50ml White wine vinegar
- 50ml Olive oil
- 100g Vegetable oil (or sunflower oil)
- 5g Dijon mustard
- 5–10g Fresh parsley, finely chopped
- 60g Roquefort cheese
- ■ Salt and pepper

1 Place the peas in boiling salted water and cook for 2–3 minutes, then refresh in ice-cold water. Drain and reserve.

2 Wash, top, tail and slice the radish and cut the beans into 3cm lengths.

3 Clean and quarter the mushrooms.

4 To make the dressing place all the ingredients in a blender or food processor and process until they make a thick creamy dressing. This is best done on pulse speed. Do not over blend.

5 Place all the ingredients in a suitable bowl and combine with the dressing.

NOTES

Serve with crisp lettuce and crusty garlic bread. Omit the cheese for vegan diets. ❏

❏ Clockwise from top: Pumpkin Soup, Mesur Dhal Soup,
Seaweed Broth Japanese style ❏

Rice and Lentil Salad — 4 covers

- 180g Long grain rice
- 100g Split yellow lentils
- 65g Fine Kenya beans
- 50g Vine cherry tomatoes
- 50g Pitted black olives
- 240g Mixed crisp lettuce (rocket, curly endive, chicory and radicchio)
- 20g Sesame seeds, toasted
- 25g Pine kernels, toasted
- 20g Purple basil, shredded

Dressing
- 30ml Virgin olive oil
- 50ml Vegetable oil
- 2.5g Dijon mustard
- 2.5ml Red wine vinegar
- 2.5ml Balsamic vinegar
- Salt and black pepper

1. Cook the rice and lentils separately and drain and refresh under cold running water.
2. Top and tail the beans then blanch and refresh in ice-cold water to retain the colour. Cut into 2–3cm lengths.
3. Wash and remove the tomatoes from the stalks then cut in half.
4. Cut the olives in half. Wash the lettuce and cut into edible sizes.
5. Mix all the vegetables, nuts, lentils, rice and seeds together in a suitable bowl.
6. Whisk all the dressing ingredients together in a suitable bowl and pour over the salad. Then gently mix with the lettuce and serve immediately.

NOTES

Suitable for vegan, coeliac, low-cholesterol and diabetic diets. ❑

Seitan Noodle Soup — 4 covers

- 150g Seitan
- 50g Rice or mung bean vermicelli noodles (glass noodles)
- 30ml Shoyu
- 50g Mange tout
- 6 Spring onions
- 1 Pak choi
- 35ml Groundnut oil

1. Roll the seitan into a cylinder shape and simmer in boiling water for 30 minutes. Remove and cool then cut into wedge shapes.
2. Soak the glass noodles in a little cold water for 5–10 minutes then remove and drain.
3. Marinade the seitan in the shoyu for 30 minutes, then drain and reserve any shoyu left over.
4. Top and tail the mange tout, peel and slice the spring onions. Wash and trim the pak choi.

→

→

- 40ml   *Rice wine or dry sherry (vegetarian)*
- 700ml *Clear vegetable stock*
- 5g   *Garlic purée*
- ■   *Salt and pepper*

5 Add the oil and garlic purée to a pan or wok and stir-fry the seitan for 3–4 minutes, then add the mange tout, pak choi, spring onions, noodles, shoyu and rice wine and cook for 2–3 minutes.

6 Add the stock and bring to the boil. Simmer for 3–4 minutes skimming the top for any debris. Correct the seasoning and serve.

NOTES

Suitable for vegan, diabetic and low-cholesterol diets. ❏

Smoked Tofu and Pistachio Nut Pâté   4 covers

- 200g   *Smoked tofu*
- 30g   *Ground pistachio nuts*
- 10g   *Groundnuts*
- 50g   *Breadcrumbs*
- 2.5g   *Caraway seeds*
- 25g   *Margarine*
- 5g   *Wholegrain mustard*
- 10-15ml *Lemon juice*
- Pinch *Ground cumin*
- 4 sprigs *Parsley*
- 8   *Whole pistachio nuts*
- ½   *Lemon (zest only)*
- ■   *Salt and black pepper*

1 Cut the tofu into rough dice and place in a food processor with the other ingredients and blend until smooth.

2 Garnish with the parsley sprigs and pistachio nuts and a little lemon zest. ❏

Spicy Parsnip Soup   Serves 4

- 40g   *Margarine*
- 70g   *Onions*
- 100g   *Potatoes*
- 400g   *Parsnips*
- 5ml   *Curry powder (mild)*
- 2.5ml *Ground cumin*

1 Peel and slice the onions, potatoes and parsnips.

2 Sauté the onions, potatoes and parsnips in the margarine. Then add the curry powder and cumin and cook for 2–3 minutes on a low heat.

3 Slowly add the flour and beat into a roux. Add the stock slowly and bring to the boil, then simmer for 30 minutes.

→

→

- 40g   Plain flour
- 1 litre Vegetable stock (white)
- 150ml Soya milk
- 25g   Fresh parsley, chopped
- ▪   Salt and ground black pepper

4 Remove from the heat, place in a liquidiser and blend until smooth. Return the soup to a clean saucepan and reheat. Add the soya milk and season. Do not boil.

5 Garnish with fresh parsley.

NOTES

This soup can be made suitable for a coeliac diet by removing the flour and increasing the parsnips to 500g.

Omitting the curry and adding other spices, such as chilli or paprika, can give a different flavour to the soup. ❑

Spicy Vegetable Salsa

- 50g   Red peppers
- 50g   Green peppers
- 50g   Onions
- 50g   Green beans
- 50g   Cucumber
- 4   Beef tomatoes
- 1tsp Olive oil
- 150ml Tomato juice
- ½   Red chilli
- ¼tsp Cumin
- 1tsp Chives, chopped
- 1tsp Fresh coriander, chopped
- 25g   Pitted black olives, chopped
- 1tsp Lime juice

1 Deseed the peppers and slice the peppers and onions. Top and tail the beans and cut into 4–5cm lengths. Wash and cut the cucumber into 4–5cm lengths. Skin and deseed the tomatoes and cut into slices.

2 Heat the oil in a suitable pan and add the peppers, green beans and onions and stir quickly over a high heat for 2–3 minutes, then add the tomato juice and cook out for 2–3 minutes.

3 Season and allow to cool. Add the chilli, cucumber, tomato, cumin, chives, coriander, olives and the lime juice and mix well.

4 Fill evenly then either steam or grill the pancakes and serve as required.

Pancakes

- 100g Plain flour
- 1   Free-range egg (med)
- 125g Milk
- 125g Water
- ▪   Nutmeg
- ▪   Salt and pepper

1 Sift the flour, nutmeg, salt and pepper into suitable bowl and whisk in the milk, egg and water.

2 Heat a suitable pan and add a touch of oil, then add the batter and tilt the pan until the batter eventually covers the base of the pan. Cook the batter until it looks dry and golden brown underneath.

3 Loosen the edges and flip over with a pallet knife. Cook for a further 2 mins and turn out onto grease proof or silicon paper and use as required. ❑

Tomato and Scallion Salsa 4 covers

- 500g   Tomatoes
- 2   Banana shallots
- 1 clove Garlic
- 4   Spring onions
- Handful Fresh coriander
- 30ml   Balsamic vinegar
-          Salt and black
           pepper

1 Skin, deseed and cut the tomatoes into quarters, saving the tomato water.

2 Peel and finely slice the shallots and garlic. Peel the spring onions and cut into quarters.

3 Roughly chop the coriander

4 Mix all the ingredients together and season with salt and freshly ground pepper.

5 Serve in a suitable dish. ❏

Triple Bean and Fungi Salad (p.138)   4 covers

- 100g   Paris mushrooms
- 100g   Small oyster
          mushrooms
- 150g   Red peppers
- 100g   Celery
- 100g   Red onions
- 150g   Red kidney beans
          (cooked or tinned)
- 150g   Black eyed beans
          (cooked or tinned)
- 100g   Flageolet beans
          (cooked or tinned)
- 90g   Fresh grated
          Parmesan cheese
          (vegetarian)
- 20g   Fresh parsley,
          chopped
-         Salt and freshly
          ground white
          pepper

Dressing
- 50ml   Extra virgin olive
          oil
- 15ml   White wine vinegar
- 15g   Pesto, vegetarian

1 Clean the mushrooms and cut into quarters. Skin and deseed the peppers then cut into 1cm × 4cm lengths. Peel the onion and celery and cut into lengths.

2 Mix the olive oil, vinegar and the pesto together and reserve the dressing.

3 Wash and drain the beans.

4 In a suitably large bowl combine the vegetables, beans, herbs, mushrooms and dressing. Check and correct the seasoning and serve with a garnish of Parmesan.

NOTES

Serve with a crisp lettuce salad. Suitable for vegans if the Parmesan is omitted. ❏

Tropical Spinach Salad — 4 covers

- 2   Papaya
- 170g   Cashew nuts
- 8   Baby corn
- 400g   Fresh baby spinach
- 12   Slices smoked tofu

Dressing

- 250g   Tofu purée
- 1   Lemon (juice only)
- 2.5g   Caster sugar
-    Seasoning

1 Peel, quarter, deseed and thinly slice the papaya.

2 Crush the cashew nuts and toast until golden brown. Blanch and refresh the corn then cut lengthways into quarters.

3 To make the dressing purée the ingredients in a liquidiser then set aside.

4 Wash the spinach, place all the ingredients in a salad bowl, add a little of the dressing, mix well and serve. ❑

Vegetable and Fungi Basil Salad — 4 covers

- 180g   Mange tout
-    Mixed lettuce (curly endive, chicory, radicchio and romain)
- 50g   Cheese, vegetarian
- 300g   Button mushrooms
- 75g   Baby corn
- 100g   Spring onions
- 200g   Red onions
- 1   Red pepper
- 1   Green pepper
- 100g   Sorrel
- 100g   Pine kernels, toasted
-    Salt and pepper

Dressing

- 50ml   White wine vinegar
- 50ml   Olive oil
- 10g   Lemon zest
- 20ml   Lemon juice
- 100g   Vegetable oil (or sunflower oil)
- 10g   Dijon mustard
- 15 leaves Basil
-    Salt and pepper

1 Blanch and refresh the mange tout, drain and cut in half. Wash and prepare the lettuce.

2 Break the cheese into bite-sized portions. Clean and slice the mushrooms, baby corn and spring onions. Peel and dice the onions and peppers, discard the seeds and stalks. Wash and dry the sorrel then shred.

3 To make the dressing place all the ingredients in a blender or food processor and process until they make a thick creamy dressing. This is best done on pulse speed. Do not over blend.

4 In a suitable container, marinade the mushrooms in the dressing for 30–40 minutes.

5 Fold in the rest of the ingredients (except the lettuce).

6 Garnish the dishes with the lettuce then add the marinated salad.

NOTES

Suitable for diabetic diets and also for low-cholesterol and vegan diets if the cheese is omitted. Omit the nuts if required for people with nut allergies. ❑

Vegetarian Kedgeree 4 covers

- 170g   Long grain rice
- 3 sprigs Parsley
- 2   Free-range eggs, large
- 250g   Smoked tofu
- 50g   Margarine
-         Cayenne pepper
- 20ml   Curry sauce, mild
-         Salt and ground black pepper

1 Cook the rice in boiling salted water with a drop of oil. Then drain/cool and refresh until required. Finely chop the parsley.

2 Hard boil the eggs, shell and finely chop one egg up.

3 Drain and cut the tofu into 1cm square dice then cook in a saucepan with the margarine for 2–3 minutes.

4 Add a pinch of cayenne pepper and continue to cook for 1 minute then add the curry sauce and cook for a further 3 minutes.

5 Add the cooked rice to the saucepan and heat through.

6 Mix in half the chopped parsley and season.

7 Place the kedgeree on a warmed serving dish and garnish with sliced egg and chopped parsley. ❏

Vegetarian Mayonnaise 4 covers

- 1   Lemon
- 100ml   Soya milk (good quality one)
- 5g   Garlic purée
- 135ml   Sunflower oil
- 60ml   Groundnut oil
- Pinch   Cayenne pepper
-          Salt and ground white pepper

1 Peel and cut the lemon rind into very fine zest, then blanch and refresh it. Remove the juice from the lemon.

2 Place the soya milk, half of the lemon juice and zest and the garlic in a processor and blend.

3 Very slowly add the oil until it begins to emulsify. Check the mayonnaise for seasoning, add a pinch of cayenne pepper on top and serve as required.

NOTES

Keep this mayonnaise in the fridge. If additional flavour is required add spices, herbs and even purées, and reduce the sunflower oil by the same amounts.

Good for vegans. ❏

- 110g Cheddar cheese, vegetarian
- 100g Banana shallots
- 15ml Fresh parsley and thyme
- 185g Breadcrumbs (fresh white)
- 2.5ml Dijon mustard
- Pinch Cayenne pepper
- 2 Medium sized eggs
- 60ml Milk
- 1 Egg white
- 100g Plain flour, seasoned
- 150ml Oil (sunflower, vegetable or olive oil)
- Salt
- Ground black pepper

1 Grate the Cheddar cheese and peel and finely chop the shallots. Wash and finely chop the herbs.

2 Place the cheese in a bowl with the breadcrumbs, shallots, mustard and herbs and mix together.

3 Season well with a little salt and plenty of black pepper and a pinch of cayenne.

4 Mix the whole eggs into the milk and stir into the sausage mixture.

5 Divide the mixture into equal amounts and roll each portion into a sausage shape.

6 Whisk the egg white and dip each sausage into the egg white and then into the seasoned flour. Shake off any excess and keep in the fridge for 15–20 minutes to harden.

7 Heat the oil in a pan and shallow fry for about 10 minutes. Turn frequently to ensure an all-round golden colour.

NOTES

This is an excellent alternative to meat-based sausages. Add a coat of breadcrumbs to give more fibre content or use half the amount of white breadcrumbs and the same amount of brown breadcrumbs when mixing together.

For a different taste use coarse grain mustard and change the cheese to suit, although it must be a semi-hard cheese. ❑

Veggi Breakfast Rashers   4 covers

- *200g   Smoked tofu*
- *90ml   Tamari sauce*
- *70ml   Oil (sunflower, vegetable or soy)*
- *Salt and pepper*
- *Pinch of Cayenne pepper*

1 Drain the smoked tofu, cut into thin slices (rashers) and place in a suitable dish.

2 Marinade the rashers in tamari and leave for 50–60 minutes.

3 Remove the rashers and gently touch dry with kitchen paper. Lightly dust with salt, pepper and Cayenne.

4 Place the oil in a pan and fry off the rashers for 4–5 minutes, until golden brown.

5 Drain off any excess oil and serve.

NOTES

These rashers can be used as a substitute for bacon, as part of a cooked vegetarian breakfast, or as a filling for a sandwich. ❏

❏ Clockwise from top: Egg-free Scrambled egg, Vegetarian Sausages, Vegetarian Kedgeree, Veggi Breakfast Rashers ❏

Warm Mixed Green Salad with Toasted Sunflower Seeds and Orange (p.123)

4 covers

- ■ *200g*   *Mixed green leaves (watercress, romaine, rocket)*
- ■ *2*   *Red peppers*
- ■ *200g*   *Onions*
- ■ *100g*   *Spring onions*
- ■ *30ml*   *Olive oil*
- ■ *350g*   *Mixed mushrooms (button, shitake, cepe or Paris brown)*
- ■ *60ml*   *Orange juice*
- ■ *10g*   *Orange zest*
- ■ *80g*   *Sunflower seeds, toasted*
- ■ *80g*   *Pine nuts, toasted*
- ■ *5ml*   *Tamari*
- ■   *Salt and freshly ground black pepper*

1 Wash and prepare the green leaves. Skin and deseed the peppers and cut into slices. Peel and slice the onions and spring onions. Clean the mushrooms and cut in half.

2 Sweat off the onions in the olive oil until tender then add the peppers and continue to cook for a further 2 minutes.

3 Add the mushrooms and continue to cook until tender, then add the orange juice, zest, seeds, nuts and Tamari. Stir and toss so all ingredients are coated.

4 Season with salt and pepper, pour over the greens, toss and serve.

NOTES

Suitable for vegans, diabetic and low-cholesterol diets. ❑

Warm Seitan and Black Bean Salad

4 covers

- ■ *450g*   *Black beans, tinned*
- ■ *1*   *Red pepper*
- ■ *230g*   *Iceberg lettuce*
- ■ *450g*   *Fresh seitan*
- ■ *20–30ml*   *Balsamic vinegar*
- ■ *20g*   *Fresh coriander, chopped*

Dressing
- ■ *50ml*   *Olive oil*
- ■ *1*   *Lime (juice only)*
- ■ *10g*   *Garlic purée*
- ■ *5g*   *Ground cumin*
- ■ *120g*   *Onions (peeled and sliced)*
- ■   *Salt and ground black pepper*

1 Wash and drain the black beans.

2 Skin and deseed the red pepper and cut into thin slices. Wash, de-core and shred the lettuce.

3 To make the dressing extract the juice from the lime, peel and slice the onions then mix together.

4 Slice the seitan and pan-fry for 3–4 minutes in hot oil, then the vinegar reduce by one-third, season and keep warm.

5 Place the lettuce in a suitable bowl, mix in the dressing, toss and place the seitan on top. Garnish with coriander and serve immediately.

NOTES

Suitable for vegan, low-cholesterol and nut-free diets. ❑

main course dishes

A Spinach Ensemble with Coconut — 4 covers

Sundried Tomato Sauce
- 113g   Shallots
- 113g   White wine
- 280g   Vegetable stock
- 113g   Sundried tomato
- 1 quart Tomato juice
- 50g   Margarine

Sweat off 113g finely chopped shallots in a little margarine, then de-glaze with half of the wine.

Now add half of the stock and reduce by half. Then add the chopped sundried tomato and the juice, reduce by half, season and correct the consistency. Then strain out and keep hot until required.

Sauce Anise
- 113g   Chopped Shallots
- 50g   Margarine
- 113g   Dry white wine
- 2   Star anise
- 283g   Stock (vegetable)
- 350g   Double cream

Sweat off 113g finely chopped shallots in a little margarine, then de-glaze the pan with the rest of the white wine, add the anise and reduce by half. Add 283g stock and again reduce by half. Add the double cream and reduce until it coats the back of the spoon. Season and strain then keep hot until required.

Cordon of Vegetables
- 100g   Finely diced shallots
- 2 bunch Spring onions
- 2   Beef tomato (concasse)

Sweat off, fine diced shallots, spring onion, tomato concasse, chopped chives, salt, pepper and a dash of spiced coriander. Then keep hot until required.

Make separate 4 × 4 yellow leaf tomatoes for garnish. Cut in 4 into quarters.

→

- 50g   Margarine
- 10g   Chop chives
- Pinch   Coriander
- Pinch   Salt/pepper
- 16   yellow tomatoes

Spinach Ensemble
- 680g   Spinach
- 128g   Shallots (diced)
- 2   Sliced spring onions
- 50g   Margarine
- Pinch   Corriander
- Pinch   Salt and pepper
- 5   Beef tomato cut
          into concasse
- 1   Purple basil

Glaze
- 238g   Coconut milk
- 6   Kaffir lime leaves
- 100ml   Double Cream

→ Pick, wash, then cook the spinach in a very hot pan with no medium but with a tight-fitting lid for 1–2 minutes. Remove from the pan then add spinach to sweated shallots (in margarine), season with salt, pepper and spiced coriander and cook for a further 1–2 minutes.

Sweat off the spring onions and shallots (in rings) in a little margarine. Add the tomato concasse, season and add a little chopped basil. Cook out in the oven for 5 minutes.

Now put half of the spinach into a mould, then add the tomato, then add the rest of the spinach, and compress.

Glaze

Simply boil the coconut milk and the chopped Kaffir lime leaves. Cool the milk then add to the cream and spoon it over the top of the mould and then glaze it under the grill. ❑

Almond and Coriander Spiced Couscous   4 covers

- 2   Banana shallots
- 1 clove Garlic
- 105g   Flaked almonds
- 50g   Dried currants
- 5-6 sprigs Coriander
- 550ml   Vegetarian stock
          (strong)
- 400g   Couscous
- 50ml   Olive oil
-         Salt and white
          pepper

1 Peel and finely chop the shallots and garlic. Then toast the almonds. Wash the currants in warm water.

2 Chop the coriander and keep to one side.

3 Bring the stock to the boil, then a little to cover the currants, allowing them to swell.

4 Place the couscous in a bowl, then pour the remaining stock over. Stir once then let it stand covered for 12 minutes or until the stock is absorbed. Fluff couscous with a fork.

5 Sweat off the garlic and shallots in the oil.

→

❏ A Spinach Ensemble with Coconut ❏

→ 6 Add the couscous to the pan and stir in the toasted almonds, currants and coriander over a low heat. Check seasoning and serve.

NOTES

To spice this up a little add 10g ground turmeric when sweating off the shallots. ❏

Aubergines with Mediterranean Herbs and Tomato Sauce

4 covers

Tomato sauce

- 820g Italian plum tomatoes
- 16 leaves Fresh basil
- 100ml Extra virgin olive oil
- 25g Caster sugar
- Salt and black pepper

1 Blanch the tomatoes in boiling water and refresh. Peel, deseed and cut into small dice (concasse). Then shred the basil leaves.

2 Heat the oil in a suitable pan then add the tomatoes and basil. Cook for 15–20 minutes until the tomatoes have broken down, then season with sugar, salt and pepper.

- 900g Aubergines (large)
- 225g Mozzarella cheese
- 15 leaves Basil
- 10g Marjoram or oregano
- 50g Pesto sauce (vegetarian)
- 50ml Olive oil
- Parmesan cheese, grated (vegetarian)
- Salt and pepper

1 Wash and top and tail the aubergines then cut lengthways into thin slices. Sprinkle generously with rock salt and leave to drain in a colander for at least 30 minutes. Then rinse under cold water and dry.

2 Drain the mozzarella cheese and cut into slices. Shred the herbs.

3 Fry the aubergines for 4 minutes each side in hot oil, cooking through, adding olive oil between each batch.

4 Drain well on kitchen paper. Lightly brush slices with Pesto.

5 Place half the tomato sauce in the base of a suitable dish.

6 Overlay with half the aubergine slices and then with the mozzarella. Add tomatoes to mixture. Cover with the remaining aubergine slices and the herbs. Season with salt and pepper.

7 Dust the top with vegetarian Parmesan cheese. Bake in a preheated oven at 200°C/Gas Mark 6 for 30–40 minutes.

8 Leave to cool slightly for 3–5 minutes before serving.

NOTES

For vegan diets leave out the cheese. For extra flavour add vegetable stock to the sauce or brush the aubergine slices with vegetarian pesto sauce. ❑

Baked Mushrooms with Sour Cream and Nuts 4 covers

- 80g   Fresh wholemeal breadcrumbs
- 55g   Ground almonds
- 35g   Pistachio nuts, peeled
- 60g   Ground cashew nuts
- 100g   Onions
- 1–2 cloves Garlic
- 90g   Margarine
- 300g   Button mushrooms
- 200g   Field mushrooms
- 20ml   Extra virgin olive oil
- 280ml Soured cream
- 10g   Fresh parsley, chopped
- 5g   Oregano leaves
- 5g   Paprika
- Salt and freshly ground pepper

1 Chop the pistachio nuts. Clean and slice the mushrooms. Peel and finely slice the garlic and onions.

2 Place the breadcrumbs, nuts, onions, garlic, margarine, salt and pepper in a mixing bowl. Mix until it looks like pastry.

3 Place the mixture in a 20cm flan tin with removable bottom and press down to form a firm base. Bake for 15 minutes at 180°C/Gas Mark 4-5 in a preheated oven.

4 Sauté the mushrooms in the oil. Drain off any excess oil.

5 Add the soured cream, parsley, oregano and salt and pepper to the mushrooms, fully mixing in the cream.

6 Pour the mushroom mixture into the baked breadcrumbs. Sprinkle with the paprika and bake in a preheated oven for a further 15–20 minutes.

7 Remove from the tin and serve, garnished with a sprinkling of chopped herbs. ❑

Baked Tempeh in a BBQ Sauce (p.271)   4 covers

- 200g   Onions
- 1   Green pepper
- 5g   Chilli powder
- 5g   Ground coriander
- 5g   Ground cumin
- pinch Cayenne pepper
- 2g   Garlic purée
- 30ml   Vegetable oil
- 16   Button mushrooms
- 450g   Tempeh
- 1   Red pepper
- 120g   Courgettes
- 150g   Pineapple chunks
- 8   Vine tomatoes
- Fresh parsley, chopped

1 To make the sauce bring to the boil the vinegar, lemon juice and the sugar, cook for 2–3 minutes then add the tomato purée, pineapple juice and cook for a further 1 minute. Then add the tamari, mustard, brown sauce and stock. Skim any debris from the surface and discard. Reserve the sauce.

2 Deseed the peppers and cut into 1cm squares. Peel and cut the onions into 1cm dice, cut the tomatoes in quarters, clean and remove the stalks from the mushrooms and cut in half. Wash, top, tail and slice the courgettes.

3 Sweat off the onions, peppers, spices and garlic in the oil for 2 minutes then add the mushrooms and tempeh and cook for a further 3–4 minutes over a low heat.

→

Sauce

- *30ml Cider vinegar*
- *30ml Lemon juice*
- *50g Brown sugar*
- *200g Tomato purée*
- *30ml Pineapple juice*
- *40ml Tamari*
- *5g Dijon mustard*
- *50ml Brown sauce (condiment)*
- *200ml Light vegetable stock or water*

➜

4 Pour the tempeh mixture into a suitable baking dish and add the tomatoes, courgettes and pineapple chunks. Cover with the sauce and tin foil and bake in a preheated oven at 180°C/Gas Mark 4 for 40 minutes, then remove foil and cook for a further 20 minutes.

5 Garnish with chopped parsley and serve.

NOTES

Suitable for vegan, coeliac and nut allergy diets. ❑

Banana and Apple Curry   4 covers

- *200g Yellow lentils*
- *½l White vegetable stock*
- *150g Onions*
- *75g Spring onions*
- *30ml Ghee (vegetable)*
- *15ml Mild curry powder (Korma)*
- *2 cloves Garlic*
- *3cm Ginger*
- *1 Green chilli*
- *75g Leeks*
- *2 Apples (Royal Gala)*
- *2 Bananas*
- *50g Sultanas*
- *30g Fresh parsley*
- *10g Almonds*

1 Peel and dice the onions, spring onions and leeks, and purée the garlic. Peel and finely chop the ginger and chillies. Cut and decore the apple and cut into large dice. Peel the bananas and cut into large dice. Toast the almonds in a pan under the grill until golden brown. Wash and chop the parsley.

2 Place the lentils in half the stock and bring to the boil. Cook until nearly all the stock has been absorbed. Then allow to cool and drain.

3 Cook off the spring onions and onions in the ghee until lightly golden brown. Add the curry powder, garlic, ginger, chilli and leeks and cook for 5 minutes.

4 Add the lentils and the rest of the stock and cook for approximately 15 minutes.

5 Add the sliced apple, bananas and sultanas and cook for a further 3–5 minutes.

6 Garnish with parsley, toasted almonds and serve with Basmati rice, mango chutney, desiccated coconut, minted yoghurt and poppadums.

➜

□ Banana and Apple Curry □

→ | NOTES

This recipe can be used for vegan, coeliac (omit poppadums), low-cholesterol and diabetic diets.

When working with fresh chillies, always wash the hands after use. Never touch your eyes or sensitive areas as the chillies will burn. □

Barbecued Seitan in a Plum and Honey Sauce (p.239)
4 covers

- 40ml *Sunflower oil*
- 100g *Onions*
- 5g *Garlic purée*
- 5g *Ginger purée*
- 20ml *Water*

1 To make the sauce, combine all the ingredients in a suitable pan and bring to the boil. Simmer for 3–4 minutes and remove any debris from the surface.

→

■ 8 × 100g Seitan strips
■ 10g Fresh coriander, chopped

Sauce
■ 50ml Dark soy sauce
■ 30ml Dry sherry or rice wine
■ 15ml White wine vinegar
■ 45ml Plum sauce (vegetarian)
■ 45ml Clear honey
■ 10g Garlic purée
■ 10g Ginger purée
■ 5g Five spice powder
■ 2.5g Cinnamon
■ 50g Shallots, finely chopped

2 Heat the oil in a suitable pan and sweat off the onions garlic and ginger for 3–4 minutes then add approximately 20ml water and stir.

3 Add the seitan strips and cook for a further 2 minutes, at which stage add the sauce. Bring to a simmer and cook for 2–3 minutes, carefully stirring so as not to break up the seitan. Correct the seasoning and add half the coriander.

4 Serve with chopped coriander.

NOTES

Serve with noodles or rice. ❑

Basic Seitan Recipe

■ 1300g Stoneground wholewheat bread flour or high gluten (unbleached white flour)
■ 750ml Water (more or less may be needed depending on gluten content in flour)
■ 3l Water

Stock
■ 110g Water
■ 110ml Tamari
■ 10 slices Fresh peeled ginger
■ 7cm Kombu

1 Put the flour in a mixing bowl and add three-quarters of the water. Slowly mix until it forms a stiff dough, adding more water as required.

2 Knead the dough for approximately 10–12 minutes on a lightly floured board; this is essential to help develop the gluten.

3 Rest the dough for 30 minutes in a bowl of cold water.

4 Wash out the starch in the dough either by i) kneading in a bowl of water and when the water is a milky colour replacing with clean water. This could take 8–10 bowls of water until it is clear and the gluten is tight, or ii) kneading under cold running water for approximately 15 minutes. First the water will run off milky in colour but the longer it is kneaded the clearer it will be. When it is the consistency of a soft chewy gum it will be much smaller than when you started (500–650g).

➔

→ 5 Mould the seitan into the required shape and rest for 10 minutes to relax the gluten. After resting the seitan will shape well and become more flexible.

6 Boil 3 litres of water, add the seitan and cook for 30 minutes or until it floats, then remove and allow to cool. Cut into the required shape. Place the seitan into the cold tamari stock and simmer for 1½ hours.

7 Store in the stock in the fridge for 8–10 days.

NOTES

There are numerous seitan recipes as well as ready-to-use flours that just require mixing, or ready-made commercial seitan. During the kneading process flavour the seitan with herbs and spices, such as garlic, ginger, paprika, parsley, thyme.

Seitan freezes well. ❏

Bean Cup Casserole   4 covers

- 200g   Haricot beans
- 50g   Butter beans
- 200g   Plum tomatoes
- 120g   Carrots
- 1 stick Celery
- 120g   Swede
- 120g   Turnip
- 110g   Onions
- 25g   Wholewheat breadcrumbs
- 4 slices Bread
- 55g   Margarine
- 200ml Vegetable stock
- 5–10g Yeast extract
- 10g   Fresh parsley, chopped
- 200g   Potatoes
- ■   Salt and black pepper

1 Soak the beans overnight in a covered bowl of water. Remove the greyish skins from the beans.

2 Skin, deseed and cut the tomatoes into 2cm dice, strain and keep the juice. Peel and cut the carrots, celery, swede, turnip and onions into 2 cm dice.

3 Cut the crusts off each slice of bread and then roll out the slices flat, brush with melted margarine, then mould each into a cup shape and bake in a preheated oven at 180°C/Gas Mark 4–5 for 10–15 minutes until golden brown.

4 In a suitable pan sweat off the carrots, celery, swede, turnip and onions without colour for 3–4 minutes. Add the beans, potatoes, stock, yeast extract, parsley and tomatoes and season.

5 Bring to the boil then transfer to a casserole dish. Sieve the breadcrumbs. Cook in a preheated oven at 180°C/Gas Mark 4–5 for 60 minutes until the dish is cooked.

6 Divide the casserole between the cups and serve with a sprinkling of parsley. ❏

Bulgar Wheat Mexican Style (p.188)

4 covers

- 150g   Onions
- 250g   Bulgar wheat
- 40g   Margarine
- 100g   Courgettes
- 1   Red pepper
- 2   Red chillies
- 100g   Celery
- 500ml Vegetable stock
- 10g   Fresh coriander, chopped
-        Salt and ground black pepper

1 Peel and chop the onion and celery. Deseed and chop the pepper into small dice. Deseed and chop the chillies into fine julienne (strips). Wash and dice the courgette.

2 Sweat off the onions and bulgar wheat in the margarine. Cook until the onion is transparent.

3 Add all the vegetables to the bulgar wheat mixture. Cook and stir for 2–3 minutes.

4 Pour the stock into the mixture and cook with a lid on for some 15 minutes until all the liquid has been absorbed. Season with salt and pepper.

5 Use a fork to stir in the coriander and loosen the bulgar wheat.

6 Serve with chopped coriander as a garnish.

NOTES

Suitable for vegan, low-cholesterol, diabetic diets.

Add 5g chilli powder for extra spice and heat to the dish if required. ❑

Bulgar Wheat and Nut Pilaff

4 covers

- 20ml   Groundnut oil
- 150g   Bulgar wheat
- 150g   Carrots
- 100g   Leeks
- 100g   Onions
- 250ml Vegetable stock
- 120g   Walnuts and almonds, chopped
-        Salt and pepper

1 Peel the onions, leeks and carrots and cut into small dice.

2 Pour the oil into a suitable saucepan, add the bulgar wheat, stir and cook for 4–5 minutes.

3 Add the vegetables and cook for a further 2–3 minutes, stirring to prevent anything sticking to the pan.

4 Stir in the stock, cover and cook for a further 15 minutes, then add half the nuts using a fork to fold them in.

5 Serve with a garnish of nuts on top. ❑

Bulgar Wheat Tabouli   4 covers

- *150g   Onions*
- *140ml Virgin olive oil*
- *250g   Bulgar wheat*
- *360ml Vegetable stock*
- *2   Lemons (juice and zest)*
- *150g   Cucumber*
- *4   Plum tomatoes*
- *10g   Parsley, chopped*
- *Salt and freshly ground black pepper*

1 Remove the zest from one lemon and extract the juice from both lemons. Peel the onions and tomatoes then cut into concasse (small dice).

2 Wash and dice the cucumber.

3 Sweat off the onions in a little oil until transparent then add the buglar wheat and stir for 1–2 minutes. Add the stock and bring to a simmer, cover and cook out for 15 minutes on a low heat.

4 Mix together the oil, lemon juice, zest and seasoning.

5 Off the heat add the cucumber, tomatoes and parsley and stir in the lemon dressing with a fork. Check and correct the seasoning if required.

6 Chill in a fridge for 2–3 hours before serving.

NOTES

Suitable for vegan, low-cholesterol and diabetic diets. ❑

Cannelloni with Sweet Pepper Ragout (p.172)   4 covers

- *300g   Tofu*
- *112g   Mushrooms*
- *1 clove Garlic, crushed*
- *15g   Flat parsley, chopped*
- *5g   Tarragon, chopped*
- *1   Free-range egg, beaten*
- *1   Lemon, freshly squeezed*
- *8   Cannelloni tubes, fresh*
- *Salt and ground black pepper*

1 Preheat the oven to 200°C/400°F/Gas Mark 6.

2 Place the tofu in a food processor and process until finely minced. Transfer to a bowl.

3 Place the mushrooms, garlic, parsley and tarragon in a blender and process until finely minced.

4 Beat the mushroom mixture into the tofu with the egg, salt and ground black pepper using the lemon juice to taste.

5 Cook the cannelloni in plenty of salted boiling water. Drain well and pat dry on a clean towel.

6 Place the filling in a piping bag fitted with a large plain nozzle, and fill each tube of pasta.

→

❑ Cannelloni with Sweet Pepper Ragout ❑

➜

Sweet Pepper Ragout

- ■ *20ml* *Olive oil*
- ■ *2* *Shallots, finely chopped*
- ■ *2 cloves Garlic, crushed*
- ■ *Pinch Cayenne pepper*
- ■ *1* *Plum tomato*
- ■ *65g* *Red pepper*
- ■ *65g* *Yellow pepper*
- ■ *Pinch Saffron*
- ■ *100ml Dry white wine*
- ■ *1tsp* *Flat parsley, chopped*
- ■ *1tsp* *Fresh basil, chopped*
- ■ *Seasoning*

1 Skin, deseed and slice the peppers. Skin, deseed and cut the tomatoes into concasse (small dice).

2 Heat the oil in a pan and add the shallots, garlic and cayenne pepper. Cook for 5 minutes or until softened.

3 Stir in the tomato, peppers, saffron and wine. Cook out uncovered for about 15 minutes until reduced by half.

4 Stir in the herbs and season to taste.

➜

Salsa

- 20ml   Olive oil
- 50g   Shitake mushrooms
- 50g   Button mushrooms
- 50g   Chanterelle mushrooms
- ½   Red chilli
- ¼tsp   Fresh cumin
- 1tsp   Fresh chives, chopped
- 1tsp   Fresh coriander, chopped
- 25g   Pitted black olives, chopped
- 1tsp   Lime juice
- 3tsp   Double cream
- 25g   Margarine

→

1 Clean and finely chop the mushrooms. Deseed and finely chop the chilli.

2 Heat the oil in a suitable pan, adding the chopped mushrooms and stir quickly over a high heat for 2–3 minutes.

3 Season and allow to cool. Add the chilli, cumin, chives, coriander, olives and lime juice and mix well.

4 Add the double cream and bind the ingredients together.

5 Stir in the margarine.

6 Assemble the dish. Place the ragout on the plate, put the cannelloni on top and then drop the salsa over the cannelloni. Garnish with chervil sprigs. ❏

Cappelletti Pasta Combo   4 covers

- 120g   Dried Cappelletti pasta
- 1   Green pepper
- 150g   Onions
- 30ml   Extra virgin olive oil
- 10g   Garlic
- 5g   Chilli powder
- 20ml   Balsamic vinegar
- 265ml   Tomato passata (tinned or bottled acceptable)
- 200g   Pinto beans (tinned is acceptable)
- 200g   Kidney beans (tinned is acceptable)
- 120g   Mozzarella or Parmesan cheese (vegetarian)
- ▪   Salt and freshly ground black pepper

1 Cook the pasta in boiling salted water and a little oil, then drain in cold running water. Drain and reserve.

2 Drain the beans, wash under cold water and reserve.

3 Deseed the green pepper and cut into small dice. Peel the onions and cut into small dice. Finely slice the garlic.

4 Sweat off the peppers and onions in a little oil for 2–3 minutes then add the garlic and chilli powder and continue to cook for 1–2 minutes. Add the balsamic vinegar and the passata sauce, and season with salt and pepper.

5 Stir in the pasta and beans, simmer for 8–10 minutes then serve with the cheese.

NOTES

Omit the cheese to cut down on the fat content. This recipe is suitable for vegan, low-cholesterol, diabetic and nut-free diets. ❏

Chard Rolls

- 20ml   Olive oil
- 100g   Pumpkin
- 1   Red pepper
- 100g   Shallots
- 10g   Garlic purée
- 220g   Paris brown mushrooms
- 120g   Risotto rice (Arborio)
- 550ml Vegetable stock
- 20g   Oregano
- 20g   Parmesan cheese (vegetarian))
- 4 leaves Chard, large
- 15g   Palm sugar
- 50g   Spring onions
-    Salt and freshly ground black pepper

1 Wash and remove the bottom stalk of the chard. Blanch first the stalk and then the leaf and refresh in ice-cold water. Cut the stalk into 1cm dice.

2 Skin and deseed the pepper and cut into 1cm dice. Peel and cut the spring onions, pumpkin and shallots into 1cm dice.

3 In oil sweat off without any colour the pumpkin, pepper and shallots, then add the garlic and the mushrooms and cook for 3–4 minutes. Add the palm sugar.

4 Add the rice and stir for 1–2 minutes, then pour in half the stock and bring to the boil. Simmer for 10 minutes until the rice has absorbed the stock and then add a little extra until all the stock has been absorbed. Check the seasoning and stir in the oregano and Parmesan cheese. Remove from the heat and cool.

5 Roll out the chard leaves, divide the mixture between them and roll up like a spring roll.

6 To reheat either steam for 5 minutes or place in a pan with a tight-fitting lid with stock or a tomato or pepper sauce for 5 minutes and serve with the sauce.

NOTES

Chinese lettuce or silver beet leaves may be used instead of chard.

Suitable for vegan, coeliac and low-cholesterol diets. ❏

Chickpea and Tacos Sauce

- 180g   Chickpeas, dried
- 450ml Vegetable stock
- 100g   Onions
- 1 clove Garlic
- 140g   Red pepper
- 140g   Yellow pepper
- 1   Red chilli

1 Peel and cut the onions and garlic into 2cm dice. Skin, deseed and cut the pepper and tomatoes into 2cm dice. Wash, de-core and cut the cucumber into 2cm dice. Wash, deseed and cut the chilli into very fine dice.

2 Soak the chickpeas overnight. Drain (reserve soaking liquid for extra stock) and cook until tender in the vegetable stock.

→

- 30ml   *Olive oil*
- 500g   *Plum tomatoes*
- 15g   *Fresh coriander, chopped*
- 10g   *Fresh parsley, chopped*
- 50g   *Cucumber*
-    *Salt and ground black pepper*

→

3   Sweat off the onions, garlic, peppers and chilli in the oil. Add the tomatoes and cook out for 20 minutes adding two-thirds of the herbs.

4   Add the chickpeas and cucumber and fry for a further 2–3 minutes.

5   Check the seasoning and serve garnished with a sprinkling of herbs.

6   Serve with fragrant rice. Recover with clingfilm if necessary.

NOTES

Suitable for vegan and coeliac diets. Serve with rice, EBLY® or potatoes. If served with EBLY® not suitable for coeliacs.

Increase the chilli content to make the dish hotter. ❏

Chickpea Curry   4 covers

- 225g   *Chickpeas, dried*
- 2 cloves *Garlic*
- 5cm   *Fresh ginger*
- 20ml   *Korma curry paste (or a mild curry powder)*
- 200g   *Onions*
- 40ml   *Vegetable oil*
- 3   *Beef tomatoes*
- 200ml *Vegetable stock*
- 200g   *Button mushrooms, sliced*
- 4   *Spring onions*
- 30g   *Fresh coriander*
- 30g   *Desiccated coconut, toasted*
- 60g   *Creamed coconut*
- 60g   *Flaked almonds, toasted*
- 2   *Bay leaf, small*
-    *Salt and white pepper*

1   Soak the chickpeas overnight in plenty of water. Cover with clingfilm or a clean cloth.

2   Drain the chickpeas, run cold water over them and pick through to remove any debris.

3   Peel and finely chop the onions, ginger and garlic. Peel and cut the spring onions into diamond shapes.

4   Sauté the garlic, ginger, curry spices and half the onions in a little oil without any colour.

5   Add the tomatoes and stock and cook for a further 10 minutes. Add the bay leaf. Blend the ingredients in a liquidiser or food processor until smooth.

6   Fry the remaining onions in the remaining oil for 3 minutes, add the sliced mushrooms and half the spring onions and cook for a further 3 minutes.

7   Pour the curry purée over the onions and mushrooms and add the drained chickpeas and most of the coriander. Heat gently for 20 minutes.

→

→ 8 Stir in 20g desiccated coconut, the creamed coconut and toasted almonds, reserving a few, and season to taste. Garnish with the remaining spring onions, coriander, toasted almonds and coconut.

NOTES

Serve with basmati rice, poppadoms, naan bread, mango chutney and mint flavoured yoghurt and cucumber. ❏

Chinese-style Chow Mein 4 covers

- ■ 120g *Chinese noodles*
- ■ 50ml *Sesame oil*
- ■ 100g *Onions*
- ■ 1 clove *Garlic*
- ■ 4cm *Fresh ginger*
- ■ 50g *Carrots*
- ■ 1 *Red pepper*
- ■ 1 *Green pepper*
- ■ 60ml *Shoyu sauce*
- ■ 200ml *Vegetable stock*
- ■ 50g *Beansprouts*
- ■ 50g *Mushrooms*
- ■ 20g *Fresh coriander*
- ■ 10g *Sugar*
- ■ 15g *Corn flour*
- ■ 250g *Tofu*
- ■ 15g *Salt*

1 Peel and cut the carrots and onions into julienne (fine strips). Peel and cut the ginger into very fine strips. Skin, deseed and cut the peppers into strips. Peel and purée the garlic. Clean the mushrooms and cut them into quarters.

2 Blanch the noodles in boiling salted water until cooked then, refresh in ice-cold water.

3 Heat half of the oil in a wok and stir-fry the onions, garlic, ginger, then the carrots and peppers for 4–5 minutes.

4 Add the shoyu sauce, reduce a little, then add the stock, beansprouts, mushrooms, half the coriander and a little sugar. Cook for a further 2–3 minutes.

5 When almost cooked sprinkle with corn flour and stir until it thickens and shines.

6 Drain the tofu, cut into 1cm × 5cm strips and put in a frying pan, colour on all sides and add to the vegetables. Keep hot.

7 Pour the remaining oil in a pan, sweat off the noodles with a little seasoning and the remaining coriander. Serve with the tofu.

NOTES

When catering for vegan diets ensure the noodles are egg-free, and for coeliac diets use rice noodles and replace the shoyu sauce with tamari. ❏

- *60ml   Peanut oil*
- *2 cloves Garlic*
- *150g   Shallots*
- *3cm   Ginger*
- *150g   Pak choi*
- *100g   Asparagus*
- *100g   Shitake mushrooms*
- *50g   Chinese*
  mushrooms, dried
- *3 drops Sesame oil*
- *10g   Sesame seeds,*
  toasted
- *20ml   Shoyu sauce*
- *100g   Spring onions*

1 Soak the Chinese mushrooms for one hour in warm water, then remove the stalk and slice along with the shitake mushrooms. Save the mushroom water.

2 Peel and slice the shallots. Peel and purée the ginger and garlic. Trim the asparagus. Trim and slice the pak choi.

3 Heat the peanut oil in a suitable wok and add the garlic, shallots and ginger. Add shoyu sauce and spring onions. Stir-fry for 2–3 minutes then add the pak choi and the asparagus. Stir-fry for a further 2–3 minutes then add the shitake mushrooms and a little mushroom water. Cook for 2 minutes then add the Chinese mushrooms and sesame oil.

4 Serve with a garnish of sesame seeds.

→

❑ Chinese-style Stir-fried Mushrooms ❑

→ NOTES

Serve with steamed rice flavoured with pandanus essence or coconut.

Suitable for vegan and diabetic diets. If Tamari is used instead of shoyu this will also be suitable for coeliac diets. ❏

Classic Stew with Seitan   4 covers

- 200g Carrots
- 150g Onions
- 100g Turnips
- 100g Parsnips
- 30ml Sunflower oil
- 350g Potatoes
- 300ml Vegetable stock
- 250g Seitan, diced
- 2 sprigs Thyme
- 1 sprig Rosemary
- 1 sprig Parsley
- 100g Button mushrooms
- 100g Paris brown mushrooms
- 20g   Miso
- 10g   Fresh parsley, chopped
- Salt and black pepper

1 Peel and cut into 1–2cm dice all the carrots, potatoes, onions, turnips and parsnips. Clean and quarter the mushrooms.

2 Sweat off the vegetables in the oil until golden brown.

3 Add the potatoes and stock (just enough to cover) and all other ingredients (except the mushrooms, miso and chopped parsley). Simmer for 30 minutes, removing any debris from the surface.

4 Remove the sprigs of herbs, correct the seasoning and add the mushrooms and miso. Cook for a further 10 minutes and garnish with chopped parsley.

NOTES

The potato starch should help to thicken the stew, but adding 10–15g potato or arrowroot powder will achieve a thicker consistency if required.

Suitable for vegan, diabetic and low-cholesterol diets. ❏

Creamed Spinach Parcels (p.180)   4 covers

- 150g Onions
- 30ml Sunflower oil
- 150g Mushrooms
- 150g Pine nuts
- 500g Frozen spinach (or cooked fresh)
- 10g   Parsley
- Pinch Ground nutmeg

1 Cook the spinach according to the instructions then drain and squeeze out and roughly chop.

2 Clean and slice the mushrooms, then peel and finely slice the onions.

3 Purée the tofu.

→

- *120ml Silken tofu*
- *8 sheets Filo pastry*
- *30g   Margarine*
- *   Salt and black*
  *   pepper*

4 Toast the pine nuts under the grill in a dry pan until golden brown.

5 Sweat off the onions in the oil over a medium heat until they are transparent.

6 Add the mushrooms and continue to cook for a further 5 minutes, then add pine nuts, remove from the heat and add the spinach. Season and add the parsley and nutmeg.

7 Pour into a bowl and stir in the tofu. Allow to cool slightly.

8 Remove two sheets of filo pastry, keeping the other sheets covered with a damp towel to prevent drying.

9 Lay one sheet on top of the other and place a quarter of the cool mixture on top, approximately 5cm from the edge. Brush the edges with cold water and roll firmly to half way then fold in the edges and brush again with a little water and continue to roll tightly.

10 Repeat this process with the remaining ingredients. Brush the tops of the parcels with a little melted margarine.

11 Bake in a preheated oven at 190°C/Gas Mark 5 for 15–20 minutes until golden brown and crisp.

NOTES

Suitable for vegan, diabetic and low-cholesterol diets. Serve with a light salad. ❏

Crisp Deep-fried Tofu with Spicy Peanut Dip   4 covers

- *600g   Fresh tofu*
- *150g   Corn flour*
- *15g   Five spice powder*
- *1   Free-range egg*
- *50g   Water*

Alternative batter

- *70g   Plain flour*
- *2   Free-range eggs*

1 Drain the tofu and cut into 2–3cm cubes.

2 Mix the corn flour and five spice powder together.

3 Mix the egg and water together and dip the tofu in, coating it entirely, then dip into the corn flour and spice mixture.

4 Remove any excess flour and place in the deep-fat fryer until golden brown. Remove and drain on kitchen paper.

5 Place on skewers and serve with the sauce.

→

❏ Top: Creamed Spinach Parcels Bottom: Spiced Yellow Pumpkin ❏

- 2.5g Baking powder
- 2.5g Cayenne pepper

Sauce
- 20g Red curry paste (commercial Thai curry paste is acceptable)
- 15ml Groundnut oil
- 15ml Rice vinegar
- 50g Palm sugar
- 70g Dry roasted peanuts
- 50ml Tamarind water
- 450ml Coconut milk
- 20ml Shoyu
- ■ Salt

6 For the alternative batter, sieve the flour, baking powder and cayenne together and stir in the eggs. Rest the batter in the fridge for 20 minutes before using. Then proceed as in steps 4 and 5.

1 Fry off the curry paste for 2–3 minutes in the groundnut oil, then add the vinegar, sugar, nuts, tamarind water, shoyu and coconut milk. Cook for a further 4–5 minutes and add a little salt to taste if required. ❑

Deep-fried Tofu in a Spicy Peanut Sauce (p.182) 4 covers

- 550g Marinated tofu

Sauce
- 65g Mirin (Rice wine vinegar)
- 65g Honey
- 130g Peanut butter
- 15ml Chilli sauce
- 20ml BBQ sauce

Batter
- 5g Chilli powder
- 5g Baking powder
- 113g Plain flour
- 2 Free-range eggs
- 113ml Milk, ice cold
- ■ Salt and pepper

1 Drain the tofu and cut it into either triangles or squares. Dry with a clean cloth.

2 To make the spicy peanut sauce pour the mirin into a pan and heat to boiling point then add the honey then the peanut butter. Remove from the heat and add the chilli and BBQ sauces.

3 To make the batter sieve the chilli powder, baking powder and flour into a suitable bowl, then mix in the ice-cold milk and eggs to form a smooth batter.

4 Place the tofu onto wooden skewers, dip into the batter and slide off the skewers into a hot fryer 180°C for 5–6 minutes until golden brown.

5 Remove and dry off any excess fat on kitchen paper then serve with the warm peanut dipping sauce.

NOTES

This recipe is not suitable for vegan diets, unless vegan peanut butter is used and the tofu is coated only in chilli flour. ❑

❏ Deep-fried Tofu in a Spicy Peanut Sauce ❏

Eastern Mushroom and Tofu Kebabs   4 covers

- 350g Fresh tofu
- 300g Button mushrooms
- 450g Aubergines
- 8   Vine tomatoes
- 450g Red peppers
- 8   Large spring onions
- 25g   Fresh coriander, chopped
- 1   Fresh lime

Dressing

- 200g Clear, light honey
- 2g   Cinnamon powder
- 5g   Cumin seeds
- 50g   Garlic purée

1 Roast the cumin seeds in a dry pan until fragrant.

2 To make the dressing warm the honey over a gentle heat. Then add the garlic, cinnamon and cumin seeds.

3 Wash the tomatoes and cut them in half. Segment the limes and reserve.

4 Wash and cut all the other ingredients into 2.5 cm dice, then thread on 20–23cm skewers, with half a tomato at each end.

5 Coat the kebabs in the warm dressing and place on a pre-heated griddle or under a grill. Brush with the dressing every few minutes, reserving the residue.

6 Cook for 6–8 minutes until golden brown. Garnish with chopped coriander and wedges of lime.

NOTES

Serve with couscous or rice and the cooking liquor and dressing. ❏

EBLY® Pilaf

- 60ml *Sunflower oil*
- 225g *Onions*
- 2.5g *Turmeric*
- 2.5g *Ground cumin*
- 2.5g *Ground coriander*
- 2–3 *Red chillies (optional)*
- 1–2 cloves *Garlic*
- 5g *Ginger*
- 300g *EBLY®*
- 600ml *Vegetable stock, hot*
- 20g *Fresh coriander, chopped*

1 Peel and finely dice the onions and ginger. Deseed and finely slice the chillies.

2 Heat the oil and sauté the onions for approximately 1 minute then add the spices, chillies, garlic and ginger.

3 Cook for a further 1 minute, add the EBLY® and coat well with the mixture.

4 Add the hot stock, mix well, add a little seasoning, cover and gently simmer for 16–20 minutes.

5 Remove from the heat, allow to rest and add half the coriander. Correct seasoning and serve, garnished with the remainder of the coriander.

NOTES

A variety of vegetables could be added, for example, peas, sweet cornkernels, mushrooms. If plain pilaff is required, leave out the Indian spices. ❑

Farfalloni with Shitake Mushrooms

- 250g *Farfalloni pasta (Farfalle bow tie pasta can be substituted)*
- 50g *Margarine*
- 50g *Plain white flour*
- 280ml *Vegetable stock (white)*
- 120ml *Dry white wine*
- 150g *Shitake mushrooms*
- 20ml *Olive oil*
- 2 cloves *Garlic*
- 10g *Chives, dropped*
- 10g *Parsley*
- 120ml *Double cream*
- *Salt and ground white pepper*

1 Cook the pasta in boiling salted water with a little oil for 15 minutes, drain and refresh under cold running water. Drain and reserve.

2 Clean and slice the mushrooms. Peel and very thinly slice the garlic.

3 Place the margarine in a thick-bottomed pan and melt over a gentle heat.

4 Add the flour and cook out until a light sandy texture has been achieved, making a roux. Remove from the heat and cool slightly.

5 Bring the stock almost to the boil and simmer.

6 Gradually add the white wine then the stock to the roux, stirring until a smooth sauce is achieved. Simmer for 45–60 minutes and pass through a strainer to remove any debris. Add double cream. Cover with greaseproof paper brushed with margarine to prevent a skin forming.

→

7 Sweat off the mushrooms in the oil for 2–3 minutes then add the garlic and cook for 2–3 minutes, then drain and add to the sauce.

8 Add the pasta to the sauce and simmer for 2–3 minutes until the pasta has reached the required temperature (do not re-boil). Add half the chives and all the parsley, stir and add seasoning.

9 Garnish with the remaining chives. ❑

Field Mushrooms Filled with Spinach, EBLY® and Glazed Cheese Sauce
4 covers

- 500g   Fresh spinach
- 75g   EBLY®
- 60ml   Olive oil
- 350g   Onions, Spanish or red
- 10   Field mushrooms (medium)
- ▪   Salt, pepper, nutmeg
- 150g   Mozzarella and Cheddar, grated (50/50) (vegetarian)

Cheese Sauce
- 45g   Butter ⎱ combine to
- 45g   Flour ⎰ a Beurre Meunière
- 350ml   Milk, hot
- 15g   English mustard
- 85g   Cheddar cheese (vegetarian)
- 1   Onion clouté (onion, bay leaf, 6 cloves)

1 Blanch, refresh, drain and chop the spinach.

2 Cook the EBLY® in plenty of boiling salted water for 15–20 minutes depending on the consistency required. Drain and leave to one side.

3 To make up the cheese sauce (optional – infuse the milk with the onion clouté), pour the hot milk on the Beurre Meunière to form a sauce. Add the mustard. Cook out on a low heat for 5 minutes then stir in the Cheddar cheese and adjust the seasoning.

4 Heat the oil and sweat the onions so that they begin to caramelise, then remove from the heat.

5 De-stalk the mushrooms, chop the stalks and cook with the onions. Brush the outside of the mushroom with olive oil then place in a non-stick or greased tray, dome side down and season.

6 Season the spinach with salt, pepper and nutmeg, place evenly in and around the inner mushroom and add the caramelised onion and the seasoned EBLY®. Carefully spoon the cheese sauce over the EBLY®, top with the grated cheese and place in a preheated at oven 200°C/Gas Mark 6 for 20–25 minutes, until cooked and glazed.

7 Place under a hot grill if further glazing is required.

8 Serve with garlic bread and a crisp salad. ❑

Filled Chinese Rolls and Tomato Sauce (p.255)   4 covers

- *180ml Vegetable stock*
- *60g   Cracked wheat*
- *283g   Tofu (fresh)*
- *50g   Peanuts*
- *20g   Fresh parsley, chopped*
- *10g   Fresh coriander, chopped*
- *10g   Fresh mint, chopped*
- *60ml   Natural yoghurt*
- *8 leaves Chinese lettuce*
- *   Salt and ground black pepper*
- *Pinch Cinnamon*

Tomato sauce
- *25g   Shallots*
- *20ml   White wine*
- *500g   Tomatoes*

1 Skin, deseed and chop the tomatoes into small dice (concasse). Peel and dice the shallots. Crush the peanuts.

2 Blanch the lettuce leaves very lightly, refresh in ice-cold water and drain.

3 Boil 150ml stock and pour over the cracked wheat and cover with a lid. Level for 12 minutes then season with salt and pepper.

4 Mash up the tofu and mix with the cracked wheat, nuts, herbs and yoghurt and check the seasoning. Add the cinnamon.

5 Lay out the leaves and trim accordingly. Divide the filling up between the eight leaves and roll like a spring roll.

6 Place the rolls in a shallow pan.

7 To make the sauce sweat the shallots off in a pan for 1–2 minutes without colour, then add the white wine and reduce by half. Add the tomatoes and the remaining stock, cook out for 10–15 minutes and season.

8 Place tomato sauce in a liquidiser and blend. Check the seasoning then pour over the rolls. Place a lid on top of the pan and bring the rolls back to a simmer for 25 minutes. Serve in a suitable dish with the sauce and chopped parsley.

NOTES

Serve with new or mid potatoes and fresh vegetables.

Suitable for vegans if soya bean yoghurt is used. It is also suitable for low-cholesterol and diabetic diets. ❑

Garlic and Olive Bread Pudding   4 covers

- *100g   Margarine*
- *20g   Garlic purée*
- *100g   Onions*
- *100g   Leeks*
- *8 slices White bread*

1 Melt the margarine and stir in the garlic purée. Cut the crusts off the slices of bread and process the crusts into crumbs.

→

- 50g   Black pitted olives
- 150g   Artichoke bottoms
- 10g   Fresh marjoram,
           chopped
- 180g   Cheddar cheese,
           grated (vegetarian)
- 500g   Milk (skimmed)
- 2   Free-range eggs,
           medium
-          Salt and ground
           white pepper

2 Peel and finely dice the leeks and onions. Roughly chop the artichoke bottoms and the olives.

3 Sweat off the onions and leeks in a little margarine until limp then remove from the heat.

4 Brush the garlic margarine onto the bread slices then cut into triangles.

5 Brush a suitable baking dish with the garlic margarine and put one layer of overlapping bread (4 slices) into the bottom of the dish.

6 Lay the onions, leeks, olives, artichokes and half of the marjoram on top of the bread. Season with salt and pepper and sprinkle the breadcrumbs over.

7 Place the final layer of bread on top of the filling and cover with grated Cheddar cheese.

8 Mix the milk and eggs together with a little seasoning and slowly pour over the top of the bread pudding.

9 Let the dish soak for 10–15 minutes then place in a preheated oven at 190°C/Gas Mark 5–6, for 30–40 minutes, until golden brown.

10 Remove from the oven and let stand for 3–4 minutes then sprinkle the remaining marjoram over the top and serve. ❏

Greek-style Stuffed Vine Leaves   4 covers

- 100g   Basmati rice
- 2tbsp   Olive oil
- 25g   Pine kernels
- 100g   Onions
- 25g   Currants
- 20g   Chestnuts
- 10g   Fresh mint, chopped
- 10g   Fresh parsley,
           chopped
- 10g   Fresh basil, chopped
-          Ground cinnamon,
           ground allspice,
           nutmeg

1 Blanch the vine leaves in boiling water for 5 minutes, no salt. Rinse in cold water and leave to drain in a colander.

2 Cook the rice in boiling salted water with a drop of oil. Then rinse and refresh until required.

3 Roast the pine kernels in a pan. Peel and chop the onions and then sauté until soft. Add the currants, chestnuts and pine kernels, then seasoning.

4 Now add the freshly chopped herbs and spices to the onion mixture. Add the cooked rice and mix in well. Check the seasoning.

→

- ■ 8   *Vine leaves*
- ■   *Salt and pepper*

Stock

- ■ *30ml*   *Olive oil*
- ■ *1*   *Lemon (juice only)*
- ■ *1 litre* *Light stock*
- ■   *Salt, pepper and sugar*
- ■ *1 sprig* *Fresh parsley, chopped*

→

5 Place a vine leaf with the vein facing upwards. Then place a small amount of filling onto it. Roll the vine up, tucking in the sides as you roll. (It is best to roll from the stalk end.)

6 Put the prepared vines tightly in a dish. Mix the stock ingredients together and pour, just covering the leaves. Cover with tin foil.

7 Place on the top of the stove and cook slowly for 1 hour. Serve 2 per portion, hot with a little chopped parsley. Serve with a fresh tomato and basil sauce. ❏

Hot Buttered EBLY® with Herbs   4 covers

- ■ *350g*   *EBLY®*
- ■ *65g*   *Margarine*
- ■ *75g*   *Fresh herbs with combinations of parsley, chives, basil, tarragon, chervil and sage*
- ■   *Salt and pepper*

1 Cook the EBLY® in plenty of boiling salted water for 15–20 minutes depending on the consistency required. Drain and leave to one side.

2 Melt the margarine in a pan. Add the cooked EBLY® and coat with the margarine.

3 Correct seasoning, add the fresh herbs and serve. ❏

Hot Red Cabbage and Russet Apples (p.207)   4 covers

- ■ *30g*   *Margarine*
- ■ *120g*   *Onions*
- ■ *½*   *Medium red cabbage*
- ■ *2*   *Russet apples*
- ■ *100g*   *Sultanas*
- ■ *5g*   *Ground cassia bark*
- ■ *150ml* *Vegetable stock*
- ■   *Salt and pepper*

1 Wash and shred the cabbage, de-core and dice the apples, and peel and dice the onions. Wash the sultanas in warm water, then soak for 15 minutes.

2 Melt the margarine over a medium heat then add the onions and the cabbage and cook for 6–8 minutes. Then add the stock and cook for a further 6–8 minutes then add the apples, sultanas and cassia powder and cook for a further 3–4 minutes.

3 Serve immediately.

NOTES

This recipe is suitable for vegan, low-cholesterol, diabetic, coeliac and nut-free diets. ❏

❏ Top: Jamaican-style Jerk   Bottom: Bulgar Wheat Mexican Style ❏

Jamaican-style Jerk — 4 covers

- 700g Seitan
- 50ml Tamari
- 20g All spice
- 20g Thyme leaves
- 5–10g Freshly ground black pepper
- 5g Cinnamon
- 5–10g Cayenne pepper
- 20g Garlic purée
- 20g Palm sugar
- 60ml Coconut oil

Sauce
- 1 Scotch bonnet pepper
- 100g Onions
- 100g Green peppers
- 80ml Orange juice
- 50ml Pineapple juice
- 150ml Vinegar
- ▪ Arrowroot powder
- ▪ Salt and black pepper

1 Drain and cut the seitan into 1½cm dice. Place all the ingredients (except the oil) in a bowl and thoroughly blend them together. Marinade the seitan for 20–25 minutes, then remove.

2 To make the sauce, skin and deseed the peppers and then cut the onions and pepper into fine dice.

3 Put all the ingredients in a pan and bring to the boil. Simmer over a low heat for 20 minutes and then thicken with a little arrowroot powder and water until the required consistency is achieved. Check the seasoning.

4 Heat the oil in a suitable pan and add the seitan. Seal all the edges of the seitan then tip off any excess oil. Add to the sauce, cook for 3–4 minutes and serve.

NOTES

Serve with plain or coconut-flavoured rice. To make this dish less hot or more hot adjust the chilli pepper and cayenne accordingly or add some Tabasco sauce.

Suitable for vegan diets. ❑

Laver Bread, Samphire and Mushroom Lasagne (p.268) — 4 covers

- 200g Green lasagne
- 50g Vegetable oil
- 1 Onion
- 130g Button mushrooms
- 500g Laver bread (frozen or cooked)
- 1 Lemon (juice)
- 225g Cottage cheese (or smoked tofu or tempeh)

1 Cook the lasagne in boiling salted water, refresh in ice-cold water and reserve until required.

2 Peel and finely dice the onions and wipe clean and slice the mushrooms.

3 Sweat off onions in vegetable oil, then add mushrooms and cook for 2-3 minutes.

4 Add the laver bread, nutmeg and salt and pepper and simmer for approximately 6 minutes.

5 Mix the cottage and Cheddar cheese with seasoning. Add together with chopped samphire.

→

- 100g Cheddar cheese
       (vegetarian)
- 100g Samphire, chopped
-       Nutmeg, grated
-       Salt and pepper

Sauce
- 25g   Margarine
- 15g   Plain flour
- 225g Soya milk
- 25g   Parmesan cheese
       (vegetarian)

6 To make the sauce make a roux with melted margarine and flour.

7 Heat the milk, slowly add to the roux and beat to a smooth paste.

8 Simmer for 2–3 minutes until thick and creamy. Do not boil as the soya milk could split.

9 Add the Parmesan cheese. Check the seasoning.

10 Place a layer of the cooked pasta in an ovenproof dish, and put half of the cottage cheese mix on top, spreading evenly. Lay half of the laver bread on top of the cheese mix, spreading evenly. Repeat. Finish with pasta covering the top. Spread the sauce over the lasagne and bake in a preheated oven at 200°C/Gas Mark 6 for 30–35 minutes. ❑

Leek and Broccoli Strudel 4 covers

- 350g Broccoli
- 113g Margarine (1)
- 20ml Olive oil
- 50g   Onions
- 340g Leeks
- 3 cloves Garlic
- 113g Plain flour
       (unbleached)
- 250ml Vegetable stock
- 50g   Peas
- 300g Sweet corn, kernels
- 10g   Chives
- 10g   Whole grain
       mustard
- 50g   Walnuts, broken
- 60g   Margarine (2)
- 8 sheets Filo pastry

1 Wash the broccoli and cut into florets. Peel the garlic and the onions, cut the onions into 2cm dice, then purée the garlic. Top and tail the leeks, cut in half, then wash and cut into 2cm dice.

2 Steam off the broccoli and refresh in ice-cold water, then drain and keep until required. Finely chop the chives.

3 Heat the margarine (1) and a little oil in a suitable pan and sauté off the onions, leeks and garlic without any colour.

4 Gradually stir in the flour and cook out for 2–3 minutes then gradually add the stock. Stir until it becomes a smooth sauce.

5 Add the broccoli, peas, sweetcorn, chives, mustard and 30g walnuts. Simmer for 5 minutes, season and allow to cool.

6 Melt the remaining margarine, lay out the filo pastry sheets and brush with margarine.

7 Place one filo sheet on top of another and divide the filling between the four portions. Roll the filo sheets into spring roll shapes, 15cm × 8cm.

8 Place the rolls on a greased baking sheet, seam side down, and brush with the remaining margarine. Spread the remaining walnuts on top.

9 Bake the strudels in a preheated oven at 220°C/Gas Mark 8 for 20–25 minutes until golden brown.

NOTES

Serve with a pepper sauce and new rosemary scented potatoes.

Suitable for vegans if vegan margarine is used. ❑

Leek and Parsnip Pie   4 covers

- 750g   Potatoes
- 2   Egg yolks
- 50g   Vegetable oil
- 225g   Parsnips
- 128g   Peas
- 50g   Turnips
- 50g   Carrots
- 110g   Onions
- 50g   Celery
- 225g   Leeks
- 28g   Parsley
- 10g   Thyme
- 300g   Velouté

1 Peel and cut the parsnips, turnips, carrots, onions and celery into 1cm dice. Top and tail the leeks and cut in half, then wash and cut into 1cm dice. Wash, pick and finely chop the parsley and thyme.

2 Peel and dice the potatoes, then place in cold salted water and boil until cooked. Remove from the heat and drain off the water. Put back on the stove and gently allow to dry out a little.

3 Place the potatoes into a food processor and purée adding the egg yolks. Add seasoning and keep to one side.

4 Sweat off the vegetables in a little oil with no colour. Tip off any excess oil and add three-quarters of the herbs and all of the velouté. Correct any seasoning.

5 Put the mixture in a suitable ovenproof dish and allow to cool slightly. Top with the mashed potato mixture.

6 Place in a preheated oven at 200°C/Gas Mark 7 for 20–25 minutes. Garnish with chopped herbs.

Velouté

100g   Margarine
100g   Plain white flour
1l   Vegetable stock
       (white)

1 Place the margarine in a thick-bottomed pan and melt over a gentle heat. Add the flour and cook out until a light sandy texture has been achieved, making a roux. Remove from the heat and cool slightly.

→

→ 2 Bring the stock almost to the boil and simmer.

3 Gradually add the stock to the roux, stirring until a smooth sauce is achieved. Simmer for 45–60 minutes and pass through a strainer to remove any debris. Cover with greaseproof paper brushed with margarine to prevent a skin forming. ❑

Lemongrass and Potato Crumble   4 covers

- 365g   Potatoes
- 100g   Plain flour
- 10g   Fresh coriander
- 10g   Fresh parsley
- 100g   Margarine
- 60ml   Vegetable oil
- 100g   Onions
- 100g   Leeks
- 1   Lemongrass
- 150ml Velouté
- ■   Salt and pepper

1 Chop the herbs. Peel and slice the leeks and onions. Top and tail the lemongrass and remove the stalk, then finely dice.

2 Wash, peel, skin and cut the potatoes into 2cm dice. Steam until just cooked.

3 Sieve the flour into a bowl and add the herbs, seasoning and the margarine. Mix until the ingredients are a biscuit-type consistency. Do not over-mix.

4 Heat the oil in a suitable saucepan and then add the onions and leeks, and cook without colour.

5 Add the lemongrass to the onions and leeks, tip off any excess margarine and add to the velouté.

6 Add the velouté to the potatoes and season and stir until fully mixed together.

7 Place the potato in an ovenproof dish and allow to cool a little then put the crumble mixture on top.

8 Bake in a preheated oven at 180°C/Gas Mark 4, for 15–20 minutes until golden brown.

Velouté

- 100g   Margarine
- 100g   Plain white flour
- 1l   Vegetable stock (white)

1 Place the margarine in a thick-bottomed pan and melt over a gentle heat. Add the flour and cook out until a light sandy texture has been achieved, making a roux.

2 Remove from the heat and cool slightly. Bring the stock almost to the boil and simmer. Gradually add the stock to the roux, stirring until a smooth sauce is achieved. Simmer for 45–60 minutes and pass through a strainer to remove any debris. Cover with greaseproof paper brushed with margarine to prevent a skin forming. ❑

❏ Lemongrass and Potato Crumble ❏

Lentil Daal   4 covers

- *110g Pye Lentils*
- *230ml Vegetable stock*
- *1   Green chilli, small*
- *5g   Turmeric*
- *5g   Ground coriander*
- *3   Plum tomatoes*
- *1   Onion*
- *1 clove Garlic*
- *1   Red chilli, small*
- *50g   Margarine*
- *10g   Fresh coriander, chopped*

1 Peel and finely dice the onion and the garlic. Wash and deseed the chillies, then very finely slice.

2 Blanch and refresh the tomatoes, then deseed and chop in to concasse (small dice).

3 Put the lentils into the stock, bring to the boil and simmer for 5 minutes.

4 Add the green chilli, turmeric, ground coriander and tomato concasse. Cook for a further 3–4 minutes.

5 Sweat off the onion, garlic and red chilli in the margarine then add the lentil mixture.

6 Add half of the chopped coriander and season to taste.

7 Garnish with the rest of the coriander and serve.

➔

→

NOTES

Suitable for vegan and various other diets.

Serve with rice or as an extra to curry. Do not touch any sensitive parts of the body while preparing the chillies. Wash hands thoroughly after touching chillies. ❏

Linguine with Olives and Capers   4 covers

- 250g   Linguine pasta
- 40ml   Olive oil
- 150g   Onions
- 1   Red pepper
- 1   Green pepper
- 20g   Garlic purée
- 5g   Mixed herbs
- 30ml   Tomato purée
- 340g   Chopped tomatoes, canned
- 120g   Courgettes
- 50–100g Black olives, pitted
- 20g   Capers
- 20g   Fresh parsley, chopped
- 100g   Baby button mushrooms
-          Salt and ground black pepper

1 Peel and slice the onions, clean and leave the mushrooms whole. Skin and deseed the peppers and then cut into 1–2cm dice. Wash, top and tail and dice the courgettes. Wash the olives and capers then cut the olives into quarters.

2 Cook the pasta in boiling salted water with a little oil for 15 minutes then refresh under cold running water. Drain.

3 Sweat off the onions in a little oil until transparent.

4 Add the peppers and garlic and fry gently for 2–3 minutes.

5 Add the herbs, tomato purée, tomatoes and courgettes and cook for 5–6 minutes. Add mushrooms. Stir well, bring to the boil and then simmer covered for 15–20 minutes.

6 Add the linguine, the olives and capers. Toss and stir the pasta in well and season to taste. Cook for a further 3 minutes.

7 Serve sprinkled with chopped parsley.

NOTES

Add ricotta or mozzarella cheese can be added. It may be necessary to add a little sugar to sweeten the tomatoes. ❏

❏ Linguine with Olives and Capers ❏

Linguine with Roasted Peppers and Garlic (p.205) 4 covers

- 225g   Linguine pasta
- 150g   Onions
- 20ml   Extra virgin olive oil
- 2   Red peppers
- 340g   Mixed mushrooms
          (chanterelle, Paris
          brown, button or
          oyster)
- 2 cloves Garlic
- 10g   Fresh sweet basil
- 227g   Garlic croûtons
- 165g   Fresh grated
           Parmesan cheese
           (vegetarian)
- ■   Salt and freshly
           ground black pepper

1 Skin, deseed and dice the peppers, clean, de-stalk and slice the mushrooms. Peel and thinly slice the garlic and onions.

2 Cook the pasta in boiling salted water for approximately 10 minutes then drain and reserve. Keep 140ml of the cooking water.

3 Sweat off the onions in a little oil then add the peppers and mushrooms. Cook for 2–3 minutes then add the garlic.

4 Add the pasta and toss until incorporated. Season then add the reserved liquid.

5 Add the basil and the croûtons and serve with the Parmesan cheese sprinkled over the top.

NOTES

Suitable for vegan, diabetic and low-cholesterol diets. ❏

Low-fat Vegetarian Chilli Beans

- 113g   Red kidney beans, tinned
- 113g   Haricot beans, tinned
- 1   Green pepper, small
- 120g   Onions
- 20g   Low-fat margarine
- 5g   Chilli powder
- 5g   Cumin seeds
- 5g   Garlic purée
- 110g   Tomato purée
- 15ml   Cider vinegar
- 250ml   Vegetable stock
- 2   Beef tomatoes
- 4   Spring onions
- 10g   Fresh marjoram, chopped
- 10g   Fresh parsley, chopped
-   Salt and ground black pepper

1 Skin, deseed and cut into 1cm dice (concasse) the tomatoes and pepper. Skin and cut the onions into 1 cm dice.

2 Remove the root and dry leaves from the spring onions and cut into 1cm lengths, including the green tops.

3 Wash and drain the beans in a colander.

4 Sweat off the pepper and onions in a little margarine, add the spices and the garlic purée and cook for 2–3 minutes.

5 Stir in the beans, tomato purée, vinegar and the stock and cook for 10–15 minutes.

6 Incorporate the tomato concasse, spring onions and marjoram and cook for a further 5–10 minutes.

7 Check seasoning and serve garnished with chopped parsley.

NOTES

Serve with basmati rice. Suitable for vegan and diabetic diets. ❑

Masaman Curry

- 400g   Carrots, leeks, courgettes, celery
- 120g   Onions
- 110g   Potatoes
- 30ml   Sunflower oil
- 650ml   Coconut milk
- 40ml   Demerara sugar
- 45ml   Shoyu
- 50ml   Tamarind water
- 40g   Peanuts
- 10g   Methi

Red curry paste
- 4   Red chillies, ground

1 To make the paste blend all the spices in a processor or pestle and mortar.

2 Peel and dice the shallots, lemongrass, galangal, ginger and garlic. Then blend all the ingredients until they form a paste.

3 Fry the paste in a little oil for 2–3 minutes until it becomes fragrant.

4 Peel and dice the carrots, leeks, courgettes, celery, onions and potatoes, sauté in hot oil and stir. Add methi. Add them to the paste and cook for 2–3 minutes.

→

- ■ *3cm stick Cinnamon*
- ■ *2*   *Star anise*
- ■ *4*   *Cloves*
- ■ *6*   *Cardamom pods*
- ■ *12g*   *Coriander seeds*
- ■ *5g*   *Pimento powder*
- ■ *15g*   *Cumin seeds*
- ■ *2.5g* *Bay leaf, powdered*
- ■ *4 cloves Garlic*
- ■ *4*   *Shallots*
- ■ *1*   *Lemongrass*
- ■ *3cm*   *Galangal*
- ■ *3cm*   *Ginger*

→ 5 Add the coconut milk, demerara sugar, shoyu sauce and tamarind water and bring to the boil. Stir in the peanuts and simmer for 20–30 minutes.

6 Serve with rice.

NOTES

Serve with basmati rice, poppadoms, naan bread, mango chutney and mint flavoured yoghurt and cucumber. ❑

Mediterranean EBLY®   4 covers

- ■ *160g*   *EBLY®*
- ■ *120ml Olive oil*
- ■ *140g*   *Aubergine*
- ■ *160g*   *Onions*
- ■ *140g*   *Courgettes*
- ■ *140g*   *Plum Italian tomato*
- ■ *10g*   *Garlic purée*
- ■ *30ml* *Basil, shredded*
- ■ *1*   *Green pepper*
- ■ *1*   *Red pepper*
- ■ *1*   *Yellow pepper*
- ■ *15g*   *Parmesan cheese, (vegetarian)*
- ■   *Salt, pepper and caster sugar*

1 Cook the EBLY® in plenty of boiling salted water for 15–20 minutes depending on the consistency required. Drain and leave to one side.

2 Skin and deseed the peppers and the tomatoes, then cut into 1–2cm pieces. Peel and cut the onions into 1–2cm pieces. Wash and slice the aubergine and courgettes.

3 Heat a little olive oil in a sauté pan. Brown the sliced aubergine on both sides, remove and place on a roasting tray. Place into a preheated oven at 190°C/Gas Mark 5 until cooked. Allow to cool slightly and cut each round into four pieces.

4 Pan-fry the onions in a little oil then add the courgettes and cook until a nice even colour is achieved.

5 Heat a little oil in a pan until very hot, add the tomatoes and garlic purée with a little salt and sugar. Cook for 5–10 seconds then add the basil and gently mix.

6 Add the EBLY® and all the vegetables. Cook for another minute and then add the Parmesan cheese.

7 Correct the seasoning and serve. Garnish with basil leaves. ❑

Mediterranean-style Bean Casserole   4 covers

- 200g   Onions
- 1   Red pepper
- 1   Green pepper
- 3 cloves Garlic
- 40ml   Olive oil
- 100ml Strong vegetable stock
- 15ml   Fresh marjoram, oregano, thyme
- 30ml   Tomato purée
- 450g   Plum Italian tomatoes
- 320g   Flageolets beans (use tinned for quick recipe)
- 50g   Black olives, stoned
- 30ml   Fresh parsley, chopped
- 100g   Yellow courgettes
-    Salt and Pepper

1 Skin, deseed and dice the peppers and tomatoes (reserve tomato liquid). Peel and dice the onions and purée the garlic.

2 Halve the olives and wash and dice the courgettes. Finely chop the herbs, keeping the parsley separate.

3 Sweat off the onions, peppers and garlic in a little oil.

4 Add the stock, mixed herbs, courgettes, tomato purée, tomatoes, tomato water and beans.

5 Stir well and bring to the boil, then simmer for 15–20 minutes.

6 Add the olives. Cook for 2 minutes and then check the seasoning.

7 Garnish with chopped parsley and serve with Italian bread and olive oil.

NOTES

Dried beans can be used as can tinned chopped tomatoes.

This recipe can be used for vegan, coeliac (omit bread), low-cholesterol and diabetic diets. ❏

Mixed Nut Burgers   4 covers

- 60g   Margarine
- 100g   Onions
- 50g   Spring onion
- 50g   Celery
- 100g   Leeks
- 20g   Mixed herbs (rosemary, thyme and parsley)
- 20g   Wholewheat flour
- 130ml Vegetable stock (white)
- 20ml   Tamari

1 Peel and finely dice the onions, spring onions, celery and leeks and then sauté with the margarine. Add the roughly chopped herbs.

2 Then add the flour and cook out for 1–2 minutes.

3 Add the stock and stir in until thick.

4 Mix in the tamari, yeast extract, finely ground nuts and breadcrumbs well, season to taste and allow to cool.

5 Divide the mixture equally into four burgers and shape by hand. (Use a burger press to give a firm shape.)

6 Fry the burgers in vegetable oil until golden.

→

❏ Top: Mushroom and Seitan Stroganoff   Bottom: Mediterranean-style Bean Casserole ❏

→   7 Serve with a tomato sauce and salad. ❏

- 80g   Ground peanuts (roasted unsalted)
- 80g   Ground roasted pinenuts
- 40g   Ground roasted almonds
- 110g   Fresh wholewheat breadcrumbs
- 80ml   Vegetable oil
-    Freshly ground black pepper

Moroccan-style Couscous 4 covers

- 160ml   Vegetable stock
- 25ml   Olive oil
-    Salt and Pepper
- 160g   Couscous
- ½   Onion, finely chopped
- 10–15g   Turmeric
- 1 small   Red pepper, finely diced
- 1 tsp   Fresh parsley
- 1 tsp   Fresh coriander
- 1 tsp   Fresh mint
- 25g   Margarine

1 Bring the stock, oil, salt and pepper to the boil.

2 Add the couscous to the hot liquid.

3 Cover with a lid and leave to swell for 12 minutes.

4 Remove from the pot and fluff with a fork.

5 Sweat off the onion, turmeric and red pepper in a suitable pan with the margarine.

6 Add the couscous with a little dash of stock, toss and stir evenly for 3–4 minutes. Add the herbs. Season and serve as required. The couscous should be yellow and light and fluffy. ❏

Moroccan-style Millet and Fig 4 covers

- 6   Spring onions
- 1   Yellow pepper
- 1 clove   Garlic
- 3cm   Ginger
- 300g   Millet seeds
- 60ml   Vegetable oil
- 20g   Turmeric
- 75g   Banana shallots

1 Peel and finely chop the spring onions, pepper, garlic, ginger and shallots.

2 Peel and finely julienne the orange, keeping the orange juice. Chop the figs into 1cm dice.

3 Sweat off the spring onions, pepper, garlic and ginger in a little oil until limp.

→

■ 600ml Vegetable stock
■ 1   Orange
■ 130g   Fresh figs
■ 60ml   Sesame oil
■ 150g   Peanuts
■ 57g   Sunflower seeds
■ 20g   Fresh coriander,
          chopped
■   Mixed lettuce
■   Salt and pepper

→

4 In a separate pan, toast the millet until it begins to crack open, then add the vegetable oil and turmeric. Add the spring onions and shallots.

5 Add the vegetable stock, orange juice and seasoning. Bring to the boil and simmer for 20 minutes

6 When the liquid has almost been absorbed add the figs, sesame oil and check the seasoning. Keep a lid on for 10–12 minutes.

7 Stir in the peanuts, sunflower seeds and the sweated vegetables. Add julienne.

8 Serve and garnish with chopped coriander and crisp lettuce. ❏

❏ Moroccan-style Millet and Fig ❏

Morroccan-style Peaches and Pears

4 covers

- 250g Onions
- 50g Margarine
- 1 Beef tomato
- 300g TVP
- 550ml Strong vegetable stock
- 2 Peaches
- 2 Pears
- 400g Potatoes
- 50g Raisins
- 10g Fresh parsley, chopped
- Salt and ground black pepper

1 Soak the TVP in the strong stock overnight until it swells up, then drain in a colander, keeping the excess stock.

2 Peel and slice the onions, peaches and pears. Skin, deseed and slice the tomato.

3 Peel and dice the potatoes. Wash the raisins in warm water, then soak them in warm stock.

4 Fry the onions in margarine until golden brown and then add the tomato. Cook for a further 3-4 minutes.

5 Add the TVP and excess stock, stirring well to incorporate the TVP. Gently cook out for 45–50 minutes.

6 Add the peaches, pears and potatoes and cook for 20–25 minutes. Season, add the raisins and cook for a further 3 minutes. Serve garnished with chopped parsley.

NOTES

Suitable for vegan, diabetic, low-cholesterol and coeliac diets.

Serve with couscous. (Couscous not suitable for coeliacs.) ❏

Mushroom and Black Olive Pizza (p.258)

4 covers

- 2 cloves Garlic
- 300g Button mushrooms
- 20g Black olives
- 150g Italian plum tomatoes
- 100g Red onions
- 1 Large red pepper
- 20g Pine nuts
- 35ml Olive oil
- 10 leaves Sweet basil
- 20g Pesto (vegetarian) (with 15ml of olive oil added)

1 Peel and slice the garlic and onions. Skin, deseed and cut the pepper and tomatoes into 2–3cm dice. Clean and slice the mushrooms and cut the olives into quarters.

2 To make the pizza mix the yeast and the warm water together in a bowl, then cover and leave in a warm place until it starts to foam.

3 Sieve the flour and warm the milk to blood heat. Place the flour in a mixer and add the yeast and water and warm milk and sugar and start to mix on slow speed until a smooth dough is achieved. Mix for 1–2 extra minutes then cover and rest in a warm place until it has doubled in volume, approximately 1 hour.

■ 220g   Ricotta cheese

Pizza
■ 2.5g   Caster sugar
■ 15g   Fresh yeast (or 7g
          dry yeast)
■ 40ml   Warm water
■ 225g   Plain flour
■ 120ml Milk

4 Roll out onto a lightly floured surface. Divide into two equal portions. Roll out the first half into a 20–22cm circle. Cover this with the ricotta cheese.

5 Roll out the second half to an 18cm circle and place this on top of the ricotta cheese.

6 Brush the exposed edges with water and fold over onto the edges of the smaller circle, pressing and crimping tightly to seal the edge.

7 Brush the top with pesto, then arrange all the other ingredients (except the olive oil and basil) on top then bake in a preheated oven at 210°C/Gas Mark 7 for 25 minutes. Remove from the oven and add basil leaves. Cut into four and drizzle with olive oil.

NOTES

Extra cheese can be added on top to glaze. ❏

Mushroom and Nut Flan   4 covers

Flan case
■ 70g   Plain flour
■ 85g   Wholemeal flour
■ 2½g   Ground cumin
■ 1   Free-range egg
■ 25ml   Vegetable oil
■ 10ml   Water

1 To make the flan case sieve both flours and cumin into a bowl and stir in the egg and oil, gradually adding the water to form a firm dough.

2 Knead the dough on a floured surface until smooth, cover with cling film and place in a fridge for 30 minutes.

3 Remove from the fridge and fill a 20cm flan ring.

Filling
■ 140g   Mixed nuts,
          ground
■ 10g   Fresh parsley,
          chopped
■ 20ml   Fresh marjoram,
          chopped
■ 10g   Sesame seeds
■ 10ml   Shoyu
■ 135g   Cashew nut pieces
■ 135g   Button mushrooms
■ 15ml   Groundnut oil

1 Clean and slice the mushrooms and leeks. Chop the marjoram and parsley. Grind the mixed nuts in a processor with water.

2 Mix the mixed nuts with the herbs, half the sesame seeds groundnut oil, shoyu and salt and pepper to taste.

3 Toast the cashew nut pieces until golden brown. Add three-quarters of the cashew nuts and all the mushrooms and leeks to the mixture and mix well. Place the mixture onto the flan case.

➜

- *50g   Leeks*
- *150ml Water*
- *Salt and ground black pepper*

→

4 Bake in a preheated oven at 190°C/Gas Mark 5 for 40–50 minutes until set. Dust with the sesame seeds and the remaining cashew nuts.

NOTES

This can be served hot or cold and is excellent for low-fat and low-cholesterol diets. ❑

Mushroom and Pepper Fajitas   4 covers

- *35ml Lime juice*
- *15g   Garlic purée*
- *20ml Sunflower oil*
- *2.5g Ground cumin*
- *2g   Dried marjoram*
- *300g Button mushrooms*
- *1   Red pepper*
- *1   Yellow pepper*
- *150g Onions*
- *150g Spring onions*
- *4   Tortillas (flour)*
- *20g   Fresh coriander, chopped*
- *2   Limes*
- *40ml Light vegetable stock*
- *Salt and pepper*

1 Clean and slice the mushrooms. Peel the spring onions and onions and cut into 4–5 cm strips. Skin and deseed the peppers and cut into 4–5 cm strips. Peel the skin of the limes and cut into zest and then segment the limes.

2 Place the lime juice, garlic purée, oil, cumin, marjoram, salt and pepper in a container with a tight lid (or a plastic bag).

3 Put all the vegetables in the marinade and shake the container to coat all the ingredients, then leave to marinate for 30–40 minutes.

4 Place the tortillas on tin foil and put in a preheated oven at 160°C/Gas Mark 2 for 8–10 minutes, just long enough to make them pliable.

5 Pour all the vegetables and the marinade and stock into a pan and cook until all the liquid has evaporated, leaving the vegetables just cooked. Add the coriander and check the seasoning.

6 Divide the mixture into four portions and roll up into the tortillas. Garnish with lime zest and segments.

NOTES

Suitable for vegan, diabetic and low-cholesterol diets. ❑

❏ Top: Mushroom and Pepper Fajitas
Bottom: Linguine with Roasted Peppers and Garlic ❏

Mushroom and Seitan Stroganoff (p.199)

Mushroom and Seitan Stroganoff (p.199) — 4 covers

- 300g Diced seitan
- 130g Carrots
- 150g Onions
- 30g Olive oil or sunflower oil
- 10g Garlic purée
- 60ml Brandy (optional or vegetarian red wine)
- ▪ Cracked black peppercorns
- 250g Button mushrooms
- 20g Fresh parsley, chopped
- 20ml Tamari
- 170g Silken tofu
- 10g Thyme leaves
- ▪ Salt
- 10g Peppercorns

1 Peel the carrots and onions and cut into strips 4cm long × ½cm wide. Clean and quarter the mushrooms.

2 Sweat off the seitan, carrots and onions in oil in a suitable pan for 3–4 minutes then add the garlic purée. Cook for a further minute then add the brandy or wine and deglaze the pan. Add peppercorns to taste.

3 Stir in the mushrooms and half the parsley and cook for 4 minutes until the mushroom liquid has evaporated. Remove from the heat.

4 Place the tamari, tofu and thyme in a food processor and liquidise. Add this to the mushrooms and seitan and stir. Correct the seasoning and serve with a garnish of chopped parsley.

NOTES

If a thick consistency is required add 10g arrowroot powder to the tofu.

Serve with rice pilaff or plain rice. Suitable for vegan, diabetic and low-cholesterol diets. ❑

Mushroom and Spinach Pastry Lattice — 4 covers

- 50g Hazelnuts
- 100g Onions
- 50–60g Red pepper
- 1–2 cloves Garlic
- 120g Button mushrooms
- 120g Mixed wild mushrooms
- 20ml Groundnut oil
- 500g Fresh spinach
- 2 Italian plum tomatoes
- 30g Fresh parsley and oregano, chopped

1 Brush a 20cm × 30cm baking tray with margarine. Chop and toast the hazelnuts in a suitable pan under the grill until golden.

2 Wash the spinach in cold water three times, removing debris and dirt. Cook in a thick-bottomed pan with the lid on for 8 minutes until wilted. Add no extra water in the cooking process. Allow to drain, leaving the spinach as whole as possible.

3 Skin, deseed and dice the pepper and tomatoes. Peel and chop the garlic and the onion. Clean and slice the mushrooms.

→

❏ Top: Mushroom and Spinach Pastry Lattice
Bottom: Hot Red Cabbage and Russet Apples ❏

- 225g Puff pastry
- 15g Pesto (vegetarian)
- 100g Cheese (vegetarian)
- 20g Margarine
- 15g Toasted sesame seeds
- Ground black pepper
- Nutmeg

4 Sweat off the onions, pepper, garlic and mushrooms in oil. Add the hazelnuts, cooked spinach, tomatoes and freshly chopped herbs. Season with nutmeg and black pepper.

5 Roll out puff pastry to about 20cm × 30cm. Place on the baking sheet and brush with pesto. Place the filling lengthways in the centre of the pastry. Break the cheese into small pieces on top of the filling.

6 Cut 6cm diagonal strips on either side of the pastry. Alternate strips from right to left. Overlap the centre. Moisten the edges with a little water.

7 Brush with margarine and sprinkle with toasted sesame seeds.

8 Place in a preheated oven at 200°C/Gas Mark 6 for 15–20 minutes until golden brown.

NOTES

For vegan diets use vegan puff pastry that contains no butter and use tempeh instead of cheese. ❏

Mushroom and Sundried Tomato Fettuccini   4 covers

- 50g Shallots
- 10g Garlic purée
- 80g Baby leeks
- 50ml Olive oil
- 120g Mixed mushrooms (oyster, Enoki, button and shitake)
- 400g Fettuccini
- 10g Fresh oregano, chopped
- 50g Fresh Parmesan cheese (vegetarian), grated
- 90g Sundried tomatoes
- 110g Pine kernels
- Salt and pepper

1 Cook the fettuccini in boiling salted water with a little oil for 15 minutes. Drain and refresh under cold running water. Drain and reserve.

2 Clean and slice the mushrooms discarding the stalks. Peel and very thinly slice the leeks and shallots.

3 Dry roast the pine kernels and purée the tomatoes.

4 Sweat off the shallots, garlic and leeks in a little oil, then add the mushrooms and cook for a further 3–4 minutes.

5 Add the fettuccini and toss. Season and add the oregano. Cook for a further 2–3 minutes, adding 20g Parmesan. Add pine kernels and tomatoes.

6 Serve and garnish with remaining Parmesan.

NOTES

Suitable for diabetic and low-cholesterol diets. ❏

□ Mushroom and Sundried Tomato Fettuccini □

Mushroom and Tempeh with Lemon Vinaigrette 4 covers

- *2 slices* *Thick bread*
- *50ml* *Olive oil*
- *5g* *Fresh parsley*
- *5g* *Thyme leaves*
- *150g* *Tempeh*
- *70g* *Pine kernels, toasted*
- *300g* *Button mushrooms*
- *1* *Red pepper*
- *1* *Yellow pepper*
- *200g* *Mixed green lettuce (watercress, romaine, rocket, chicory)*

1 Cut the tempeh into small dice. Clean and slice the mushrooms. Skin, deseed and dice the peppers.

2 Remove the crusts from the slices of bread and cut into 1.5cm dice. Toss in hot oil, add the herbs and seasoning and fry until golden brown.

3 To make the dressing place all the ingredients into a blender or food processor and process until they make a thick creamy dressing. This is best done on pulse speed. Do not over-blend.

4 Mix the dressing with all the other ingredients (except the mixed greens) and marinade for 5–10 minutes.

→

- ■ Salt and pepper

→ 5 Place the marinade on top of the greens and toss. Serve with the croûtons. ❑

Dressing
- ■ 25ml White wine vinegar
- ■ 25ml Lemon juice
- ■ 10g Lemon zest
- ■ 50ml Olive oil
- ■ 100g Vegetable oil (or sunflower oil)
- ■ 5g Dijon mustard
- ■ Salt and pepper

Mushroom Fettuccini   4 covers

- ■ 50g Margarine
- ■ 50g Plain white flour
- ■ 250ml Vegetable stock (white)
- ■ 250ml Milk or cream
- ■ 100g Onions
- ■ 10g Garlic puree
- ■ 30g Olive oil
- ■ Ground white pepper
- ■ 145g Shitake mushrooms
- ■ 450g Fettuccini, cooked
- ■ 10g Chives
- ■ 4 Nasturtium flowers
- ■ 30g Parmesan cheese (vegetarian)

1 Wash and remove the stalks from the mushrooms and slice.

2 Place the margarine in a thick-bottomed pan and melt over a gentle heat.

3 Add the flour and cook out until a light sandy texture has been achieved, making a roux. Remove from the heat and cool slightly.

4 Bring the stock almost to the boil and simmer.

5 Gradually add the stock and milk to the roux stirring until a smooth sauce is achieved. Simmer for 45–60 minutes and pass through a strainer to remove any debris.

6 Cover with greaseproof paper brushed with margarine to prevent a skin forming.

7 Sweat off the onion and garlic purée in a little olive oil then add the ground white pepper and mushrooms. Sauté until cooked.

8 Drain and add the pasta. Toss until reheated.

9 Mix in the sauce and chives while still hot.

10 Check the seasoning and serve with a garnish of grated Parmesan and nasturtium flowers. ❑

- ■ *450g*   *Button Mushrooms*
- ■ *230g*   *Onions*
- ■ *200g*   *Peas*
- ■ *240g*   *Peppers*
- ■ *340ml Velouté*
- ■ *50g*   *Vegetable oil*
- ■ *15g*   *Fresh parsley*
- ■ *10g*   *Fresh thyme*
- ■   *Salt and black pepper*

Velouté

100g	*Margarine*
100g	*Plain white flour*
1l	*Vegetable stock (white)*

1 Peel and dice the onions and the peppers.

2 Clean the mushrooms. Wash the herbs and finely chop them.

3 Heat the oil in a suitable pan then sweat off the onions and peppers without any colour.

4 Tip away any excess oil and add the peas and velouté to the mixture. Simmer for 10 minutes.

5 Add the mushrooms to the mixture, adjust the seasoning and then add half the chopped herbs.

1 Place the margarine in a thick-bottomed pan and melt over a gentle heat. Add the flour and cook out until a light sandy texture has been achieved, making a roux.

2 Remove from the heat and cool slightly. Bring the stock almost to the boil and simmer. Gradually add the stock to the roux, stirring until a smooth sauce is achieved. Simmer for 45–60 minutes any pass through a strainer to remove any debris. Cover with greaseproof paper brushed with margarine to prevent a skin forming.

NOTES

The velouté needs to be slightly thicker than normal to take account of the water content in the mushrooms.

Excellent vegan dish, suitable for low-cholesterol diets. ❑

Mushroom, Herb and Nut Crumble   4 covers

- ■ *400g*   *Field mushrooms or Paris mushroom*
- ■ *400g*   *Chestnuts*
- ■ *400ml Vegetable stock*
- ■ *2 cloves Garlic, crushed*
- ■ *1*   *Onion*
- ■ *60g*   *Margarine*
- ■ *60g*   *Plain flour*

1 Clean and slice the chestnuts and the mushrooms. Peel and chop the onions and the garlic. Pick, wash and chop the thyme, parsley and chives.

2 Cook off the mushrooms and chestnuts in the stock. Drain, reserving the stock and keep to one side. Sweat off the garlic and onions in a little margarine.

→

→

- 40ml 48% Double
         cream
- 10g   Thyme
- 20g   Fresh parsley and
         chives
-        Seasoning

Crumble

- 15g   Fennel seeds
- 2 large sprigs Parsley
- 15g   Thyme
- 90g   Oatmeal, medium
- 90g   Wholemeal flour
- 30g   Ground almonds
- 30g   Walnuts and
         hazelnuts
- 60g   Pistachio nuts,
         shelled and skinned

3 Make a roux with the rest of the margarine and flour, then add the reserved stock, stirring in slowly until a creamy consistency is achieved.

4 Add the cream and reduce a little. Add the onions, garlic, mushrooms and chestnuts to the sauce. Cook for 8–10 minutes.

5 Season the sauce, then stir in the herbs. Pour this mix into a suitable ovenproof dish.

6 To make the crumble mix all the ingredients together in a processor or blender until they resemble fine bread-crumbs.

7 Spread the crumble over the top of the sauce and place the dish in a preheated oven at 200°C/Gas Mark 7 for 25 minutes or until golden brown.

NOTES

Using field or Paris mushrooms will add better flavour, but if not available substitute with any flavoursome mush-rooms. ❏

Mushroom, Leek and Cashew Nut Platt   4 covers

- 300g Leeks
- 15ml Olive oil
- 2 cloves Garlic
- 175g Mixed mushrooms
- 50g   Ground cashew
         nuts
- 20g   Ground walnuts
- 6–8 leaves Fresh basil
- 3 sprigs Fresh parsley
- 2   Beef tomatoes
- 100g Shallots
- 20ml Shoyu
- 225g Puff pastry
         (vegetarian)
- 75g   Cheddar cheese
         (vegetarian)
- 1   Egg, beaten

1 Lightly toast the ground cashew nuts, wash and cut the shallots and leeks into 2cm dice then blanch, refresh, deseed and cut the tomatoes into concasse (small dice).

2 Grate the Cheddar cheese. Wipe the mushrooms clean and roughly chop. Peel and purée the garlic.

3 Wash and chop the parsley and shred the basil.

4 Sauté the leeks and shallots in oil in a large frying pan for 5–6 minutes. Add the garlic purée and mushrooms. Cook for a further 2–3 minutes.

5 Lower the heat and add the nuts, basil leaves, half the parsley and the tomato concasse.

6 Add shoyu, salt and pepper. Mix well then allow to cool.
→

- 10g   Sesame seeds, toasted
-      Salt and pepper

→

7 Roll out the pastry on a lightly floured surface to approximately 30cm × 20cm and place on a greased baking tray.

8 Place the filling lengthways in the centre of the pastry. Add the Cheddar cheese on top of the filling.

9 Cut 6cm diagonal strips on either side of the pastry. Alternate strips from right to left, overlaping the centre.

10 Brush with the beaten egg and sprinkle with toasted sesame seeds.

11 Place in a preheated oven at 200°C/Gas Mark 6 for 15–20 minutes.

NOTES

This recipe can work well as an individual (Wellington type) portion dish.

It can also be used for vegan diets if the cheese is replaced with tempeh or smoked tofu, and the egg replaced with 1tbsp soya flour and 2tbsp water. This will have the same effect as the egg. If cashew nuts are not available use an alternative. ❏

Mushroom, Leek and Pea Flan   4 covers

- 332g   Short pastry (vegetarian)
- 200g   Leeks
- 20g   Margarine
- 200g   Button mushrooms
- 4   Free-range eggs
- 50ml   Semi-skimmed or soya milk
- 50g   Natural yoghurt
- 400g   Cheddar cheese (vegetarian)
- 20g   Parmesan cheese (vegetarian)
- 100g   Peas, frozen
- 5g   Cayenne or paprika

1 Roll and cut out the pastry on a floured surface. Line a greased flan case with the pastry, then cover with greaseproof paper and bake blind in a preheated oven at 180°C/Gas Mark 4 for 10–12 minutes.

2 Peel and top and tail the leeks then cut into 2cm dice. Clean and slice the mushrooms.

3 Sweat off the leeks without any colour in the margarine then add the mushrooms and cook for a further 2–3 minutes.

4 In a separate bowl mix together the eggs, milk, yoghurt, Cheddar cheese and Parmesan cheese. Season then add the leeks, mushrooms and peas, thoroughly mixing together.

→

→ 5 Pour the mixture into the flan case and bake in a pre-heated oven at 160°C/Gas Mark 3–4 for approximately 40 minutes until golden brown and the filling has set.

6 Garnish with cayenne or paprika and parsley sprigs.

NOTES

The egg mixture must be set before the flan is removed from the oven. ❏

- 4 sprigs Fresh parsley
- Salt and ground white pepper

Mushroom Stroganoff   4 covers

- 50g   Onions
- 1   Red pepper
- 40g   Margarine
- 600g   Mixed mushrooms (oyster, shitake, Chanterelle)
- 34g   Paprika
- 68ml   White wine (vegetarian)
- 340ml Béchamel sauce
- Tabasco sauce
- Salt and black pepper
- 40g   Baby mange tout

Béchamel
- 100g   Margarine
- 100g   Plain white flour
- 1l   Soya milk
- 1   Onion studded with cloves and a bay leaf

1 Clean and trim any woody stalks, but leave the mushrooms whole.

2 Skin and deseed the pepper. Cut the onions and pepper into 2cm slices. Top and tail the mange tout then blanch and refresh in ice-cold water.

3 Sweat off the onions and the pepper in the margarine until soft then add the mushrooms and sweat lightly.

4 Add the paprika and cook for a further 30 seconds. Add mange tout. Add the white wine to deglaze the pan then add the béchamel. Bring to the boil and simmer gently until the mushrooms are cooked.

5 Add seasoning and Tabasco sauce to taste. Serve either with rice or in filo or pastry cups.

1 Place the margarine in a thick-bottomed pan and melt over a gentle heat. Add the flour and cook out without any colour for a few minutes, making a roux. Remove from the heat and cool slightly.

2 In a separate pan bring the milk and the studded onion almost to the boil and simmer, infusing the flavour of the onion, for 10 minutes. Strain off the milk through a fine strainer.

3 Gradually add the milk to the roux, stirring until a smooth sauce is achieved. Simmer for 15–20 minutes and pass through a strainer to remove any debris. Cover with greaseproof paper brushed with margarine to prevent a skin forming. ❏

New Potato and Wheat Grain Casserole   4 covers

- 50g   Leeks
- 2 cloves Garlic
- 70g   Onions
- 30g   Margarine
- 30g   Plain flour
- 300ml Vegetable stock, strong
- 150g   Whole wheat grains
- 100ml Milk
- 250g   New or mid potatoes
- 1   Small cauliflower
- 30g   Fresh parsley, chopped
- 1   Yellow courgette
- 1   Green courgette
-        Salt and white pepper

1 Wash and peel the leeks, onions and garlic, then cut into large dice. Wash and dice the courgettes and potatoes, then separate the cauliflower into florets.

2 Soak the wheat grains overnight and then drain them. Chop the parsley.

3 Sweat off the leeks, garlic and onions in the margarine. Add the flour and beat out then add the stock. Add the wheat grains to the onions and leeks and cook for 5–6 minutes.

4 Pour the milk into the mixture, and add the potatoes. Continue to cook for 12–15 minutes.

5 Place the cauliflower, parsley and the courgettes in the mixture and cook for a further 10 minutes. Check the seasoning and that the ingredients are cooked and tender.

6 Serve hot with French-style baguettes.

NOTES

For vegan diets change the milk to soya milk or replace it with more stock. This dish has lots of fibre and is good for low-cholesterol and diabetic diets if the milk is changed to semi skimmed or soya milk. ❑

Noodle Doodle (p.232)   4 covers

- 250g   Noodles, dried
- 80g   Onions
- ½   Red pepper
- ½   Green pepper
- ½   Yellow pepper
- 30ml   Virgin olive oil
- 60g   Mushrooms
- 30g   Spinach, cooked
- 60g   Sweetcorn kernels
- 10g   Fresh parsley, chopped

1 Cook the noodles in boiling salted water with a little oil for 10-15 minutes then refresh under cold running water. Drain and reserve.

2 Peel and cut the onions into 5mm dice. Skin and deseed the peppers and cut into 5mm dice. Clean and slice the mushrooms.

3 Sweat off the onions and peppers in the oil over a medium heat for 2–3 minutes then add the mushrooms, spinach and sweetcorn kernels and cook and stir for a further 5 minutes adding half the herbs and cheese.

→

→

- *10g*   *Fresh chives, chopped*
- *20g*   *Parmesan cheese (vegetarian)*
- *250ml Velouté*
-     *Salt and ground white pepper*

4 Toss in the noodles and pour in the velouté and cook out for a further 3–4 minutes. Add the remaining half of the Parmesan and herbs. Serve immediately.

NOTES

Suitable for vegan, low-cholesterol and diabetic diets.

The recipe for Velouté is on page 113. Adapt the ingredients accordingly. ❏

Nut and Vegetable Curry with Vegetable Pilau   4 covers

Curry

- *100g*   *Onions*
- *1 clove Garlic*
- *3cm*   *Fresh ginger*
- *30ml*   *Groundnut oil or vegetable ghee*
- *10g*   *Mild curry powder*
- *10g*   *Ground coriander*
- *15g*   *Ground cumin*
- *10g*   *Tomato purée*
- *230g*   *Potatoes*
- *100g*   *Carrots*
- *15g*   *Raisins*
- *20g*   *Ground nuts*
- *320ml Vegetable stock*

Pilau

- *100g*   *Onions*
- *15ml*   *Vegetable oil or ghee*
- *200g*   *Basmati rice*
- *55g*   *Pine nuts, toasted*
- *1*   *Red pepper*
- *50g*   *Peas*
- *350ml Vegetable stock*
-     *Salt and pepper*

1 Peel and chop the onions, garlic and ginger. Peel and dice the potatoes and carrots.

2 To make the curry fry off the onions, garlic and ginger in the oil.

3 Add all the other ingredients except the stock and cook for 1–2 minutes, then add the vegetable stock, bring to the boil and simmer for 45 minutes.

4 To make the pilau peel, dice and fry the onion in the oil until golden brown. Add the rice and toss to coat all the grains. Peel, deseed and dice the pepper.

5 Add the nuts, pepper, peas and vegetable stock. Bring to the boil and simmer for 15–20 minutes until the rice has absorbed the stock.

6 Serve and garnish with chopped coriander and pilau rice.

NOTES

Serve with naan bread, minted yoghurt, mango chutney and poppadums. This dish is suitable for vegan, diabetic and low-cholesterol diets. ❏

Oriental Vegetable Salad   4 covers

- 230g Noodles, cooked
- 45ml Tamari
- 60g Water chestnuts
- 112g Mange tout, cooked
- 60g Spring onions
- 60g Beansprouts
- 70g Ginger
- 80g Carrots
- 80g Green beans
- 25ml Hoi sin sauce
  (vegetarian)
  (optional)

1 Peel and cut the ginger and carrots into julienne (fine strips). Cut spring onions at an angle, thinly.

2 Top and tail the green beans and blanch in boiling salted water until just cooked. Refresh in ice-cold water then cut into julienne.

3 Cut the noodles into 6cm lengths and mix with tamari.

4 Cut the water chestnuts in half. Combine all the ingredients. Check the seasoning.

5 Dress neatly into a suitable container and garnish accordingly.

NOTES

Suitable for vegan diets if rice noodles are used.

Do not use Hoi sin sauce for diabetic and low-cholesterol diets because of the sugar content. ❏

Panache of Mushrooms and Greens   4 covers

- 200g Shallots
- 100g Spring onions
- 50ml Extra virgin olive oil
- 10g Garlic purée
- 350g Mixed mushrooms
  (button, shitake, cepe
  or Paris brown)
- 60ml Dry sherry
  (vegetarian, optional)
- 20g Pine nuts, toasted
- 20g Sunflower seeds,
  toasted
- 10g Chives, chopped
- 300g Mixed greens
  (watercress, romaine,
  rocket, baby spinach)
- Salt and black
  pepper

1 Clean, de-stalk and slice the mushrooms.

2 Peel and slice the shallots and spring onions. Wash and prepare the greens and place in a suitable bowl.

3 Sweat off the shallots and spring onions in the oil, without any colour for 2–3 minutes until tender.

4 Add the garlic purée and then the mushrooms. Stir and cook for 4–5 minutes.

5 Deglaze the pan with the sherry and add the nuts, seeds and chives.

6 Correct the seasoning and pour over the greens. Toss and serve immediately.

NOTES

Suitable for vegan, diabetic, coeliac and low-cholesterol diets. ❏

- *100g Baby leeks*
- *100g Onion*
- *60ml Extra virgin olive oil*
- *2 cloves Garlic*
- *500g Italian plum tomatoes*
- *50g Sultanas*
- *50g Macadamia nuts*
- *450g Purple broccoli*
- *180g Pasta, penne rigate or penne*
- *142g Cheddar cheese (vegetarian)*
- *6 leaves Basil*
- *Sea salt and ground black pepper*

1 Peel and finely chop the onion, leeks and garlic. Wash the sultanas then soak in warm water for 15 minutes until plump.

2 Skin, deseed and cut the tomatoes into concasse (small dice), save the tomato pulp and water. Push the pulp through a very fine sieve and save the tomato water.

3 Cut the purple broccoli into florets and cook in boiling salted water for 3–4 minutes. Refresh in ice-cold water and allow to drain.

4 Sauté off the onion and leeks in oil until limp, then add the garlic and cook for 2 minutes.

5 Add the tomato concasse and season. Simmer for 15–20 minutes, then add the tomato water. Add the sultanas, nuts and broccoli and cook for a further 5 minutes.

6 Put the pasta into boiling salted water with a little olive oil for 10–14 minutes until just cooked. Drain and refresh.

7 Mix the pasta and the sauce together and break the cheese into the dish. Garnish with the fresh basil leaves and serve.

NOTES

This dish can be used for vegan diets if the cheese is omitted. The pasta can also be substituted with other pastas, such as macaroni, fusilli or rigatoni.

For extra flavour add 30g vegetarian pesto sauce. ❑

Pasta and Haricot Bean Stew 4 covers

- *1 Onion*
- *50g Leeks*
- *2 cloves Garlic*
- *30g Margarine*
- *500ml Milk*

1 Three-quarters cook the pasta in boiling salted water and refresh and keep to one side until required.

2 Peel the onions and cut into 2cm dice. Blanch and refresh the tomatoes, then skin, deseed and cut into 2 cm dice. Peel and purée the garlic.

→

→

- 250ml Vegetable stock (strong)
- 200g Haricot beans, tinned
- 50g Courgettes
- 20g Fresh parsley, chopped
- 65g Fusilli pasta
- 4 Tomatoes
- Salt and ground white pepper

3 Peel the outer leaf of the leeks then top and tail, cut in half and wash. Cut the leeks and courgettes into 2cm dice.

4 Sauté the onions, leeks, and garlic in the margarine. Pour the milk over then cook for a few minutes.

5 Place the stock and one-third of the beans in a blender and purée. Then pour it in the pan of sautéed vegetables with the whole beans and courgettes.

6 Add the three-quarters of the parsley, the pasta and the tomatoes and bring back to a simmer, then cook for approximately 5 minutes.

7 Garnish with the remaining parsley. Check the seasoning and serve.

NOTES

Suitable for vegan diets if egg-free pasta is used and the milk is replaced with soya milk, but be careful not to overheat as it could split.

For low-cholesterol diets replace the milk with soya or semi-skimmed milk. ❏

Pasta with Almond Sauce 4 covers

- 210g Pasta bows (farfalle or fusilli)
- 200g Onions
- 5g Cayenne pepper
- 1 bulb Fennel
- 100g Leek
- 1 Green pepper
- 2–3 cloves Garlic
- 80g Ground almonds
- 30ml Olive oil
- 300ml Vegetable stock
- 1 Baby courgette
- 1 Carrot
- Salt and black pepper

1 Cook the pasta in boiling salted water for 10–12 minutes until just cooked. Refresh in ice-cold water and reserve.

2 Peel and finely chop the onion and fennel. Peel and purée the garlic.

3 Wash, deseed and cut the pepper into small dice. Peel, and top and tail the carrot, wash the courgette and leek, then very finely slice them both into thin ribbons.

4 Sauté the onions, cayenne pepper, fennel, pepper and garlic in the oil for 5 minutes.

5 Mix the almonds and the stock together in a blender for approximately 1 minute until smooth.

6 Pour the sauce over the onion mixture and slowly heat through, stirring until the sauce has thickened.

→

→ 7 Add the pasta bows and courgette and carrot ribbons to the dish. Cook out for 5 minutes, stirring all the time to prevent burning.

8 Season to taste and serve.

NOTES

Be careful not to over-process the sauce. Keep stirring it continually once the pasta has been added.

This is a good vegan recipe.

Serve with oven-roasted vegetables. ❑

Penne Pasta with Gorgonzola Sauce   4 covers

- *400g   Penne pasta*
- *300g   Paris brown mushrooms*
- *50ml   Extra virgin olive oil*
- *200g   Green courgettes*
- *200g   Yellow courgettes*
- *70g   Sundried tomatoes*
- *2 cloves Garlic*
- *50g   Cream cheese*
- *100g   Gorgonzola cheese (or vegetarian soft alternative)*
- *10g   Fresh parsley, chopped*
- *5g   Chives, chopped*
- *10 leaves Basil*
- *Salt and freshly ground white pepper*

1 Clean the mushrooms and cut into quarters. Dry, clean and slice the tomatoes. Wash and slice the courgettes and peel and very thinly slice the garlic.

2 Cook the pasta in boiling salted water with a little oil. Drain and refresh under cold running water. Drain and reserve.

3 Sweat off the mushrooms in a suitable hot pan with the olive oil. Cook until the liquid has nearly all evaporated.

4 Add the courgettes, tomatoes and the garlic and cook for 4–5 minutes and then add the pasta. Toss and stir adding the cream cheese and then the Gorgonzola. Stir and toss until fully melted then season. Add parsley and chives.

5 Garnish with torn basil leaves.

NOTES

Gorgonzola, Paris mushrooms and penne pasta can all be interchanged with other close ingredients if preferred. ❑

Potato Layered Pie   4 covers

- 150g TVP
- 300ml Strong vegetable stock
- 500g Potatoes
- 100g Onions
- 30g Margarine
- 10g Dried mixed herbs
- 30g Tomato purée
- 5ml Worcester sauce
- 2.5g Paprika
- 1 Free-range egg
- 125ml Natural yoghurt
- 30g Plain flour
- 20g Fresh parsley, chopped
- 20g Freshly chervil, chopped
- 2.5g Ground cumin
- Salt and ground white pepper
- 220g Tomatoes
- 1 clove Garlic

1 Soak the TVP in the strong stock overnight until it swells up then drain in a colander. Keep the excess stock.

2 Cook the potatoes in cold salted water for approximately 15 minutes, then air-dry. Peel and slice the potatoes and allow to cool.

3 Peel and slice the onions and purée the garlic. Skin and deseed the tomatoes and cut into concasse (small dice). Save the tomato water.

4 Sweat the onions off in the margarine and add the TVP, dried herbs, tomatoes, garlic, tomato purée, Worcester sauce, salt, pepper and paprika and cook for 5 minutes. Add any excess stock and cook for a further 3–4 minutes. Check the seasoning.

5 Pour half of the TVP mixture into a suitable ovenproof dish, then lay a layer of potato. Repeat this process once more.

6 Whisk the egg, yoghurt, flour, parsley, chervil, salt, cumin and pepper together and then pour this over the top of the pie.

7 Bake for a further 30 minutes in a preheated oven at 180°C/Gas Mark 5, until golden brown. Finish the dish with a dusting of paprika. ❑

Pulse Pittas   4 covers

- 40g Margarine
- 1 Onion
- 100g Button mushrooms
- 10g Ground cumin
- 250g Split red lentils
- 450ml Vegetable stock
- ½ Lemon (juice)
- 10g Fresh parsley, chopped
- 4 Pitta bread
- Salt and pepper

1 Peel and chop the onion, clean and slice the mushrooms and wash and slice the tomatoes.

2 Melt the margarine and sauté the onion. Add the mushrooms and the cumin and stir for a further 2 minutes.

3 Add the lentils and stock, bring to the boil and cook for 20–30 minutes. When the lentils are soft and the liquid has been absorbed add the lemon juice and parsley. Season to taste and keep warm, stirring occasionally until mix is thick.

→

Garnish

- Lettuce, chopped
- Cucumber, diced
- Black grapes
- 4   Tomatoes, sliced

→

4 Sprinkle (dampen) the pitta bread with cold water and toast them for 3 minutes on each side. Cut in half horizontally.

5 Divide the mixture between the pitta bread pockets and add the garnish. ❑

Pumpkin and Potato Rogan Josh   4 covers

- 50g   Vegetable ghee
- 150g   Onions
- 50g   Carrots
- 4   Cardamom seeds
- 5g   Chilli powder
- 5g   Ground coriander
- 5g   Ground cumin
- 5g   Paprika
- 2.5g   Turmeric
- 200ml   Natural yoghurt (optional)
- 300g   Chopped tomatoes (tinned acceptable)
- 50g   Courgettes
- 50g   Leeks
- 150g   Pumpkin
- 150g   Potatoes
- 50g   Green Kenya beans
- 10g   Flaked almonds
- Fresh coriander, chopped

Paste

- 20g   Ginger purée
- 20g   Garlic purée
- Pinch   Saffron and ground nutmeg
- 5   Cloves
- 10   Peppercorns
- 60g   Ground almonds
- 2   Green cardamoms
- 15g   Poppy seeds, toasted

1 To make the paste mix all the ingredients together with a little water and pound in a pestle and mortar or coffee grinder.

2 Peel the onions, pumpkin, potatoes, carrots and leeks then cut into 1½cm dice. Wash and top and tail the courgettes and beans then cut into 2.5cm dice.

3 Heat the ghee in a thick-bottomed pan and fry the onions and carrots until golden brown then add the cardamom pods and the paste, frying for a further 2 minutes. Then add all the other spices. Do not burn.

4 Stir in 150ml yoghurt, the chopped tomatoes and 150ml water. Simmer for 25 minutes, stirring to prevent sticking. Add all the other ingredients except the coriander and almonds and simmer for a further 15–20 minutes. Add chopped coriander and serve with a spoonful of yoghurt and flaked almonds to garnish.

NOTES

Serve with basmati rice, poppadoms, naan bread, mango chutney and mint flavoured yoghurt and cucumber. Suitable for vegan (omit the yogurt), diabetic and low-cholesterol diets. ❑

❏ Clockwise from top: Pumpkin and Potato Rogan Josh; Chick Pea Curry; Vegetable Balti ❏

Pumpkin Pilaff
4 covers

- 100g   Spring onions
- 2.5cm Ginger
- 1   Orange pepper
- 1 clove Garlic
- 60ml   Vegetable oil
- 300g   Millet seeds
- 550ml Vegetable stock
- 1   Orange (juice only)
- 130g   Pitted dates
- 2.5ml Sesame oil
- 150g   Cashew nuts, toasted
- 57g   Pumpkin seeds
-        Salt and pepper
-        Crisp lettuce
-        Edible flowers (nasturtiums and pansies)

1 Squeeze the juice from the orange, chop the pitted dates and peel and chop the spring onions, pepper and garlic. Peel and cut the ginger into julienne (thin slices).

2 Sweat off the spring onions, ginger, pepper and garlic in the vegetable oil.

3 In a separate pan with a lid, toast the millet seeds until they crack open and then add the onion mixture.

4 Add the stock and the orange juice to the pan. Season and bring to the boil and then allow to simmer for 20 minutes.

5 When the liquid has been absorbed add the dates and the sesame oil and check the seasoning.

6 Stir in the cashew nuts and pumpkin seeds. Serve on a suitable dish garnished with crisp lettuce and edible flowers.

NOTES

Suitable for vegan, low-cholesterol and diabetic diets. ❑

Quick Five-bean Chilli
4 covers

- 60g   Onions
- 2 cloves Garlic
- 50ml   Vegetable oil
- 5–10g Chilli powder
- 113g   Mixed vegetables (carrot, leeks, turnip)
- 250g   Beef tomato
- 113g   Broad beans (tinned)
- 113g   White haricot beans (tinned)
- 113g   Flageolet beans (tinned)

1 Drain all the beans in a colander.

2 Blanch and refresh the tomatoes, remove the skin, deseed and cut into 2cm dice (concasse). Peel and slice the garlic and the onions.

3 Peel and cut the leeks, carrot and turnips into 2cm dice.

4 Sauté the onions and garlic in oil in a suitable pan with a little colour. Add the chilli powder and cook out for a further 2 minutes.

5 Add the vegetables and cook for 5 minutes. Add the tomato concasse then add all the beans and the stock. Cook for a further 15 minutes.

- 113g Butter beans (tinned)
- 113g Kidney beans (tinned)
- 180ml Vegetable stock
- 250g Long grain rice
- 10g Arrowroot
- 20g Fresh coriander, chopped
- 60ml Sunflower oil
- Salt and ground white pepper

6 Wash then cook the rice in boiling salted water with a dash of vegetable oil for 10–15 minutes until just cooked. Refresh under cold running water, drain and keep ready to reheat when required.

7 Check the seasoning in the chilli, thicken with a little arrowroot powder and water if required.

8 Reheat the rice in either boiling water or a steamer.

9 Serve the chilli with rice and chopped coriander.

NOTES

If the chilli is too hot reduce it down then add apple or pineapple juice. This will take the heat out of the chilli. Suitable for vegan, diabetic, coeliac (omit the arrowroot) and low-cholesterol diets. ❑

Quinoa and Samphire (p.263)   4 covers

- 150g Quinoa
- 30ml Olive oil
- 400ml Vegetable stock
- 200g Samphire
- 100g Butter beans
- 10g Mint leaves
- 1 Lemon (juice and zest)
- 400g Broad beans
- 40g Sprouting beans
- 6 Spring onions
- Salt and ground pepper

1 Fry the quinoa in a little oil for 1–2 minutes, then add the stock and bring to the boil. Simmer for 15 minutes uncovered or until the stock has been absorbed.

2 Blanch and refresh the samphire in ice-cold water, then drain and trim to shape.

3 Trim and discard the grey outer skins from the butter beans.

4 Season the quinoa with salt and pepper. Chop the mint leaves, remove the zest from the lemon and squeeze out the juice. Cut the zest into small strips.

5 Gently toss the beans, lemon juice and zest, samphire, sprouting beans, spring onions and mint. Add the quinoa.

6 Present in a suitable dish or bowl and garnish with a little chopped mint.

NOTES

This is suitable for vegan, gluten-free and high-protein diets. ❑

Red Wine with Paris Mushrooms and Chestnuts 4 covers

- 120g Chestnuts, dried
- 150g Carrot and turnip
- 1 Bay leaf
- 2 sprigs Fresh thyme
- 1 sprig Fresh rosemary
- 200ml Red wine (vegetarian)
- 250ml Brown vegetable stock
- 30g Margarine
- 10 Small shallots
- 60g Button mushrooms
- 15ml Coarse ground mustard
- 30–45ml Tamari

1 Peel and dice the shallots, carrots and turnips. Soak the dried chestnuts for at least 6 hours.

2 Place the chestnuts, carrots, turnips, bay leaf, thyme and rosemary and 160ml red wine into a suitable saucepan with enough vegetable stock to cover. Simmer for approximately 50 minutes.

3 Melt the margarine and fry the shallots until lightly browned. Add the button mushrooms and the rest of the red wine, cook for 5 minutes and add to the rest of the ingredients.

4 Simmer for a further 30 minutes, reducing the liquid by approximately one-quarter.

→

❏ Red Wine with Paris Mushrooms and Chestnuts ❏

- 120g Small Paris
       mushrooms
- 20g   Fresh parsley,
       chopped
- ▪   Ground black
       pepper

5 Add the mustard, tamari and black pepper to taste. Add Small Paris mushrooms. Cook for a further 5–10 minutes.

6 Check seasoning and thicken if required. Serve garnished with chopped parsley. ❑

Ricotta and Vegetable Pie 4 covers

- 300g Carrots
- 200g Onions
- 2   Red peppers
- 10g   Margarine
- 20–30ml Semi-skimmed
       or soya milk
- 140g Ricotta cheese
- 240g Leaf spinach
       (frozen is
       acceptable)
- 15 leaves Basil
- ▪   Ground nutmeg
- ▪   Salt and ground
       black pepper

Pastry
- 140g Plain flour
- 175g Wholemeal flour
- 5g   Ground cumin,
       salt and pepper
- 2   Free-range eggs
- 50ml Vegetable oil
- 20ml Water

1 Skin, deseed and cut the red peppers into quarters. Peel and slice the onions and carrots. Drain any excess water from the spinach.

2 Cook and purée the carrots. Sweat off the peppers and onions in a little margarine.

3 Cream the milk and the ricotta, making it spreadable.

4 To make the pastry sieve both flours and the cumin into a bowl and stir in the eggs and oil, gradually adding water to form a firm dough.

5 Knead dough on a floured surface until smooth, cover with clingfilm and place in a fridge for 30 minutes.

6 Remove from the fridge and roll out just over half to line a 20cm flan ring.

7 Layer the pie first with spinach then season, then spread the ricotta over and season.

8 Add the peppers and onions and the basil. Cover the mixture with the carrot purée and season. The final layer should be spinach.

9 Roll out the remaining pastry and cover the pie. Cut a small hole into the top.

10 Bake in a preheated oven at 180°C/Gas Mark 3–4 for 1½ hrs.

11 Garnish as required. ❑

Roasted Buckwheat Salad Garnished with Aramé 4 covers

- 100g Roasted buckwheat
- 10g Arame
- 8 Spring onions
- 60g Cucumber
- 50g Carrots
- 50g Mouli
- 50g Celery
- 1 bunch Watercress
- ¼ head Curly endive
- 100g Shallots
- Salt and ground black pepper
- 5g Fennel seeds

Dressing

- 30ml Sunflower oil
- 18ml White wine vinegar
- 20ml Tamari
- 2.5cm Fresh root ginger (juice only)
- 2.5cm Galangal

1 Peel and finely slice the shallots. Top and tail the spring onions and cut into diamonds. Grate the ginger, galangal and squeeze out the juice and reserve. Throw away the pulp.

2 Soak the aramé in water for 10–12 minutes. Cut the mouli, celery, carrots and cucumber into allumettes (matchstick-size cuts).

3 Bring 250ml water to boil. Add the buckwheat, return to the boil, then simmer, with a lid for 5 minutes.

4 Whisk the oil, vinegar, Tamari, ginger juice and seasoning together, to make the dressing.

5 Transfer the cooked buckwheat and aramé to a bowl and pour the dressing while still hot and mix in well. When cool add the fennel seeds, spring onions, shallots, cucumber, mouli, celery and carrots and mix together well.

6 Garnish with spring onions, watercress and curly endive around the edges of the salad.

NOTES

Suitable for vegan and low-cholesterol diets. ❏

Roasted EBLY® Cream 4 covers

- 110g EBLY®
- 420ml Milk
- 410ml Whipping cream
- 8 Egg yolks
- 80g Sugar
- 16 Strawberries
- 16 Raspberries
- 4 sprigs Redcurrants
- 16 Blackcurrants
- 4 sprigs Mint
- 30g Icing sugar

1 Roast the EBLY® in a preheated oven at 220°C/Gas Mark 7 until evenly coloured (15–20 minutes).

2 Heat the milk and cream until boiling point, add the hot roasted EBLY®, cover the pan and infuse off the heat for 30 minutes.

3 Beat the egg yolks and sugar and stir thoroughly, and add the milk and cream.

4 Pour into a dish or individual ramekins or dariole moulds. Place in a container of hot water and bake in a preheated oven at 150°C/Gas Mark 2 for 1 to 1¼ hours if using a large dish (half the cooking time if individuals are being set), or until set.

5 Serve either hot or chilled. Once chilled, quenelle the cream and garnish with fruits, mint and icing sugar. ❏

- 120g   Puréed smoked tofu
- 450g   Long grain rice, cooked
- 60ml   Groundnut oil
- 100g   Onions
- 5–10g Garlic purée
- 1   Green pepper
- 120g   Shitake mushrooms
- 300g   Tempeh
- 110g   Cashew nuts
- 35ml   Shoyu
- 20g   Fresh coriander, chopped
- 5   Tomatoes
- 4   Spring onions
- 1   Red chilli
- 50g   Cucumber
-        Salt and black pepper

1 Cut the tempeh into 1cm dice. Drain the rice ensuring that there is no excess water.

2 Skin and deseed the pepper and chilli then cut the pepper into 1cm dice and finely slice the chilli. Peel and cut the onions into 1cm dice. De-stalk and slice the mushrooms. Dry-roast the cashew nuts under the grill or in the oven until golden brown.

3 Peel, top and tail the spring onions, wash and slice the cucumber and wash and cut the tomatoes into quarters. Remove the seeds, leaving the tomato leaf.

4 Mix the tofu with the rice ensuring that there are no lumps of rice. Season with salt and pepper.

5 Pour the oil into the pan or wok over a medium heat, add the onions chilli and garlic purée and fry for 2–3 minutes (do not burn the garlic). Add the pepper and the shitake mushrooms. Fry for a further 2 minutes then add the cucumber, tempeh, nuts and rice. Fry for 3–4 minutes then add the shoyu.

6 Toss and stir the rice to prevent it from sticking, stir in half the chopped coriander and check the seasoning.

7 Serve with a garnish of chopped coriander, tomatoes and spring onions.

NOTES

Suitable for vegan, low-cholesterol, coeliac and diabetic diets. ❑

Seaweed Broth Japanese Style (p.151)   4 covers

- 1 strip (2cm × 15cm) Kombu seaweed
- 650ml Stock or water
- 50g   Mouli
- 50g   Carrots
- 50g   Celery

1 Peel and finely dice the mouli, ginger and carrots. Peel and finely slice the garlic, celery and spring onions. Peel and slice the shallots thinly into rounds.

2 Wash and cut back the watercress stalks and finely chop.

→

- 50g   Shallots
- 50g   Spring onions
- 35ml Shoyu
- 1 clove Garlic
- 2cm   Ginger root
- 40g   Watercress

3 Wash the kombu lightly and wipe with a clean cloth then place in 650ml of water or light vegetable stock and bring to the boil. Simmer for 15 minutes and remove.

4 Add all the other ingredients (except the watercress) and simmer for a further 5–6 minutes. Skim the surface for any debris.

5 Check the seasoning and add the watercress. Cook for 1 more minute and serve.

NOTES

Suitable for vegan, low-cholesterol and diabetic diets. For coeliac diets change the shoyu for tamari. ❑

Seitan Kebabs   4 covers

- 450g Seitan
- 30ml Vegetable oil
- 1   Red pepper
- 1   Medium onion
- 8   Vine tomatoes
- 16   Button mushrooms
- 150g Pineapple chunks
- 8   Wooden skewers

Marinade
- 60g   White wine vinegar
- 200g Brown sugar
- 25g   Tomato purée
- 200g Pineapple juice
- 120g Shoyu
- 200g Tomato ketchup

1 To make the marinade bring the vinegar and sugar to the boil, cook for 2–3 minutes then add the tomato purée, pineapple juice, shoyu and ketchup. Cook for a further 2 minutes and skim any debris from the surface. Reserve.

2 Soak the seitan overnight in the marinade, then remove and drain, reserving the marinade for basting. Place the seitan on a greased tray and grill until a light golden brown (do not allow it to become dry).

3 Heat the marinade and keep hot.

4 Deseed the pepper and cut into 2cm squares. Peel and cut the onion into large dice, cut the tomatoes in half and remove and discard the stalks from the mushrooms.

5 Assemble the ingredients on the skewers starting and ending with half a tomato.

6 Brush the ingredients with oil and place under the grill. Baste with the marinade and turn regularly until all ingredients are golden brown.

7 Serve with the marinade.

NOTES

Serve with rice.

Suitable for vegan diets. ❑

Seitan Pilaff with Apricots 4 covers

- 60g   Ghee
- 700g   Seitan
- 300g   Onions
- 1 clove Garlic
- 10g   Ground cumin
- 10g   Ground coriander
- 5g   Ground turmeric
- 75g   Dried apricots
- 400g   Basmati rice
- 750ml Vegetarian stock
- 35g   Dried currants
- 60g   Peas
- 80g   Pine nuts
- 50g   Peanuts
- 10g   Fresh coriander, chopped

1 Cut the seitan into 2cm dice. Peel and chop the onions and garlic. Wash the apricots under warm water and then slice.

2 Roughly chop the peanuts and then dry toast them with the pine nuts under the grill.

3 Heat half the ghee in large pan, add the seitan in batches, and cook until lightly browned all over. Drain and remove.

4 Heat the remaining ghee in same pan, sweat the onions, garlic and spices, cook and stir.

5 Add the apricots and rice and stir over the heat until the rice is coated in spice mixture. Stir in the stock and simmer, covered with tight-fitting lid, for approximately 15 minutes.

6 Remove from the heat. Stir in the seitan, then stand, covered, for a further 15 minutes. Gently stir in currants, peas and nuts. Garnish with coriander, if desired. ❑

Seitan with Lemon, Fennel and Cashew 4 covers

- 550g   Seitan
- 10ml   Clear honey (with a pinch of cinnamon)
- 10g   Arrowroot powder
- 40ml   Shoyu
- 300ml Vegetable stock
- 1   Lemon (juice and zest)
- 60ml   Groundnut oil
- 2.5ml Sesame oil
- 5g   Ginger purée
- 5g   Garlic purée
- 1 bulb Baby fennel
- 20g   Cashew nuts

1 Roll the seitan into a cylinder shape and simmer in boiling water for 30 minutes. Remove and cool then cut into wedge shapes.

2. Remove the zest and squeeze the juice from the lemon and place the juice in a bowl with half the zest. Blanch and refresh the rest of the lemon zest and reserve for garnish.

3 Toast the cashew nuts without colour under the grill until golden brown. Cut the fennel in half. Remove root and cut into fine slices.

4 Mix the honey, shoyu and stock with the lemon juice and add the seitan. Marinate for 30 minutes. Remove and drain, keeping all the marinade.

5 Put 30 ml groundnut oil in a suitably hot pan and fry off the seitan for 3 minutes then add the fennel, ginger and garlic purée. Cook but do not brown.

→

❑ Top: Noodle Doodle   Bottom: Seitan Pilaff with Apricots ❑

→
6 Add the marinade and simmer for 20 minutes, stirring to ensure nothing sticks to the bottom of the pan.

7 Add the cashew nuts and cook for another minute. Serve with a garnish of blanched lemon zest, flavour with sesame oil.

NOTES

Serve with noodles or plain rice.

Suitable for vegan diets.

If the dish is too wet mix a lime arrowroot powder and water together and stir in to required consistency. ❏

Seitan with Szechwan and Lime (p.306)   4 covers

- 500g   Seitan
- 40ml   Groundnut oil
- 100g   Onions
- 50g   Carrots
- 100g   White cabbage
- 100g   Shitake mushrooms
- 50g   Mange tout
- 50g   Baby corn cobs

Marinade
- 40ml   Dark soy sauce
- 20ml   Dry sherry
- 2 drops Sesame oil
- 5g   Ginger purée
- 5g   Garlic purée
- 2.5g   Five spice
- 5g   Szechwan peppercorns
- 1   Lime (zest and juice)

1 Roll the seitan into a cylinder shape and simmer in boiling water for 30 minutes. Remove and let cool then cut into wedge shapes.

2 To make the marinade combine all the ingredients and use as required.

3 Place the seitan into the marinade for 30 minutes.

4 Peel the onions and cut into 2cm dice. Peel the carrot and thinly slice length ways and then cut the strips into 3cm lengths. Top and tail the mange tout. Cut the baby corn in half and thinly slice the cabbage. Clean and remove the stalk and slice the shitake mushrooms in half.

5 Remove the seitan from the marinade and drain. Reserve the marinade. Heat the oil in the pan and stir-fry the onions, carrots and cabbage for 3–4 minutes then add the seitan and cook for a further 2–3 minutes. Add the reserved marinade to the stir-fry.

6 Stir-fry the shitake mushrooms, mange tout and baby corn. Cook for 2–3 minutes and serve.

NOTES

Serve with noodles or plain rice.

Suitable for vegan, diabetic, low-cholesterol diets. ❏

Seitan with Tagine, Dates and Honey (p.271) 4 covers

- 700g Seitan
- 20ml Olive oil
- 2 Onions
- 4 cloves Garlic
- 10g Cumin seeds
- 10g Ground coriander
- 10g Ground ginger
- 10g Ground turmeric
- 10g Ground cinnamon
- 5g Chilli powder
- 5g Ground nutmeg
- 350ml Vegetarian stock
- 200ml Water
- 85g Seedless dates
- 60ml Honey
- 80g Flaked almonds
- 8 sprigs Coriander

1 Peel and finely slice the onions and peel and purée the garlic. Cut the dates in half. Toast the flaked almonds under the grill until golden brown.

2 Wash and roughly chop the coriander.

3 Drain the seitan and cut into 3cm strips. Heat 1 tablespoon oil in a pan, add the strips in batches and cook, stirring, until browned. Drain on absorbent paper.

4 Sweat the onions, garlic and spices in a little oil and cook, stirring, in a suitable pan.

5 Return the seitan to the pan with the stock and water. Simmer, covered for 1 hour. Remove the lid and simmer for about 30 minutes or until mixture has thickened slightly.

6 Stir in the dates, honey and flaked almonds. Sprinkle with fresh coriander.

NOTES

Serve with couscous or rice. An excellent meal for vegans. ❏

Shitake Mushrooms with Cider and Greens 4 covers

- 100ml Olive oil
- 10g Palm sugar or honey
- 15g Dijon mustard
- 70ml Cider vinegar
- 10g Thyme leaves
- 350g Shitake mushrooms
- 200g Small field mushrooms
- 20g Pistachio nuts, toasted
- 200g Mixed greens (watercress, romaine, rocket and curly endive)
- Salt and freshly ground black pepper

1 Clean and de-stalk the mushrooms then slice. Wash and prepare the greens into bite-sized pieces.

2 Pour 40ml oil into a bowl with the sugar, mustard, cider vinegar, thyme leaves and seasoning. Whisk the ingredients well.

3 With the remaining oil sweat off the mushrooms for 3–4 minutes, then add the pistachio nuts and season.

4 Pour the mushrooms onto the greens and toss and serve immediately.

NOTES

Suitable for vegan, coeliac and low-cholesterol diets. ❏

❏ Top: Spiced Couscous and Oyster Mushrooms
Bottom: Shitake Mushrooms with Cider and Greens ❏

Smoked Tofu, Cheese and EBLY® 4 covers

- 230g EBLY®
- 100g Onions
- 30g Olive oil
- 60ml Crème fraîche
- 120g Smoked tofu
- 100g Peas
- 60g Parmesan cheese (vegetarian)
- Salt and pepper

1 Cook the EBLY® in plenty of boiling salted water for 15–20 minutes depending on the consistency required. Drain and leave to one side.

2 Brown the onions in a little olive oil.

3 Remove any excess oil from the pan, set aside the onions and deglaze the pan with the crème fraîche.

4 Strain the EBLY®, add pepper and the crème fraîche and reheat the onion, with the tofu and peas. Cook for 2–3 minutes.

5 Serve with garnish of Parmesan cheese. ❑

Smoked Tofu on a Spiced Rice with Herb Oils 4 covers

- 113g Mixed peppers
- 113g Banana shallots, diced
- 1 clove Garlic
- 60ml Virgin olive oil
- 300g Long grain rice, cooked
- 57g Curry powder
- 250ml Vegetable stock
- 4 × 170g slices Smoked tofu
- 4 Red cherry tomatoes
- 4 Yellow cherry tomatoes
- 100g Rocket leaves

1 Skin and peel the peppers, shallots and garlic. Then finely dice them and sweat off in a little oil.

2 Add the rice to the pan then add the curry powder and stock. Cook in the oven (200°C for 15–20 minutes), covered with buttered greaseproof paper.

3 Place the smoked tofu in a pan with a little oil and pan fry until golden brown. Drain on kitchen paper.

4 Cut the tomatoes in half, cover in olive oil and seasoning then lightly grill. Keep warm until required.

5 Place the cooked rice in the centre of the plate and top with the tofu. Place rocket leaves drizzled in the green dressing on top of the tofu, surrounded by alternate red and yellow tomatoes and balsamic dressing.

Green dressing
- 1pkt Fresh coriander
- 250ml Olive oil
- 113g White wine vinegar (good quality)

1 Liquidise the ingredients, then strain and season.

→

Balsamic dressing

- ■ *300ml Balsamic vinegar (good quality)*
- ■ *30g Caster sugar*
- ■ *8 sprigs Chervil*

→ 1 Over a high heat reduce the balsamic vinegar down to 60ml, with sugar. ❑

Soured Cream, Mushroom and Tarragon Pie   4 covers

- ■ *340g Short pastry (vegetarian)*
- ■ *150g Onions*
- ■ *40g Margarine*
- ■ *300g Button mushrooms*
- ■ *3 Free-range eggs*
- ■ *5g Tarragon leaves*
- ■ *50g Pumpkin seeds, toasted*
- ■ *200ml Soured cream*
- ■ *160g Spinach*
- ■ *180g Grated cheese (mozzarella or Cheddar) (vegetarian)*
- ■ *Seasoning*

1 Line a greased 15cm or 20cm flan ring with baking parchment. On a lightly floured surface roll out the pastry and use to line the flan ring. Alternatively roll out into individual round cases. Dock the pastry and blind bake in a preheated oven at 200°C/Gas Mark 6 for 5–6 minutes. Roll out the leftover pastry into strips and reserve.

2 Clean and slice the mushrooms, peel and slice the onions. Blanch and refresh the spinach, squeeze out the remaining liquid then roughly chop it.

3 Sweat the onions off in a little margarine then add the mushrooms and cook until all the liquid from the mushrooms has evaporated. Season.

4 Whisk the eggs, tarragon, seasoning and the soured cream together.

5 Put the onions, mushrooms, spinach and cheese into the pastry pie and pour the cream mixture over. Add pumpkin seeds.

6 Place a lattice of pastry strips over the top of the pie and bake for 20–25 minutes until set.

7 Remove from the oven and rest for 5 minutes then remove from tin or ring and serve.

NOTES

Serve with crisp lettuce and salad or fresh new potatoes. ❑

Soya Bean Kebabs
4 covers

- 550g   Tempeh
- 550g   Fresh tofu
- 8   Small vine tomatoes
- 3   Green courgettes
- 3   Yellow courgettes
- 16   Button mushrooms
- 2 each Green, red and yellow peppers
- 8   Baby sweet corn
- 8   Kebab (wooden) skewers
-         Sunflower oil

Marinade

- 5ml   Dijon mustard
- 35ml   Tamari
- 35ml   Palm oil
- 40ml   Maple syrup
- 40ml   Pineapple juice
- 4cm   Ginger
- 4cm   Galangal
- 1   Lemongrass
- 3 cloves Garlic
- 12   Peppercorns
-         Sea salt

1 To make the marinade, mix the mustard, Tamari, Palm oil, peppercorns, maple syrup and pineapple juice together. Grate the ginger and squeeze the juice into the mixture, finely shred the lemongrass, purée the garlic and add the seasoning.

2 Cut tempeh and tofu into dice. Heat the marinade through and add the tempeh pieces. Bring to a simmer for 15 minutes. Remove the tempeh and reserve the liquor. Put the tofu into a cold marinade.

3 Wash the tomatoes and cut in half. Wash the courgettes and cut into 2cm dice. Wash and deseed the peppers and cut into 2cm dice. Half the sweet corn.

4 Place half a tomato onto the skewer then a tofu, pepper, courgette, mushroom, pepper, tempeh and sweet corn. Repeat this process until the skewer is full, finishing with half a tomato.

5 Brush with oil, place on a tray and grill until golden and crisp. Turn and brush regularly with oil to keep moist.

NOTES

Use the marinade to cook rice and serve with the kebabs. Also serve a Satay sauce. Suitable for vegan and gluten-free diets. ❏

Spiced Chick Pea Salad
4 covers

- 20ml   Sunflower oil
- 100g   Onions
- 1 clove Garlic
- 10g   Cumin seeds
- 10g   Turmeric
- 450g   Beef tomatoes
- 400g   Chickpeas, pre-cooked (tinned acceptable)

1 Peel and slice the onions and garlic clove. Skin, deseed and cut the tomato into concasse (small dice).

2 Sweat off the onion and garlic in a little oil until golden brown.

3 Add the spices and cook out for 2–3 minutes.

→

❏ Top: Soya Bean Kebabs   Bottom: Barbecued Seitan in a Plum and Honey Sauce ❏

- 10ml Lemon juice
- 20g Fresh coriander, chopped
- Salt and pepper

→

4 Add the tomatoes and cook for a further 2 minutes. Add the chickpeas, lemon juice, and half the coriander and cook for 2 more minutes.

5 Check the seasoning and serve, garnishing the top with the remainder of the coriander. ❑

Spiced Couscous and Oyster Mushrooms (p.235) 4 covers

- 340ml Orange juice
- 6 Cardamom seeds
- 50ml Olive oil
- 120g Onions
- 100g Spring onions
- 350g Oyster mushrooms
- 5g Ground cumin
- 2g Ground cinnamon
- 230ml Light vegetable stock
- 25g Raisins
- 220g Couscous
- 10g Fresh coriander, chopped
- 20g Flaked almonds, toasted
- Salt
- Fresh ground black pepper
- 10g Fennel, chopped

1 Clean and dice the mushrooms. Peel and thinly slice the onions and spring onions. Wash and drain the raisins.

2 Bring the orange juice and the cardamom seeds to the boil and reduce by one-third, removing any debris from the surface.

3 Heat a little olive oil in a pan and sweat off the onions, chopped fennel, and spring onions. Then add the mushrooms, cumin and cinnamon. Cook out for 3–4 minutes and season.

4 Add the orange juice to the mushroom mixture and simmer gently for 4–5 minutes.

5 Bring the vegetable stock to the boil and add the stock and raisins to the couscous. Cover with a tight-fitting lid and let stand for 12 minutes. Then stir in the coriander with a fork, check seasoning and divide into four portions.

6 Serve the orange and mushroom sauce over the couscous, garnishing with almonds.

NOTES

Suitable for vegan, diabetic and low-cholesterol diets. Most other varieties of mushroom can be used instead of oyster mushrooms. ❑

Spiced Patna Rice and Vegetables
4 covers

- 150g   TVP
- 500ml Vegetable stock
- 200g   Patna rice
- 200g   Onions
- 1–2 cloves Garlic
- 100g   Margarine
- 300g   Carrots, turnip,
         celery, leeks and
         broccoli
- 2   Beef tomatoes
- 5–10g Curry powder,
         mild
- 30ml   Shoyu
- 1   Free-range egg
         omelette
-        Salt and white
         pepper
-        Tabasco to taste

1 Soak the TVP in the strong stock overnight until it swells up then drain in a colander. Keep the excess stock.

2 Cook the rice in boiling salted water with a little dash of oil. Refresh under cold running water, drain and keep to one side.

3 Peel and slice the onions and purée the garlic. Skin and deseed the tomatoes and cut into concasse (5mm dice). Save the tomato water.

4 Sweat off the onions in a little margarine until golden brown.

5 Add the TVP with excess stock and reduce the stock right down.

6 Add extra margarine then add the rice, vegetables and tomatoes and the curry powder.

7 Add the shoyu and stir. Cut the omelette into fine strips and add this to the mixture. Check the seasoning, turn out into a dish and garnish accordingly.

NOTES

Suitable for vegans if the omelette is omitted

Suitable for coeliac, diabetic and low-cholesterol diets.

To increase the protein content add nuts or tofu to the recipe. ❑

Spiced Peanut Loaf
4 covers

- 100g   Carrots
- 185g   Onions
- 100g   Leeks
- 60g   Celery
- 3–4cm Root ginger
- 1 clove Garlic
- 40ml   Peanut oil
- 185g   Ground peanuts
- 175g   Fresh breadcrumbs

1 Finely chop the onions, leeks, ginger, celery, and garlic. Peel and grate carrots and lightly fry in the oil.

2 Mix all the dry ingredients together with coriander and the fried ingredients in a large bowl. Add the free-range eggs to bind the mixture. Season well.

3 Press in a loaf tin lined with greaseproof paper lightly brushed with margarine and bake in a preheated oven at 200°C/Gas Mark 6 for 15 minutes.

→

→

- 10g   Freshly chopped
         coriander
- 5g   Ground cumin
- 5g   Ground coriander
- 2g   Caraway seeds
- 2g   Ground turmeric
- 2   Free-range eggs
-        Salt and black
         pepper

Topping
- 210ml Milk
- 2   Eggs
-        Salt and ground
         black pepper
- 10g   Garam masala

4 Mix together all the topping ingredients. Pour over the top of the loaf and continue cooking for a further 30–35 minutes. At the end of baking time the loaf should be firm and golden brown.

5 Allow to cool a little, taking care not to break the topping.

6 Serve either hot or cold with a spicy chilli or salsa-style tomato sauce and a crisp salad. ❑

Spiced Yellow Pumpkin   4 covers

- 450g   Yellow pumpkin
- 40ml   Vegetable oil
- 60g   Brown lentils
- 20g   Black mustard seeds
- 10   Curry leaves
- 20g   Garlic purée
- 30g   Ground coriander
- 20g   Ground turmeric
- 40g   Freshly grated
         coconut
-        Salt

1 Peel and deseed the pumpkin and cut into pieces.

2 Heat the oil in a saucepan and gently fry the lentils, mustard seeds and curry leaves until the lentils are golden and the mustard seeds pop.

3 Add garlic and fry for another minute. Add the ground spices and stir well.

4 Put the pumpkin in a large pan. Put the mixture in the pumpkin with enough water to just cover the vegetables.

5 Add salt, cover the pan and simmer until the pumpkin is half cooked.

6 Sprinkle in the coconut and cook until the pumpkin is tender.

NOTES

Desiccated coconut can be used if fresh coconut is not available. ❑

St Petersburg Bake

4 covers

- 200g TVP
- 500ml Stock
- 20ml Vegetable or sunflower oil
- 300g Potatoes
- 2 Free-range eggs
- 100g Onions
- 1 clove Garlic
- 2.5g Fresh dill
- 2.5g Fresh rosemary
- 75g Smoked tofu
- 130ml Milk
- 120g Brown breadcrumbs
- 2 sprigs Parsley
- Salt and ground black pepper

1 Soak the TVP in the strong stock overnight until it swells up then drain in a colander. Keep the excess stock.

2 Peel and dice the potatoes and cook in cold salted water for approximately 20 minutes, then air dry and purée. Allow them to cool, then beat an egg yolk into the potato and add seasoning.

3 Peel and dice the onions and purée the garlic. Sweat the onions and garlic in the vegetable or sunflower oil and then add the TVP, dill and rosemary. Cook for only a few minutes.

4 Chop the smoked tofu and mix into the TVP mixture. Add any excess stock and cook out for 10 minutes.

5 Bring the milk to a simmer and pour very slowly onto a whisked egg, then add this mixture to the TVP.

6 Place half of the TVP mixture in a greased ovenproof dish then add a layer of potato, next add the other half of the TVP and top with the breadcrumbs. Bake in a preheated oven at 180–200°C/Gas Mark 5–6 for 10–12 minutes until golden brown on top.

7 Garnish and serve with parsley sprigs. ❏

Stuffed Aubergines

4 covers

- 2 Aubergines
- 15ml Oil
- 120g Onions
- 120g Celery
- 120g Green pepper
- 60g Button mushrooms
- 10g Garlic purée
- 40g Whole medium breadcrumbs
- 15g Tomato purée
- 20g Margarine

1 Peel the onions and cut into 1cm dice. Skin and cut the pepper into 1cm dice, peel the celery and clean the mushrooms and dice both.

2 Wash and cut the aubergines in half. Scoop out the flesh and chop then cook in boiling salted water for 5 minutes. Remove, drain and chop.

3 Sweat off the onions and the chopped aubergine in hot oil until a light brown colour.

4 Add the celery, pepper, mushrooms and garlic and fry for a further 5 minutes.

→

→

- 60g   Cheddar cheese
         (vegetarian)
- 20g   Thyme, parsley and
         oregano
- ■   Salt and pepper

5 Remove from the heat add the margarine and stir in the breadcrumbs, tomato purée, 30g cheese, seasoning and herbs.

6 Fill the aubergine skins, top with the remaining cheese and bake in a preheated oven at 180°C/Gas Mark 5 for 20–25 minutes, until golden brown. ❏

Stuffed Baby Pumpkin   4 covers

- 100g   Onions
- 2 cloves Garlic
- 20g   Ground cumin
- 10g   Ground coriander
- 15g   Ground paprika
- 10g   Ground turmeric
- 20g   Olive oil
- 300g   Plum tomatoes
- 10g   Caster sugar
- 150g   Long grain rice,
         cooked
- 110g   Fine Kenya beans
- 25g   Peas
- 75g   Chickpeas (cooked
         or tinned)
- 2 × 450g Pumpkins
         (golden nugget)

1 Peel and finely chop the onions and garlic. Top and tail the Kenya beans and cut into 3cm lengths.

2 Peel and roughly chop the chickpeas. Cut the pumpkins in half roundways and cut a little off the bottom. Scoop out seeds and membranes from pumpkin, leaving 1cm shell.

3 Sweat the onions, garlic and ground spices in a little oil without colour. Add the tomatoes and sprinkle with sugar. Simmer for 10 minutes.

4 Combine the tomato mixture with the rice, beans, peas and chickpeas and incorporate fully.

5 Divide the mixture equally between the four pumpkin halves.

6 Place the pumpkins in a roasting tray with water to three-quarters of the way up the pumpkins and bake in a pre-heated oven at 170°C/Gas Mark 3–4 for 1½ hours until tender.

7 Serve half per portion and garnish with sprigs of herbs.

NOTES

Suitable for vegan, low-cholesterol, gluten- and wheat-free diets. The pumpkins can be substituted with peppers, tomatoes and other types of pumpkin and squashes. ❏

- 100g   Onions
- 40ml   Olive oil
- 2.5g   Turmeric
- 2.5g   Garam masala
- 400ml Vegetable stock
- 300g   Long grain rice, cooked
- 10g   Fresh coriander, chopped
- 5g   Fresh parsley, chopped
- 8   Beef tomatoes
- 113g   Chickpeas (tinned or cooked)
- 4   Plum tomatoes
- 150g   Quinoa
- 65g   Margarine
-        Salt and pepper

1 Cut the top off the beef tomatoes and remove the pulp from the inside.

2 Chop the chickpeas. Peel and dice the onions. Skin, deseed and cut the plum tomatoes into concasse (small dice).

3 Sweat off the onions without any colour in the oil, then add the spices and continue to cook for 1–2 minutes. Then add 100ml stock and cook for another 1–2 minutes.

4 Add the rice and stir. Cook for 2–3 minutes. Add the herbs, chickpeas and concasse and cook for 4–5 minutes, stirring occasionally to prevent sticking.

5 Fry the quinoa off in margarine for 1–2 minutes, then add the rest of the stock. Bring to the boil and then simmer for 15 minutes uncovered or until the stock has been absorbed.

6 Season both the rice and quinoa mixtures. Warm through the tomato cases, then fill with the rice mixture and top with quinoa.

7 Serve with spinach and creamed potatoes. ❏

❏ Stuffed Beef Tomatoes ❏

- 30g   TVP
- 50ml   Strong vegetable stock
- 1 clove Garlic
- 2   Aubergines (medium)
- 100g   Onions
- 1   Beef tomato
- 10ml   Olive oil
- 20g   Fresh parsley, chopped
- 10g   Fresh rosemary, chopped
- 10g   Fresh chives, chopped
- 55g   Wholemeal breadcrumbs
- 30g   Chopped nuts (peanuts, walnuts or pinenuts) (optional)
- 120g   Cheddar cheese (vegetarian)
- ▪   Salt and pepper

1 Soak the TVP in the strong stock overnight until it swells up then drain in a colander. Keep the excess stock.

2 Peel and dice the onions and purée the garlic. Skin and deseed the tomato and cut into concasse (5mm dice). Save the tomato water.

3 Wash the aubergines, remove the stalks and cut lengthways, scooping out the core flesh.

4 Sprinkle with salt and olive oil and bake in a preheated oven at 200°C/Gas Mark 6 for 15 minutes.

5 Chop the aubergine flesh and grate the Cheddar cheese.

6 Sweat off the onions, aubergine flesh, garlic and tomato in olive oil. Add the stock, tomato, water and TVP. Cook for 10 minutes and add the herbs, breadcrumbs, nuts and seasoning.

7 Fill the four aubergine cases with the mixture, top with the cheese and return to the oven for 10–12 minutes until the cheese is golden brown.

NOTES

Nuts are optional, so remove for nut-free recipe.

For vegan diets omit the grated cheese. ❏

Stuffed Peppers   4 covers

- 100g   Margarine
- 100g   Onions
- 4   Red peppers
- 5g   Garlic purée
- 150g   Long grain rice
- 20g   Tomato purée
- 720ml Vegetable stock
- 10g   Fresh parsley, chopped
- 50g   Hazelnuts

1 Wash, top and deseed the peppers, keeping the top. Peel and dice the onions and garlic. Chop the hazelnuts. Skin and deseed the tomatoes and cut into concasse (small dice).

2 Melt the margarine in a suitable frying pan and sweat off the onions, peppers and garlic purée, without colour.

3 Add the rice and ensure that it is all coated in the margarine then add the tomato purée, 420ml stock and stir in half the parsley.

→

→

■ 2   Beef tomatoes
■   Salt and pepper

4 Season the rice and cook for 15 minutes. Add the hazel-nuts and concasse.

5 Spoon the mixture into the peppers and place the tops back on. Put the peppers on a greased tray and add the remaining 300ml stock. Bake in a preheated oven at 160°C/Gas Mark 4 for 15–25 minutes. Cover. Baste the peppers and continue to cook for a further 10–15 minutes.

6 Remove and drain then garnish with the remaining parsley.

NOTES

Suitable for vegan, low-cholesterol and coeliac diets. ❑

Sweet and Sour Filo Parcels   4 covers

■ 40ml   Olive oil
■ 1 large Onion
■ 3 cloves Garlic
■ 10g   Fresh ginger
■ 1 stick Celery
■ 110g   Peas
■ 1   Red pepper
■ 1   Green pepper
■ 140g   Mushrooms
■ 1   Red chilli
■ 100g   Beansprouts
■ 8 sheets Filo pastry
■ 30g   Margarine
■ 100g   Cashew nuts, roasted
■ 60g   Water chestnuts

Sauce

■ 30ml   Tamari
■ 40ml   White wine vinegar
■ 110ml   Pineapple juice
■ 30g   Brown sugar
■ 10g   Tomato purée
■ 30g   Corn flour
■ 30g   Tomato passata

1 Wash, deseed and slice the chilli and peppers. Peel and slice the onion, celery, mushrooms, garlic and ginger. Wash the beansprouts. Slice water chestnuts.

2 Heat the oil in a wok and sweat off the onion, garlic, 70g cashew nuts and ginger then add the rest of the vegetables and cook until tender.

3 To make the sauce reduce the sugar and white wine vine-gar in a separate pan by one-third then add the tamari and pineapple juice and reduce a little. Next add the tomato passata and purée and continue to cook out for 5 minutes. Thicken if required with corn flour. Cool right down.

4 Add the sauce to the stir-fry to the sauce and check the seasoning.

5 Lay two filo sheets, one on top of the other, and place one quarter of the mixture one third of the way up the filo sheet and fold over the filo pastry and roll three quarters of the way, then fold in the edges and seal. Then roll the final quarter. It should look like a spring roll. Then brush the top with a little melted margarine and add the remaining crushed cashew nuts, bake in a preheated oven at 200°C/Gas Mark 6 for 10–15 minutes, until golden brown. ❑

Sweet and Sour Vegetables

- *30ml   Vegetable oil*
- *120g   Carrots*
- *120g   Onions*
- *110g   Leeks*
- *50g   Celery*
- *100g   Spring onions*
- *150g   Red, green and yellow peppers*
- *100g   Mange tout*
- *50g   Bamboo shoots*
- *50g   Water chestnuts*
- *30g   Shoyu*
- *5cm   Fresh ginger*
- *20g   Pineapple segments, tinned*
- *20g   Arrowroot or corn flour*
- *20g   Fresh coriander, roughly chopped*

Sauce
- *100ml   Pineapple juice*
- *35g   Tomato ketchup*
- *40ml   White wine vinegar*
- *30g   Brown sugar*
- *20g   Tomato purée*
- *10ml   Worcester sauce*

1 Peel and cut the carrots, celery, onions and spring onions into 2cm dice. Wash, deseed and cut the peppers into 2cm dice and top and tail the mange tout then cut in half. Top and tail the leeks, then cut in half, wash and cut into 2cm dice.

2 Wash and drain the bamboo shoots then halve the water chestnuts. Peel and finely dice the ginger.

3 To make the sauce mix the pineapple juice, white wine vinegar, sugar, tomato purée, Worcester sauce, shoyu and ginger and ketchup together and bring to the boil, removing any debris that comes to the surface. Simmer for 15–20 minutes.

4 Strain the sauce and thicken with arrowroot or corn flour.

5 Sweat off the vegetables in the oil, without colour. Drain and remove any excess oil. Add the pineapple segments.

6 Add the cooked vegetables to the sauce and cook for a further 5 minutes.

7 Garnish with the coriander.

NOTES

Serve with either rice or noodles. Suitable for vegan diets. ❏

Sweet Potato Tart
4 covers

- *340g   Short pastry (vegetarian)*
- *200g   Onions*
- *40ml   Vegetable or sunflower oil*
- *10 leaves Basil*
- *2   Beef tomatoes*
- *150g   Sweet potatoes*

1 Peel, slice and cook the sweet potatoes in boiling salted water. Drain off the water once cooked and allow to air dry.

2 Line a greased 15cm or 20cm flan ring with baking parchment. On a lightly floured surface roll out the pastry and use to line the flan ring. Alternatively roll out into individual rounds and dock the rounds.

→

248   wholefood and vegetarian cookery

→
- ■ *180g*   *Cheese (mozzarella or Cheddar) (vegetarian)*
- ■   *Salt and ground white pepper*

3 Peel and cut the onions and the tomatoes into slices and then wash and cut the basil leaves into chiffonade (very fine strips).

4 Sweat off the onions in a little oil and then drain off any excess.

5 Brush the flan or individual rounds with a little oil, season and sprinkle with a little basil. Put a layer of onions onto the basil, followed by a layer of tomato and a layer of potatoes and cheese.

6 Repeat this process once more, finishing with a layer of cheese.

7 Bake in a preheated oven at 200°C/Gas Mark 7 for 10–15 minutes. Remove when golden brown and serve.

NOTES

Replace the cheese with tempeh for vegan diets and ensure that vegan pastry is used.

For extra flavour serve a pepper sauce or a spicy tomato sauce. ❏

Tamari EBLY®   4 covers

- ■ *300g*   *EBLY®*
- ■ *120g*   *Onions*
- ■ *20ml*   *Ground nut oil*
- ■ *15ml*   *Tamari*
- ■   *Salt and pepper*

1 Cook EBLY® in plenty of boiling salted water for 15–20 minutes depending on the consistency required. Drain and leave to one side.

2 Peel and dice the onion.

3 Heat the oil in a suitable pan then add the onion and cook without colour. Add the EBLY® and stir then add the tamari and season.

4 Serve immediately. ❏

❏ Top: Sweet Potato Tart   Bottom: Mushroom Pepper Pot ❏

Tempeh Risotto   4 covers

- 150g   Onions
- 1   Green chilli
- 5g   Garlic purée
- 40ml   Olive oil
- 320g   Arborio rice
- 800ml   Vegetable stock
- 180g   Tempeh, diced
- 100g   Tomatoes
- 4   Spring onions
- 20g   Fresh parsley, chopped
- 20g   Fresh basil, finely shredded

1 Peel the onions and spring onions and cut into fine dice. Skin and deseed the tomatoes and cut into small dice. Deseed and very finely shred the chilli.

2 Sweat off the onions, chilli and garlic purée in a little oil without colour.

3 Add the rice and coat all the grains, stirring to prevent sticking.

4 Gradually add the stock and bring to the boil, skimming any debris from the surface. Simmer for 12–15 minutes.

➔

❏ Tempeh Risotto ❏

→

- *100ml Double cream (optional)*
- *15g Ground Parmesan cheese (vegetarian)*
- *Salt and pepper*

5 Stir in the tempeh, tomatoes, spring onions, parsley and half the basil. Add the double cream and simmer for a further 3–4 minutes. Stir in the Parmesan, correct the seasoning and serve with the remaining basil as a garnish.

NOTES

If the cream is omitted this recipe is suitable for vegan, low-cholesterol, diabetic and coeliac diets. ❑

Teriyaki Mushroom   4 covers

- *200g Shallots*
- *200g Spring onions*
- *30ml Sunflower oil*
- *200g Pak choi*
- *400g Shitake mushrooms*
- *200g Button mushrooms*

1 Clean and slice the mushrooms and pak choi. Peel and quarter the shallots and cut the spring onions into 3–4cm lengths.

2 Sweat off the shallots and spring onions in the oil for 2–3 minutes on a medium heat then add the pak choi and mushrooms and cook for a further 2–3 minutes.

→

❑ Teriyaki Mushroom ❑

Teriyaki-style sauce

- *120ml Mirin*
- *60g   Brown sugar*
- *120ml Shoyu*
- *3 drops Sesame oil*

→

3 To make the sauce pour the mirin into a pan then add the sugar and dissolve. Add the shoyu and reduce by a third. Add the 3 drops of sesame oil.

4 Add the teriyaki sauce to the mixture and cook for a further 2–3 minutes then serve.

NOTES

Suitable for vegan diets. If tamari is used in place of shoyu it will also be suitable for coeliac diets. ❑

Thai Green Curry with Tempeh   4 covers

- *500g   Marinated tempeh*
- *150g   Sunflower oil*
- *2 bunches Spring onions, sliced*

1 Cut the tempeh into squares and reserve until required.

2 To make the paste peel the garlic, shallots and galangal, deseed the chillies then finely chop them all.

→

❑ Thai Green Curry with Tempeh ❑

→

- 250ml Coconut milk
- 2   Limes (zest only)
- 200g   Fresh basil, shredded
- 200g   Green Thai Curry Paste
- 40g   Shallots, sliced

Curry Paste (green)

- 20   Black peppercorns
- 6   Chillies
- 4   Shallots
- 4 cloves Garlic
- 1 bunch Coriander
- 2   Limes (zest only)
- 5cm   Galangal
- 10g   Ground turmeric
- 20g   Coriander seeds
- 10g   Cumin seeds
- ■   Palm oil
- ■   Salt

3 Grind the coriander, cumin and black peppercorns together in a processor or pestle and mortar, then add all the other paste ingredients except the Palm oil and continue to grind until it becomes smooth.

4 Fry the tempeh in the sunflower oil for 2 minutes on both sides. Add the shallots and sliced spring onions and fry for a further 2 minutes. Drain and keep to one side.

5 Fry off the paste in a little Palm oil until it begins to smell fragrant, then add the coconut milk.

6 Boil the coconut milk mixture and add the lime zest and tempeh and onions. Add the shredded basil and cook for 10 minutes.

NOTES

Serve with Jasmine rice or noodles that are either plain or coconut flavoured. ❑

Thai-style Fried Rice   4 covers

- 113g   Tofu
- 30ml   Vegetable oil
- 340g   Jasmine rice, cooked
- 50g   Carrots
- 2   Yard-long beans
- 6   Baby corn cobs
- 20ml   Shoyu
- 10g   Palm sugar
- 5   Red chillies
- 100g   Cucumber
- 1   Lime
- 8 leaves Purple basil (holy basil)
- 4   Spring onions, trimmed

1 Peel and chop the carrots into 1cm dice. Trim and chop the yard-long beans and baby corn cobs into 2cm dice. Remove the seeds and stalk from one of the chillies and cut into a fine dice.

2 Drain and chop the tofu.

3 Place the oil into a hot pan or wok and add the rice. Stir to prevent it from sticking.

4 Add the carrots and yard-long beans and cook for 1–2 minutes then add the baby corn cobs. Mix well.

5 Add the tofu, shoyu, basil, sugar and the chilli. Stir-fry for 2–3 minutes.

6 Serve on a suitable plate and garnish with sliced cucumber, lime, cut into quarters, spring onions and chillies.

→

❏ Top: Thai-style Noodles
Bottom: Filled Chinese Rolls and Tomato Sauce ❏

→ | NOTES

Suitable for vegan diets. If holy basil or purple basil is not available use sweet basil. Palm sugar is better than refined white sugar but if it is not available use either a light honey or brown sugar. ❏

Thai-style Noodles (p.255)   4 covers

- 260g   Rice noodles
- 40ml   Vegetable stock
- 80ml   Tamarind juice
- 60ml   Vegetable oil
- 2   Free-range eggs (optional)
- 30ml   Shoyu
- 1tsp   Dried ground chillies
- 100g   Smoked tofu
- 300g   Beansprouts
- 4   Spring onions
- 20g   Ground roasted peanuts
- 30g   Palm sugar

1 Wash the beansprouts in cold water and drain. Cut the tofu into thin slices. Cut the spring onions into large diamond shapes.

2 Soak the noodles in the stock and tamarind water until the noodles begin to soften. Drain.

3 Place 50–60ml oil in a suitable pan or wok and fry off the noodles for 1–2 minutes. Do not allow them to stick to the pan, turn and stir continually.

4 Scramble the eggs in a clean pan with a little oil. When cooked add to the noodles.

5 Add all the other ingredients (except sugar and nuts, and keep some beansprouts and chillies for garnish) and cook out for 2–3 minutes then add the nuts and sugar.

6 Garnish with beansprouts and chillies.

NOTES

Vermicelli noodles, which are often called glass noodles, can be used. They are made from mung beans.

This recipe is good for vegan diets if the eggs are omitted and extra tofu is added. ❏

Tofu with Stir-fried Vegetables   4 covers

- 100g   Yard-long beans
- 1   Red pepper
- 3cm   Ginger
- 2 cloves Garlic
- 90ml   Peanut oil

1 Drain the tofu and cut into 2cm squares. Skin, deseed and cut the pepper into 3–4cm slices.

→

→
- 100g Broccoli
- 150g Shitake mushrooms
- 100g Cauliflower
- 40ml Water
- 400g Tofu
- 60g Spring onions
- 10g Purple basil leaves (holy basil)
- 20ml Mirin
- 15ml Shoyu
- 20g Palm sugar
- ■ Salt and pepper

2 Peel and slice the garlic, ginger and spring onions. Clean and slice the mushrooms, cut the beans into 3–4cm lengths and separate the cauliflower and broccoli into small florets.

3 Fry off the yard-long beans, pepper, ginger and garlic in the peanut oil (without burning the garlic) for 2–3 minutes. Add the mirin and palm sugar.

4 Add the broccoli, mushrooms and cauliflower and stir-fry for 1–2 minutes. Add about 40ml water and continue to cook for a further 2 minutes. Add the shoyu.

5 Carefully add the tofu and the spring onions and cook for another 2 minutes, then add the basil leaves and check the seasoning.

NOTES

Suitable for vegan diets. ❏

Tofu with Apricots and Pilaff Rice   4 covers

- 60g Ghee
- 500g Tofu
- 200g Onions
- 1 clove Garlic
- 10g Ground cumin
- 10g Ground coriander
- 5g Ground turmeric
- 75g Dried apricots
- 250g Basmati rice
- 1l Vegetable stock
- 35g Dried currants
- 60g Peas
- 80g Pine nuts
- ■ Fresh coriander, chopped

1 Drain the tofu and cut into 3cm dice. Peel and slice the onions and garlic. Wash the dried apricots under warm water and then slice them.

2 Heat 30g ghee and add the tofu in batches, cooking lightly until golden brown all over, then drain and reserve.

3 In the same pan heat the remaining ghee. Sweat off the onions, garlic and spices. Add the apricots and rice and stir over the heat until the rice is coated in the spice mixture. Stir in the stock and simmer, covered with tight-fitting lid, for 15 minutes.

4 Remove the pan from the heat and very carefully stir in the tofu and let it stand for 15 minutes. Stir in the currants, peas and pine nuts. Garnish with chopped coriander.

NOTES

A good dish for vegan diets. If the nuts are omitted this recipe can also be used for nut-free diets. ❏

❏ Top: Mushroom and Black Olive Pizza   Bottom: Tofu with Apricots and Pilaff Rice ❏

- ■ 6   *Spring onions*
- ■ 1   *Red onion*
- ■ 10ml   *Vegetable oil*
- ■ 25g   *Ground walnuts*
- ■ 25g   *Chopped mixed nuts*
- ■   *Pesto sauce*
- ■ 80g   *Cheddar cheese (vegetarian)*
- ■ 2   *Beef tomatoes*
- ■ 4 sprigs Oregano
- ■ 30ml   *Tomato purée*
- ■ 2   *Free-range eggs*
- ■ 30ml   *Milk (or soya milk)*

Flan case
- ■ 100g   *Margarine*
- ■ 50g   *Rolled oats*
- ■ 100g   *Plain wholemeal flour*
- ■   *Salt and pepper*

1 Peel, wash and slice the onion and spring onions. Grate the Cheddar cheese.

2 Blanch and refresh the tomatoes, then peel, deseed and slice. Remove the leaves from the sprigs of oregano.

3 Sweat off the onions and spring onions in a little oil then season and mix in the nuts. Remove from the heat and add the cheese, tomatoes, oregano and tomato purée. Beat the eggs and milk and add to the mixture when suitably cooled. Keep to one side.

4 To make the flan case mix the margarine into the flour and rolled oats. Add a little water to make the mixture moist and then press into a greased and lined 23–25cm flan tin. Spread the mixture evenly over the base and around the sides.

5 Place greaseproof paper on top of the pastry flan, fill with baking beans and blind bake in a preheated oven at 190°C/Gas Mark 5 for 15 minutes. Brush bases with Pesto.

6 Pour the mixture into the flan case and cook in a preheated oven at 150°C/Gas Mark 3 for 45 minutes or until set.

NOTES

This can be used as a starter or as a main meal. Serve warm or cold with salad Russe or potato salad and coleslaw and a crisp green salad. Garnish with parsley sprigs. For vegan

- ■ 350g   *Potatoes*
- ■ 1   *Egg yolk*
- ■ 30g   *Margarine*
- ■ 350g   *Beef tomatoes*
- ■ 220g   *Onions*
- ■ 1 clove Garlic
- ■ 30g   *Plain flour*

1 Soak the TVP in the strong stock overnight until it swells up then drain in a colander. Keep the excess stock.

2 Peel and dice the potatoes and cook in cold salted water for approximately 20 minutes, then air dry and purée. Allow to cool, then beat an egg yolk and add seasoning.

→

- 200g   TVP
- 500ml Strong vegetable stock
- 1   Bay leaf
- 8g   Thyme leaves (fresh if possible)
- 50g   Flaked almonds
- 2 sprigs Parsley
- 50g   Celery
-        Salt and ground black pepper

3 Peel and slice the onions, chop the celery, and purée the garlic. Skin and deseed the tomatoes and cut into concasse (5mm dice). Save the tomato water.

4 Place a knob of margarine in a hot pan and add the concasse and cook out until it has turned into a thick purée, this should take 10–15 minutes.

5 Sweat the sliced onions, celery and garlic purée in the remainder of margarine then add the flour and cook for 2–3 minutes.

6 Add the TVP and stir. Then add the excess stock, bay leaf, thyme leaves and tomato water and stir well to remove any lumps of flour. Cook for 30 minutes. Add seasoning.

7 Add one-third of the tomato purée, stir in and correct the seasoning.

8 Place the TVP mixture in a suitable dish. Allow to cool, pipe potato around the edges then spoon the remaining tomato purée into the centre. Sprinkle with the flaked almonds and bake in a preheated oven at 180–200°C/Gas Mark 5–6 for 10–12 minutes until golden brown.

9 Garnish with parsley sprigs and serve. ❑

Tomato, Bean and Onion Tart   4 covers

- 40ml   Vegetable oil
- 340g   Short pastry (vegetarian)
- 360g   White beans, tinned
- 180g   Plum tomatoes
- 2 cloves Garlic
- 100g   Onions
- 12 leaves Basil
- 100g   Pine nuts
- 150ml Velouté
- 180g   Cheese, grated (mozzarella or Cheddar) (vegetarian)
-        Seasoning

1 Line a greased 15cm or 20cm flan ring with baking parchment. On a lightly floured surface roll out the pastry and use to line the flan ring. Alternatively roll out into individual round cases.

2 Peel and slice the onion. Peel and purée the garlic. Wash and shred the basil. Wash and slice the tomatoes.

3 Lightly sweat off the onions and garlic in the vegetable oil. Then add the pine nuts.

4 Drain and purée half the beans and add to the onions. Add half of the basil to this mixture and the rest of the beans. Cook for 2–3 minutes and season. Add the velouté and adjust the seasoning if required.

5 Pour the mixture into the pastry case, place sliced tomatoes on top and cover with the grated cheese.

→

→

6 Bake in a preheated oven 200°C/Gas Mark 6–7 for approximately 40 minutes until golden brown. Serve with a sprinkling of chopped basil.

Velouté

- ■ *100g Margarine*
- ■ *100g Plain white flour*
- ■ *1l Vegetable stock (white)*

1 Place the margarine in a thick-bottomed pan and melt over a gentle heat. Add the flour and cook out until a light sandy texture has been achieved, making a roux.

2 Remove from the heat and cool slightly. Bring the stock almost to the boil and simmer. Gradually add the stock to the roux, stirring until a smooth sauce is achieved. Simmer for 45–60 minutes and pass through a strainer to remove any debris. Cover with greaseproof paper brushed with margarine to prevent a skin forming.

NOTES

For vegan diets, ensure the pastry and margarine are vegan. Also use tempeh or tofu, instead of the cheese. ❏

Tri-colour Pasta Bake   4 covers

- ■ *50g Onions*
- ■ *60ml Vegetable oil*
- ■ *2 cloves Garlic*
- ■ *200g Courgettes*
- ■ *200g Aubergines*
- ■ *1 Red pepper*
- ■ *1 Green pepper*
- ■ *250g Beef tomatoes*
- ■ *20g Fresh parsley*
- ■ *113g Tri-colour pasta*
- ■ *35g Margarine*
- ■ *10g Dried mixed herbs*
- ■ *90g Breadcrumbs*
- ■ *Salt and white pepper*

1 Blanch and refresh the tomatoes, remove the skin, deseed and cut into concasse (small dice). Peel and slice the garlic and the onions.

2 Skin and deseed the peppers and cut them into 2cm dice.

3 Trim the ends of the aubergine and courgettes then cut into 5mm thick slices. Wash and finely chop the parsley.

4 Sauté the onions in hot oil then add the garlic, courgettes, aubergines and peppers. Season lightly and cook for 5 minutes.

5 Add the concasse and the parsley and stir.

6 Cook the pasta in boiling salted water for 15–20 minutes. Refresh under ice-cold water and drain in a colander.

7 Mix the vegetables and pasta together. Check the seasoning.

→

→ 8 Melt the margarine in a pan, add the mixed dried herbs and breadcrumbs and stir until fully incorporated. Season.

9 Pour the vegetables into an ovenproof dish and cover evenly with the breadcrumb mixture.

10 Bake in a preheated oven at 180°C/Gas Mark 4 for 15–20 minutes until or golden brown.

NOTES

Suitable for vegan and low-cholesterol diets. To add more fibre use wholemeal breadcrumbs. For more protein use nuts in the topping or diced tofu in the vegetable filling. ❏

Tuscan Bean and Basil Ragout   4 covers

- 110g   Onions
- 100g   Leeks
- 100g   Celery
- 30g   Olive oil
- 400g   Button mushrooms
- 10–15g Pesto (vegetarian)
- 397g   Chopped Italian tomatoes, tinned
- 397g   Borlotti beans or rose coco beans, tinned (or haricot beans)
- 20g   Sweet basil leaves
- 113g   Parmesan cheese (vegetarian)
- Salt and freshly ground black pepper

1 Clean the mushrooms and cut into quarters. Wash the leeks and cut into 1cm dice. Peel and dice the celery and onions.

2 Drain and wash the beans. Reserve.

3 Sweat off the onions, leeks and celery in a little olive oil without colour.

4 Add the mushrooms, cook for a further 3–4 minutes then stir in the pesto.

5 Stir in the tomatoes and beans and cook for a further 6–8 minutes. Season and add 10g basil leaves and three-quarters of the Parmesan. Cook for a further 1–2 minutes.

6 Serve garnished with the remaining basil and Parmesan. ❏

❑ Top: Tuscan Bean and Basil Ragout   Bottom: Quinoa and Samphire ❑

Vegetable Balti
4 covers

- 5g Fennel seeds
- 50ml Palm oil or vegetable ghee
- 200g Onions
- 5g Cumin seeds
- 5g Chilli powder
- 5g Ground coriander
- 20g Garlic purée
- 20g Ginger purée
- 120g Potatoes
- 120g Carrots
- 120g Green peppers
- 400g Tomatoes, chopped, tinned
- 80ml Strong vegetable stock
- 120g Courgettes
- 4 Tomatoes
- 100g Baby corn cobs
- 100g Peas
- 2 Green chillies
- 25g Fresh coriander, chopped
- 50ml Natural yoghurt

1 Peel and dice the onions, potatoes and carrots. Wash the courgettes and cut into 1–2cm dice. Skin and deseed the peppers and cut into 1–2cm dice. Cut the baby corn cobs into 1–2cm cubes. Wash the tomatoes and cut into quarters.

2 Heat a thick-bottomed pan and fry off the fennel seeds in a little oil and stir, then add the onions and fry until brown.

3 Add all the dry spices and stir for 1 minute, then add the garlic and ginger purée stirring for a further minute.

4 Stir in the potatoes, carrots and peppers and cook for a further 5 minutes, stirring constantly.

5 Pour in the tinned tomatoes and the vegetable stock and simmer uncovered for 10 minutes.

6 Add the courgettes and quartered tomatoes. Cook for a further 10 minutes then add the baby corn cobs, peas, chillies and half the coriander.

7 Cook for 5 more minutes then check seasoning. Serve garnished with a spoonful of natural yoghurt topped with chopped coriander.

NOTES

Suitable for vegan, diabetic, low-cholesterol and nut-free diets. Serve with naan bread, rice, poppadoms and raitas. Not suitable for coeliacs. ❑

Vegetable Curry
4 covers

- 400g Onions
- 60g Vegetable ghee
- 1 Red pepper
- 1 Green pepper
- 90g Leeks
- 100g Carrots
- 30g Garlic purée

1 Peel the onions, celery, leeks and carrots and cut into 2cm dice. Skin and deseed the tomatoes and peppers and cut into 2cm dice. Clean and quarter the mushrooms. Peel and finely dice the ginger.

2 Top and tail the courgettes and cut into 2cm dice together with the baby corn.

→

→

- *30mm Ginger*
- *100g Celery*
- *30g Mild curry powder*
- *200ml Vegetable stock*
- *6–8 Cardamom seeds (green)*
- *30g Turmeric, ground cumin and ground coriander*
- *100g Tomatoes*
- *70g Courgettes*
- *70g Button mushrooms*
- *70g Baby corn*
- *Fresh coriander, chopped*
- *Salt and ground black pepper*

3 Sweat 200g onions in the ghee with the peppers, leeks, carrots, garlic purée, ginger and celery in a suitable pan.

4 In a separate pan fry 200g onions until golden brown, then add 15g curry powder and a little stock. Cook for 15 minutes then liquidise.

5 Add the cardamom seeds and the spices. Cook for 3 minutes then add the tomatoes and cook out for a further 10 minutes.

6 Add the stock and the onion purée and cook out for 20 minutes then add the courgettes, mushrooms and baby corn and cook for a further 10 minutes. Stir regularly and check the seasoning.

7 Garnish with chopped coriander and serve with rice.

NOTES

Serve with basmati rice, poppadoms, naan bread, mango chutney and mint flavoured yoghurt and cucumber.

Suitable for vegan, diabetic and low-cholesterol diets. Not suitable for coeliacs. ❏

Vegetable Strudel   4 covers

- *30g Vegetable oil*
- *150g Carrots*
- *200g Yard-long beans*
- *6 Baby corn cobs*
- *100g Celery*
- *150g Spring onions*
- *10–20ml Shoyu*
- *10g Palm sugar*
- *1–2 Red chillies, to taste*
- *30ml Plum sauce*
- *50ml Sweet chilli sauce*
- *240g Jasmine rice, cooked*
- *8 sheets Filo pastry*
- *Margarine*
- *10g Sesame seeds, toasted*

1 Peel and chop the carrots into slices. Trim and chop the celery, spring onions, yard-long beans and baby corn into slices. Remove the seeds and stalk from one of the chillies and cut into fine slices.

2 Heat the oil in a hot pan or wok and stir-fry the carrots and yard-long beans for 1–2 minutes then add the baby corn cobs, celery, spring onions and holy basil. Mix well.

3 Add the shoyu, sugar, chilli, the juice of the lime and the plum and chilli sauces. Stir-fry in.

4 Pour this mixture into a bowl, stir in the rice and check the seasoning. Leave to cool for 10–15 minutes.

5 Remove two sheets of filo pastry, keeping the other sheets covered with a damp towel to prevent drying.

→

- ➜
- ■ 8 leaves Holy basil (purple basil)
- ■ 1 Lime

6 Lay one sheet on top of the other and place one-quarter of the cool mixture on top, approximately 5cm from the edge. Brush the edges with cold water and roll firmly to half way then fold in the edges and brush again with a little water and continue to roll tightly.

7 Repeat this process with the remaining ingredients. Brush the tops with a little melted margarine and dust with sesame seeds.

8 Bake in a preheated oven at 190°C/Gas Mark 5 for 20 minutes until golden brown and crisp.

NOTES

Suitable for vegan, diabetic and low-cholesterol diets. Serve with a light salad. ❏

Vegetables with Polenta   4 covers

- ■ 1 Red pepper
- ■ 1 Green pepper
- ■ 120g Onions
- ■ 100g Spring onions
- ■ 5g Garlic purée
- ■ 80g Leeks
- ■ 80g Celery
- ■ 30ml Olive oil
- ■ 220g Field mushrooms
- ■ 20g Fresh parsley, chopped
- ■ 10g Fresh thyme leaves
- ■ 4 slices Polenta (1.5cm thick)
- ■ Salt and pepper

1 Clean the mushrooms and cut into quarters. Wash the leeks and cut into slices. Peel and slice the celery, spring onions and onions. Skin, deseed and slice the peppers.

2 Sweat off the peppers, onions, spring onions, garlic purée, leeks and celery in the olive oil over a medium heat and without colour for 5–10 minutes. Then add the mushrooms and cook for a further 4–5 minutes.

3 Add 10g parsley and all the thyme and season with salt and pepper.

4 Pan-fry or grill the polenta until golden brown and heated through.

5 Place the polenta on the serving dish and spoon the vegetable mixture over.

6 Garnish with the remaining chopped parsley.

NOTES

Suitable for vegan, diabetic and low-cholesterol diets. ❏

Vegetable Yorkshire Pudding (p.268)

4 covers

- 80ml   Vegetable oil
- 50g   Carrots
- 50g   Onions
- 25g   Cherry tomatoes
- 50g   Baby button
          mushrooms
- 50g   Kenya beans

Batter
- 113g   Plain flour
- 113g   Milk
- 2 medium Free-range eggs
-         Pinch of salt and
          ground black
          pepper

1 Peel and thickly slice the carrots and onions. Wash and remove the stalk from the tomatoes and leave whole.

2 Clean the mushrooms and leave whole. Top and tail the beans and cut into 3cm lengths.

3 To make the batter sieve the flour into a bowl with the milk, eggs and seasoning. Whisk until you have a smooth batter. Let stand for some 20 minutes.

4 Divide the vegetable oil between four large Yorkshire pudding moulds (minimum 10–12cm) and place into a preheated oven at 210°C/Gas Mark 7 until the oil is smoking.

5 Divide the vegetables equally into four and add to the hot oil, then pour the batter into the moulds and over the vegetables.

6 Quickly place the moulds back in the oven and cook for 30 minutes.

7 Remove carefully as there could be very hot oil inside the Yorkshire puddings. Drain for 1–2 minutes before serving. ❏

Vegetarian Polenaise

4 covers

- 250g   TVP
- 500ml   Strong vegetable
          stock
- 100g   Onions
- 1 clove Garlic
- 80g   Margarine
- 20g   Tomato purée
- 250g   Breadcrumbs
- 20g   Fresh parsley,
          chopped
- 2   Free-range eggs,
          hard boiled

1 Soak the TVP in the strong stock overnight until it swells up then drain in a colander. Keep the excess stock.

2 Peel and dice the onions and purée the garlic. Peel and finely chop the eggs. Grate the cheese.

3 Sweat the onions and garlic in a little of the margarine then add the tomato purée. Add the TVP and season.

4 Add the excess stock and cook for 25 minutes.

5 Sieve the breadcrumbs and then fry in the remaining margarine until golden brown. Add 10g parsley, the chopped eggs and the cheese.

→

❑ Top: Vegetable Yorkshire Pudding
Bottom: Laver Bread, Samphire and Mushroom Lasagne ❑

- 55g Cheddar cheese (vegetarian)
- 50g Sunflower oil
- Salt and ground white pepper

→

6 Place the TVP mixture in a suitable dish, cover with the breadcrumb mixture and then bake in a preheated oven at 200°C/Gas Mark 6 for 15 minutes until golden brown.

7 Garnish with the remaining parsley and serve. ❑

Walnut and Fig Couscous 4 covers

- 600ml Vegetable stock
- 400g Couscous
- 60ml Olive oil
- 10g Garlic purée
- 120g Shallots
- 1 Fig
- 8 Dried stoned dates
- 105g Walnuts
- 50g Sultanas
- Fresh coriander, chopped
- Salt and ground white pepper

1 Peel and dice the shallots, chop the walnuts, and dice the fig and the dates. Wash the sultanas and soak in warm water.

2 Boil the stock, add the couscous and stand for 8–10 minutes or until the stock has been absorbed. Fluff the couscous with fork.

3 Heat the oil in a suitably large pan and cook the garlic purée and shallots until soft.

4 Add the couscous to the shallots. Stir in the fig, dates, walnuts, sultanas and coriander and season.

NOTES

Suitable for vegan, diabetic and low-cholesterol diets.

For added texture and protein add either tempeh, seitan or tofu. ❑

Watercress, Nettle and Vegetable Crumble (p.271) 4 covers

- 25g Margarine
- 25g Wholewheat flour
- 300ml Soya milk
- 20ml Creamed horseradish
- 150g Watercress
- 150g Nettles
- 100g Broccoli
- 100g Cauliflower
- 50g Spring onions

1 Peel and cut the shallots, celery and peppers into 2cm dice. Top and tail the leeks and spring onions, then wash and cut into dice. Wash and chop the watercress and nettles. Peel and purée the garlic.

2 Blanch all the vegetables in boiling salted water and then refresh in ice-cold water. Drain and keep to one side.

3 Melt the margarine in a suitable saucepan. Add the flour and make a roux. Add the milk and stir into a smooth sauce, then add the creamed horseradish.

→

- ■ 50g Shallots
- ■ 50g Celery
- ■ 1 clove Garlic
- ■ 75g Peppers (red or green)
- ■ 100g Leeks
- ■ Salt and black pepper

Topping

- ■ 20g Sesame seeds
- ■ 40g Barley flakes
- ■ 40g Millet flakes
- ■ 30g Cheddar cheese, grated (vegetarian)

4 Add the watercress and nettles to the sauce. Season then add the vegetables and transfer to ovenproof dish.

5 To make the topping put the sesame seeds in a pestle and mortar or blender and grind to a powder. Add to the other ingredients, mix together and spread over the top of the vegetable mixture.

6 Place in a preheated oven 190°C/Gas Mark 5, for approximately 30 minutes until golden brown.

NOTES

For vegan diets, ensure vegan margarine is used. Also replace the cheese with margarine and ensure that the horseradish is egg-free and contains no milk or cream.

When picking and working with the nettles use plastic gloves to avoid stings. ❑

Wheat and Vegetable Fricassee   4 covers

- ■ 175g Leeks
- ■ 2 cloves Garlic
- ■ 60g Onions
- ■ 100g Broccoli
- ■ 75g Cauliflower
- ■ 1 Green pepper
- ■ 2 sticks Celery
- ■ 150g Carrots
- ■ 60g Margarine
- ■ 60g Plain wholemeal flour
- ■ 600ml Soya milk
- ■ 100g Cheshire cheese, grated (vegetarian)
- ■ 10g Cayenne pepper
- ■ 100g Wholewheat grains
- ■ 6 sprigs Parsley
- ■ 20g Fresh thyme leaves
- ■ 50g Wholemeal breadcrumbs
- ■ Salt and black pepper

1 Peel the onion, garlic, carrots and celery and chop into 2cm dice.

2 Wash the broccoli and cauliflower, then trim into neat florets.

3 Wash and chop the parsley. Remove the outer leaves from the leeks, then split and wash any dirt and debris, top and tail then cut into 2cm dice. Skin and deseed the pepper then cut into 2cm dice.

4 Soak the wholewheat overnight, then drain and cook in boiling salted water for 30 minutes until soft.

5 Sauté the leeks, garlic and onion in 20g of margarine, then steam the remaining vegetables until tender. Melt the remaining 40g of margarine in a pan, stir in the flour and cook over a low heat for about 2 minutes.

6 Take pan off the heat and gradually add the milk, a little at a time, stirring thoroughly. When all the milk has been added, bring to a simmer (be careful as soya milk can split easily if over-heated), stirring all the time. Simmer for 3–5 minutes.

→

❏ Clockwise from top: Watercress, Nettle and Vegetable Crumble,
Seitan with Tagine, Date and Honey and Baked Tempeh in a BBQ Sauce. ❏

7 Add two-thirds of the grated cheese to the sauce. Season to taste with salt, pepper and cayenne. Add the wheat, herbs and cooked vegetables to the sauce. Put mixture in an ovenproof dish.

8 Mix the breadcrumbs and remaining cheese, and sprinkle this over the top of the dish. Place in a preheated oven at 190°C/Gas Mark 5 and cook until golden.

NOTES

This can be used as a vegan dish. The protein content can be increased by adding nuts instead of breadcrumbs, and sautéed diced seitan. ❏

Wheat Chilli	4 covers

- 50g   Mouli
- 75g   Onions
- 100g   Celery
- 1–2   Red peppers
- 50g   Carrots
- 20ml   Olive oil
- 2 cloves Garlic
- 5ml   Ground cumin
- 5ml   Ground coriander
- 5ml   Cayenne pepper
- 450g   Beef tomatoes
- 15ml   Tomato purée
- 50ml   Red wine (vegetarian)
- 300ml Vegetable stock
- 10g   Thyme leaves
- 2   Bay leaves
- 250g   Red kidney beans (tinned)
- 50g   Bulgar wheat
- 30ml   Miso
- 15ml   Shoyu

1 Peel the onions, celery, mouli and carrots and cut into 1cm dice. Blanch, refresh, skin and deseed the peppers and tomatoes, then cut into 1cm dice. Skin and purée the garlic.

2 Drain the beans in a colander and reserve until required. Wash and remove the thyme leaves, leave whole.

3 Sweat the onions and vegetables in the olive oil. Add the garlic purée and spices and cook out for 2 minutes.

4 Add the tomatoes, tomato purée, wine, stock, herbs, beans and the bulgar wheat. Simmer gently for 15–20 minutes until the liquid has reduced and the dish has thickened.

5 Add the miso and shoyu and check the seasoning. Cook for a few more minutes then serve.

NOTES

Suitable for vegan diets. Serve with long grain rice. ❏

White Bean Stew with Sundried Tomato 4 covers

- 200g   *Onions*
- 30ml   *Olive oil*
- 10g   *Garlic purée*
- 300g   *Button mushrooms*
- 60ml   *Dry white wine (vegetarian)*
- 397g   *Chopped tomatoes (tinned acceptable)*
- 5g   *Thyme leaves*
- 5g   *Fresh rosemary, chopped*
- 10g   *Fresh parsley, chopped*
- 500ml   *Vegetable stock*
- 400g   *Cannellini beans (soaked weight)*
- 60g   *Courgettes*
- 50g   *Celery*
-    *Salt and freshly ground black pepper*
- 40g   *Sun-dried tomatoes*

1. Soak the beans overnight, then drain and cook for 15 minutes in water. Drain and refresh.

2. Peel the onions and celery and cut into 1cm dice. Wash and dice the courgettes, clean the mushrooms and cut into quarters.

3. In a large pot sweat off the onions and celery with olive oil until limp, then add the garlic purée and cook for a further minute.

4. Add the mushrooms and cook out for 4–5 minutes until a light golden colour has been achieved. Deglaze the pan with the wine and reduce until almost all the wine has evaporated.

5. Stir in all tomatoes, thyme, rosemary and half of the parsley.

6. Add the stock and cook for 10 minutes.

7. Purée half of the beans then add to the stew with the remaining beans and courgettes and cook for 10 minutes. Check the seasoning.

8. Garnish with the remaining chopped parsley.

NOTES

Tinned beans can be used for this recipe. If cannelloni beans are not available use haricot beans or flageolet beans. Serve with new potatoes or rice.

Suitable for vegan, diabetic and low-cholesterol diets. A little sugar may need to be added if the tomatoes are tart. ❑

Wholewheat Pancakes Layered with Ratatouille 4 covers

Ratatouille

- 30ml   *Virgin olive oil*
- 100g   *Onion*
- 2 cloves *Garlic*
- 180g   *Aubergine*
- 180g   *Courgettes*
- 75g   *Red pepper*

1. Peel and dice the onion, garlic, red pepper and tomatoes. Cut the aubergine and courgettes into dice. Finely chop the herbs.

2. Sauté the onion and garlic in the oil then add the aubergine, courgettes and pepper and cook for 10 minutes.

→

→

- *3   Beef tomatoes*
- *25g   Tomato pasatte*
- *1 sprig Basil*
- *1 sprig Parsley*
- *10g   Caster sugar*
- *   Salt and ground
        black pepper*

Pancakes
- *120g Wholewheat flour*
- *310ml Semi-skimmed
        milk*
- *1   Free-range egg*
- *10ml Vegetable oil*
- *10g   Fresh parsley*
- *   Salt*
- *5g   Cayenne pepper*

Nettle Layer
- *400g Fresh nettle
        (washed)*
- *   Salt and ground
        black pepper*

Mushroom Sauce
- *70g   Margarine*
- *250g Button or Paris
        mushrooms*
- *50g   White flour*
- *470ml Milk*
- *100ml Dry white wine
        (vegetarian)*
- *1   Onion studded
        with cloves and a
        bay leaf*
- *2 sprigs Marjoram,
        chopped*
- *   Salt and ground
        black pepper*

3 Add the tomatoes, tomato passatte, sugar and aniseeds. Season.

4 Simmer for 20 minutes, add the herbs and check the seasoning.

1 Place all the ingredients in a liquidiser and blend. Leave to stand for 30 minutes.

2 With the mixture make 7–8 pancakes 15–18cm in diameter.

1 Wash the nettle in cold water three times, removing any debris and dirt. Cook in a thick-bottomed pan with the lid on for 8 minutes until wilted. Do not add water in the cooking process. Allow to drain and then roughly chop. Season with salt and pepper.

2 Make a béchamel sauce with the flour, 50g margarine, milk and onion. Add marjoram (see page 108).

3 Clean and slice the mushrooms, then sauté in the remaining margarine.

4 Add the wine to the mushrooms and then add to the béchamel sauce. Season to taste with salt and pepper.

5 Grease a 18–20cm ovenproof dish. Trim the pancakes to size if necessary and place a pancake in the bottom of the dish followed by half the mushrooms and sauce. Place another pancake on top and spread half the nettle over the pancake. Add a third pancake and half of the ratatouille mixture. Repeat this process, finishing with a pancake.

6 Preheat the oven to 180°C/Gas Mark 4. Cover the dish with tin foil and cook for 20–30 minutes. Garnish with chopped parsley and serve. ❏

- 120g   Wholegrain rice
- 60g   Wild rice
- 150g   Aramé
- 15ml   Vegetable oil
- 100g   Onions
- 5g   Garlic purée
- 100g   Celeriac
- 100g   Carrots
- 8   Spring onions
- 150g   Red peppers
- 140g   Button mushrooms
- 10g   Fresh parsley, chopped
- 5g   Thyme leaves
- 15ml   Shoyu

1 Wash the arame and reserve. Skin and deseed the peppers and beef tomatoes. Peel and dice the onions, celeriac, carrots and spring onions. Clean the mushrooms and cut in half.

2 Cook the rice separately in boiling salted water with a little oil for 10 minutes because the wild rice takes a little longer.

3 In a large frying pan, fry the onion, garlic purée, celeriac and carrots in hot oil on a medium heat for 8–10 minutes until the carrots are tender.

4 Add the spring onions, red peppers and mushrooms and fry for a further 5 minutes.

→

❑ Wild Rice and Aramé Paella ❑

→

■ *100ml White wine*
■ *120g Peas*
■ *4 Beef tomatoes*
■ *Salt and pepper*

5 Add the fried vegetables to the part cooked rice, together with the arame, herbs, shoyu, white wine, peas and tomatoes. Cook uncovered for a further 10 minutes.

6 Check and adjust the seasoning.

NOTES

Suitable for vegan, low-cholesterol and diabetic diets. For coeliac diets use tamari in place of shoyu. ❏

desserts

Arabic Cake

- 100g Unsalted margarine
- 320g Semolina
- 2.5g Ground cinnamon
- 110g Self-raising flour
- 110g Desiccated coconut
- 15g Baking powder
- 50g Brown sugar
- 225ml Warm water
- 15ml Rose water
- 100ml Natural yoghurt
- 70g Flaked almonds
- 170g Sugar syrup (with 5g ground cinnamon)
- 20g Icing sugar

1 Melt the margarine and mix into the semolina, cinnamon, flour, coconut, baking powder and sugar.

2 Slowly add the warm water, rose water and yoghurt to make a smooth runny paste. Pour the mixture into a greased silicone-lined tray. The mixture should be 1.5–2 cm deep.

3 Spread the almonds over the surface and stand the mixture for 15 minutes, to rest.

4 Gently warm up the sugar syrup. Do not boil just keep warm.

5 Place the cake mixture in a preheated oven at 200°C/Gas Mark 6 for 15–20 minutes. When golden brown remove and pour the hot sugar syrup over and allow to cool. Then divide evenly and garnish with icing sugar. ❑

Brandy Date Cake 4covers

- *125g Margarine*
- *250g Oatmeal biscuits*
- *20ml Brandy*
- *155g Dates*
- *500g Tofu (firm or silken)*
- *100ml Soya milk*
- *½ Lemon*
- *½ Lime*
- *100ml Apple juice concentrate*
- *5ml Vanilla essence*
- *4 sprigs Mint*
- *1 Fig*
- *15 Gooseberries*
- *10g Icing sugar*

1 Wash the fig and gooseberries and cut in half. Keep for garnish. Blend the biscuits in a processor. Remove the zest from the lemon and lime. Remove the juice and reserve.

2 Place the margarine in a suitable saucepan and melt, then add the biscuit crumbs and moisten with the brandy.

3 Grease a 15–18cm flan tin with a loose bottom. Line the bottom of the tin, for ease of removal, and press the base mixture evenly into the tin.

4 Put the dates in a little water and simmer until soft then place all the ingredients (except the strawberries, gooseberries, half of the mint leaves and the icing sugar) in the blender and purée until smooth. Add the juice to taste.

5 Place the purée on the base and bake in a preheated oven at 180°C/Gas Mark 4 for 50 minutes until golden brown.

6 Decorate with sliced fig, gooseberries and mint leaves. Dust with icing sugar. ❑

Banana and Caramel Rice Pudding (p.280) 4 covers

- *3 Bananas*
- *10ml Lemon juice*
- *40g Muscovado sugar*
- *80ml Water*
- *700ml Milk*
- *100g Short grain rice*
- *1 Vanilla pod*
  or
- *10–15ml Vanilla essence*
- *2 Free-range eggs, medium size*
- *20g Angelica*

1 Separate the eggs and split the vanilla pod and remove the seeds. Peel and slice half of the bananas and dice the rest.

2 Place the bananas in the lemon juice to prevent browning.

3 Simmer the sugar and half of the water until it has caramelised. Place the bottom of the pan into cold water.

4 Add the caramel to the rest of the water and the milk.

5 Add the rice and the vanilla seeds and bring to the boil, then reduce to a simmer for 20 minutes until the rice has absorbed the liquid.

6 Pour the rice slowly onto the egg yolks. Whisk the yolks vigorously until fully incorporated into the rice. Add the diced bananas.

→

❏ Top: Brandy Date Cake   Bottom: Tofu Fruit Mousse ❏

□ Banana and Caramel Rice Pudding □

→ 7 Whisk the egg whites until very stiff then fold into the mixture to give it a little lightness.

8 Pour the mixture into a presentation glass or coups and place the sliced bananas on top. Decorate with strips of angelica. □

Bramley Apple, Peach and Apricot Strudel   4 covers

- *400g Bramley apples*
- *50g   Apricots*
- *50g   Dates*
- *50g   Peaches*
- *50g   Plums*
- *30ml Water*
- *1   Orange (juice and zest)*
- *30g   Flaked almonds*

1 Peel, core and chop the apples, peaches, plums and apricots. Chop the dates. Remove the rind from the orange and cut into julienne (very fine strips). Reserve the juice.

2 Toast the almonds under the grill until golden brown.

3 Place the apples, peaches, plums, apricots, dates, orange zest and juice, water, 20g flaked almonds and the Cointreau in a pan and simmer for 5 minutes. The apples should still be in chunks.

→

→

- 15ml   Cointreau
- 6 sheets Filo pastry, frozen
- 50g   Margarine
-         Icing sugar
- 75g   Almonds

4 Brush each sheet of filo pastry with melted margarine and lay them on top of each other (6 sheets overlapping) on a greased tray. Trim as necessary.

5 Place the filling down the centre of the sheets, going right to the top and bottom of the sheets and leaving a gap of 2cm at each side.

6 Fold the pastry sides over to meet and seal with a little water. Then roll the strudel over so the seam is underneath. Add any spare strips of pastry to garnish the top.

7 Brush with melted margarine and sprinkle with the remaining flaked almonds.

8 Bake in a preheated oven at 200°C/Gas Mark 6 for 20–25 minutes.

9 Finish by dusting with icing sugar. ❏

Chocolate and Coconut Fudge Cake   4-6 covers

- 400g   Self-raising flour
- 20g   Desiccated coconut
- 5g   Baking powder
- 250g   Brown sugar
- 600ml Water
- 125g   Creamed coconut
- 175ml Peanut oil
- 60g   Cocoa powder
- 100ml Coconut cream

Fudge Icing
- 50g   Margarine
- 15ml   Semi-skimmed milk (for vegan use soya milk)
- ½   Vanilla pod
- 200g   Icing sugar

1 Sieve the flour, dessicated coconut and baking powder in a bowl with the sugar.

2 Boil 700ml water and pour over the creamed coconut. When the water has cooled slightly pour in the oil and cream.

3 Pour this liquid on the flour mixture and mix thoroughly. Line two 20cm cake tins with greaseproof paper.

4 Add the mixture equally to the two cake tins and bake in a preheated oven at 180°C/Gas Mark 4 for 60–70 minutes until the cake is springy. Allow to cool before turning out onto a cooling wire.

5 To make the fudge icing split the vanilla pod and scrape out the seeds. Then melt the margarine and add the milk over a gentle heat. Add the vanilla seeds and let them infuse.

6 Sieve the icing sugar and stir into the mixture.

7 Fill and cover the cakes with the fudge and dust with cocoa powder or desiccated coconut.

NOTES
This is a rich cake. Other flavours can be used, for example, coffee essence, ground walnuts and brandy instead of desiccated coconut and cocoa powder. Good dessert for vegans. ❏

Coconut Tart   4 covers

- 210g   Flour
- 130g   Margarine
- 2   Eggs, medium size
- 55g   Sugar
- 150ml Milk
- ½   Lemon (juice only)
- 2.5ml Almond essence
- 70g   Desiccated coconut
-         Salt

1 Sieve the flour into a bowl and add the salt and 110g margarine. Rub together and add sufficient water to make a dough, then rest in the fridge for 20 minutes.

2 Line a greased 20cm tin. Roll out the dough onto a lightly floured surface then press into the tin. Firm the corners and trim the edges.

3 Separate the eggs. Whisk the sugar and egg yolks together then add the milk, lemon juice and essence. Melt the remaining margarine and add this to the milk mixture.

4 Whisk the egg whites until they peak. Then fold into the mixture together with 55g coconut.

5 Pour this mixture on the pastry flan and sprinkle the remaining coconut on top. Place in a preheated oven at 180°C/Gas Mark 4–5 for 30 minutes until set.

6 Remove from the oven, allow to cool slightly then serve. ❏

Cranberry and Orange Cake   4–6 covers

- 160g   Sugar
- 170g   Margarine
- 3   Free-range eggs, medium size
- 180g   Self-raising flour
- 1   Orange (juice and zest)
- 28g   Icing sugar
- 113g   Cranberries

1 Grease and lightly flour a 15–18cm tin.

2 Crush the cranberries, remove the zest from the orange and squeeze the juice. Blanch and refresh the zest and chop into small dice.

3 Mix the sugar and margarine together until white.

4 Whisk the eggs well in a separate bowl, then incorporate into the sugar mixture fully.

5 Sieve the flour and fold into the mixture slowly and carefully with the zest and cranberries. Slowly add the orange juice.

6 Pour into the tin and bake in a preheated oven at 180°C/Gas Mark 4–5 for 25 minutes. The cake should feel firm and springy to the touch.

7 Remove and allow to cool before turning out on to a cooling wire.

8 Dust with icing sugar and serve. ❏

❏ Cranberry and Orange Cake ❏

EBLY® and Orange Custard with Caramelised Sugar

4 covers

- ■ *90g*   *EBLY®*
- ■ *1*   *Orange (zest and juice)*
- ■ *300ml* *Milk*
- ■ *2*   *Free-range egg yolks*
- ■ *75g*   *Sugar*
- ■ *20g*   *Corn starch*
- ■ *60ml* *Whipping cream*
- ■   *Light demerara for glazing*

1 Cook the EBLY® in 360ml boiling water and the orange zest for 15–20 minutes depending on the consistency required. Drain and leave to one side, discarding the zest.

2 Warm the milk gently. Beat the egg yolks, sugar and corn starch together then slowly beat in the simmering milk.

3 Return to the heat and bring back to the boil, whisking continually.

4 When thickened and cooked out remove from the heat. Add the orange juice and the cream.

5 Add the drained EBLY®, mix well and pour into either a large ovenproof serving dish or individual ramekin dishes. Chill at this stage until cold.

6 Sprinkle the top with demerara or caster sugar and glaze either by using a blow torch or an extremely hot grill. Serve. ❏

Fruit and Muesli
4 covers

- 560ml Milk
- 78g Rolled oats
- 100g Strawberries
- 30g Hazelnuts
- 2 Russet apples
- 25g Raisins
- 50g Dried apricots
- 25g Coconut shavings
- 25g Peaches

1 Wash all the fruit and remove any stalks or stones.

2 Dice the strawberries, apples and peaches. Slice the apricots. Chop the hazelnuts.

3 Place the milk in a suitable bowl.

4 Stir in all the other ingredients, keeping a little coconut for garnish.

5 Place into a serving bowl and garnish the top with the coconut shavings.

NOTES

This recipe can be used for vegan and low-cholesterol diets if semi-skimmed or soya milk is used. ❏

Mango and Papaya Slice
4 covers

- 350g Puff pastry (vegan)
- 10g Fresh mint, chopped
- 200g Almond paste
- 1 Yellow ripe mango
- 1 medium Papaya
- 20g Margarine
- 20g Macadamia nuts
- 25g Brown sugar (optional)

1 Grind the nuts in a coffee grinder or blender. Peel the mango and the papaya, remove the seeds then slice.

2 Roll out the pastry to 32 × 48cm then cut into four 8 × 12cm slices and place on a greased baking tray.

3 Brush the pastry with a little water and sprinkle half the chopped mint over.

4 Divide the almond paste into four then roll out slightly smaller than the pastry slices. Place one on each of the pastry slices.

5 Lay the slices of mango and papaya alternately on top of the almond paste then lightly brush with melted margarine. Sprinkle with the nuts and sugar.

6 Bake in a preheated oven at 200°C/Gas Mark 6 for 20 minutes until golden brown. Sprinkle on the remaining mint as a garnish.

NOTES

Suitable for vegan and low-cholesterol diets. If the sugar is omitted it is also suitable for diabetic diets. ❏

→

❑ Mango and Papaya Slice ❑

Orange and Pecan Muffins
20 muffins

- 60g Margarine
- 200g Caster sugar
- 2 medium Free-range eggs
- 1 large Orange
- 220g Soured cream
- 2g Nutmeg
- pinch Cinnamon
- 120g Pecan nuts, chopped
- 10g Baking powder
- 220g Wholewheat flour
- 220g Plain flour
- 2.5g Salt

1 Remove the zest and segment the orange. Place the segments on a tray under the grill and lightly dry out, then chop. Cut the zest into small dice.

2 Cream the margarine and the sugar together until it is a whitish colour then add the eggs, orange zest and segments and soured cream.

3 Gently fold in the spices, nuts, baking powder and flour.

4 Pour gently into the muffin cases or mould and bake in a preheated oven at 190°C/Gas Mark 5–6 for 20 minutes until the top is springy to the touch. ❑

Orange Chocolate Mousse 4 covers

- 300g Silken tofu
- 1 Orange (juice and zest)
- 15–20ml Maple syrup or honey
- 15ml Grand Marnier
- 135g Dark chocolate (vegetarian)
- 4 sprigs Fresh mint

1 Grate a little chocolate and keep for garnish. Melt the rest of the chocolate in a bowl over a pan of hot water.

2 Remove the skin from the orange, cut into very fine strips and blanch in boiling water. Refresh. Cut the orange in half and squeeze the juice.

3 Put the tofu, orange juice and half of the zest, maple syrup and liqueurs in a processor and blend until smooth, while slowly adding the melted chocolate.

4 Place the mousse into four glasses or dishes and then refrigerate for 1–2 hours.

5 Garnish with grated chocolate and orange zest with a sprig of mint.

NOTES

This is an excellent vegetarian sweet, containing no animal fats. Liqueurs and flavourings can be replaced to give many different mousses, such as: curaco, brandy, rum, etc. White or milk chocolate can be used but the amount should be increased to 150g. Alter the amount of syrup used to suit. ❑

Orange Chocolate Roll 4–6 covers

Sponge
- 4 Eggs
- 3 Egg whites
- 180g Caster sugar
- 60g Cocoa powder
- 60g Milk chocolate (vegetarian)
- 30g Icing sugar
- 20g Groundnuts

Filling
- 40g Maple syrup
- 25g Margarine
- 80ml Double cream

1 Line a 33 × 23cm tray with silicone paper.

2 Melt the chocolate. Take two of the eggs and separate them and adding the whites to the three other egg whites. Keep the yolks separate.

3 Whisk 2 whole eggs and 2 yolks with the caster sugar over a pan of simmering water. This will slowly cook the eggs and become thick and creamy.

4 Remove the bowl from the pan and allow to cool a little, then gently fold the cocoa powder and groundnuts into the mixture.

5 Whisk the remaining egg whites in a clean bowl until stiff and white, then gently fold the melted chocolate into this mixture.

→

→

- 60ml Grand Marnier
- 2 Oranges (zest and juice)
- 220g Milk chocolate (vegetarian)
- 320ml Double cream, whipped

6 Pour the mixture evenly on the lined tray and place in a preheated oven at 190°C/Gas Mark 5 for 20 minutes until cooked.

7 To make the filling place all of the ingredients (except the chocolate and the whipped cream) in a saucepan, boil and stir constantly for 3 minutes. Take off the heat and grate the chocolate into the mixture, saving a little for decoration, then pass through a sieve and allow to go cold.

8 When the sponge is cooked, remove from the oven and turn out onto silicone paper dusted in icing sugar. Peel off the lining paper, then trim the edges of the sponge.

9 Spread the chocolate filling over the surface of the roulade to 1cm from the edge. Spread the whipped double cream over the filling. Roll the roulade, dust with icing sugar and decorate with grated chocolate.

NOTES

Cover and place in the fridge until required. This can be made with white or dark chocolate and the liqueur can be replaced with rum or brandy, for example. ❑

Orange Liqueur   4 covers

- 2 Free-range eggs, medium size
- 25g Caster sugar
- 250ml Milk
- 15g Gelatine (vegetarian)
- 30ml Cointreau
- 2 Oranges (zest and segments)
- 40ml Water

1 Remove the zest from the oranges then blanch and refresh it. Segment the orange and reserve until required. Soak the gelatine in the water.

2 Separate the eggs. Beat the sugar and egg yolks, then add the milk until a creamy consistence is achieved. Add the gelatine and Cointreau.

3 Whisk the egg whites to a soft peak and then fold into the mixture.

4 Divide the orange segments into four glasses or coups (keep some for decoration) then add the mousse mixture and leave to set for 2 hours in a fridge.

5 Decorate the tops with the remaining orange segments and zest.

→

→ | NOTES

For variations use tangerines or pink grapefruits. The protein content can be increased by adding macadamia nuts to garnish the tops. ❑

Peach and Apple Pudding   4 covers

- 10g   Low-fat margarine
- 4 slices Wholemeal bread
- 170ml Soya milk
- 10g   Walnuts, chopped
- 45g   Brown sugar
- ¼tsp Mixed spice
- 85g   Tofu (silken)
- 2   Apples
- 2   Peaches
- 30g   Ground nuts
- 10g   Icing sugar
- 200g Natural yoghurt
- 2ml   Vanilla essence

1 Cut the crusts off the sliced bread and cut the slices into 2 triangles. Break the crusts into breadcrumbs and keep separate.

2 Select a suitable baking dish and grease the inside with the margarine. Place 2 slices of bread (4 triangles) in the dish, overlapping.

3 Mix the milk, walnuts, sugar, spices and tofu together in a separate bowl.

4 Peel and chop the apples and peaches, then add these to the sugar and milk mixture.

5 Spoon half of the mixture into the dish and neatly overlap with the remaining bread. Finish by adding the remaining apple and peach mixture.

6 Bake in a preheated oven at 180°C/Gas Mark 4 for 15 minutes then remove and dust with 15g ground nuts. Cook until golden brown (approximately 5 minutes). Remove from the oven and allow to cool for 5 minutes then remove from the dish and dust in icing sugar.

7 Mix the yoghurt, breadcrumbs, vanilla essence and remaining ground nuts and serve with the pudding.

NOTES

Suitable for vegan and low-cholesterol diets. If the walnuts are replaced with other nuts remember that some nuts contain high amounts of fat. ❑

□ Strawberry, Hazelnut and Cassia Torte □

Strawberry, Hazelnut and Cassia Torte   4 covers

- *160g   Margarine, melted*
- *160g   Caster sugar*
- *1   Free-range egg,*
          medium size
- *160g   Ground hazelnuts*
- *160g   Self-raising flour*
- *5g   Ground cassia bark*
- *2.5g   Ground star anise*
- *230g   Strawberries*

Garnish

- *235ml Whipped cream or*
          fromage frais
- *tsp   Vanilla essence*
- *8   Strawberries*

1 Sieve the flour and spices. Remove the stalks from the strawberries and cut into 1cm dice.

2 In a bowl mix the margarine, sugar, egg, nuts, flour and spices.

3 Line and grease four single moulds or a 21.5cm spring release cake tin.

4 Carefully pour half of the mixture over the base of the tin and spread evenly.

5 Spread the strawberries over the mixture, then pour the remaining mixture over.

6 Bake in a preheated oven at 180°C/Gas Mark 4–5 for 40–45 minutes.

→

→

■ *113g Hazelnuts, ground*
or chopped

7 Allow the torte to cool in the tin for 45 minutes. Then remove and cover with whipped vanilla-flavoured double cream, fromage frais or icing sugar.

8 Garnish with ground or chopped nuts and strawberry quarters.

NOTES

Not suitable for vegan diets. ❏

Rose Apple and Apple Strudel   4 covers

■ *250g Raisins*
■ *30ml Cider*
■ *4   Pink rose apples*
■ *4 medium Cooking apples*
■ *40ml Lemon juice*
■ *160g Brown sugar*
■ *50g   Ground almonds*
■ *60g   Chopped hazelnuts*
■ *Pinch Cinnamon*
■ *100ml Soured cream*
■ *8 sheets Filo pastry*
■ *30g   Margarine*

1 Wash and then soak the raisins in the cider. Peel, de-core and dice the apples and then soak in the lemon juice and a little water to cover.

2 Mix the soaked raisins, sugar, nuts (save a little for garnishing), cinnamon and soured cream.

3 Drain the apples then combine with the raisin mixture in a suitable bowl.

4 Remove two sheets of filo pastry, keeping the other sheets covered with a damp towel to prevent drying.

5 Lay one sheet on top of the other and place a quarter of the cool mixture on top, approximately 5cm from the edge. Brush the edges with cold water and roll firmly to half way then fold in the edges, brush again with a little water and continue to roll tightly.

6 Repeat this process with the remaining ingredients. Brush the tops with a little melted margarine and garnish with the remaining nuts.

7 Bake in a preheated oven at 190°C/Gas Mark 5 for 15–20 minutes until golden brown and crisp. ❏

❏ Rose Apple and Apple Strudel ❏

recipes for coeliac diets

Avocado, Cheese and Spinach Salad · 4 covers

- *15ml* *Lemon juice*
- *120g* *Cottage cheese*
- *2* *Avocadoes*
- *5ml* *Tamari*
- *Pinch* *Cayenne pepper*
- *20ml* *Virgin olive oil*
- *150g* *Vine cherry tomatoes*
- *120g* *Fresh baby spinach (or red mustard cress)*
- *10g* *Chives*
- *10g* *Fresh thyme leaves*
- *50g* *Flaked almonds*
- *Salt and white pepper*

1 Wash the spinach and toast the almonds under the grill, Peel the avocados then cut into quarters and slice.

2 Wash the tomatoes, remove from the stalk and cut in half. Chop the chives.

3 Stir half of the lemon juice with salt and a little white pepper into the cottage cheese and spoon a quarter of the mixture into a ring in the centre of a serving plate. Arrange a quarter of the avocado on top. Repeat with the remaining ingredients.

4 Whisk the remaining lemon juice, tamari, cayenne pepper, salt and a little pepper and olive oil together then mix in the tomatoes, spinach, chives and thyme. Carefully mix evenly.

5 Place a handful of the spinach mixture on top of each portion of avocado and cheese and arrange some tomatoes around the edge.

6 Garnish with toasted flaked almonds. ❑

□ Avocado, Cheese and Spinach Salad □

Cepe Mushroom Soup   4 covers

- 100g   Onions
- 50ml   Olive oil
- 20g   Fresh rosemary, chopped
- ½   Red pepper
- 220g   Cepe mushrooms
- 380g   Paris brown mushrooms
- 20g   Garlic purée
- 500g   Beef tomatoes
- 40g   Tomato purée
- 20ml   Dry sherry
- 450ml Vegetable stock
-        Salt and pepper

1 Peel the onions and cut into 2cm dice. Clean and quarter the mushrooms.

2 Skin, deseed and cut the tomatoes and pepper into 2cm dice.

3 Sweat the onions, rosemary and pepper off in oil, until lightly coloured.

4 Add the mushrooms and fry off until golden brown. Add the garlic purée, tomatoes and tomato purée.

5 Deglaze the pan with the sherry and then add the stock. Bring to the boil and simmer for 10 minutes. Skim the surface, removing any debris.

6 Correct the seasoning and serve. □

Chapattis

- *230g Chickpea flour*
- *20g Arrowroot*
- *85ml Water*
- *pinch Ground cumin*
- *10ml Virgin olive oil*
- * Salt*

1 Place all the ingredients except the oil in a suitable bowl and mix well, until they form a dough.

2 Divide into 2½cm balls and roll them on a lightly floured surface into a round shape.

3 Place the oil in a hot frying pan then put the chapattis in the pan and cook for 1–2 minutes each side. Serve either hot or cold after cooking.

NOTES

Use as a substitute for bread.

Good with rice and spicy Asian foods. Also suitable for vegan diets. ❑

Chilli Potatoes

- *30ml Sunflower oil*
- *10g Black mustard seeds*
- *10g White split peas*
- *15g Yellow split peas*
- *200g Onions*
- *2 Red chillies*
- *2 cloves Garlic*
- *500g Potatoes*
- *500ml Vegetable stock*
- *10g Fresh coriander, chopped*
- *5g Turmeric powder*
- *10g Lemon zest*
- * Salt*

1 Peel the potatoes and onions and cut into 2cm dice. Top, tail, deseed and finely dice the chillies. Peel then purée the garlic.

2 Place the oil in a suitable pot with a tight-fitting lid and add the mustard seeds. Cook with the lid on until all the seeds have popped without burning, then add the peas and cook until lightly golden brown.

3 Add the onions, chillies, turmeric, lemon zest, garlic and then the potatoes. Cook for 2-3 minutes then add the stock. Bring to the boil with the lid on and simmer for 20 minutes, stirring every 5 minutes to prevent sticking.

4 When cooked serve in a suitable dish garnished with chopped coriander. ❑

Deep-fried Soya Sticks 4 covers

- 500g   Tofu or tempeh
- 113g   Cornmeal
- 5g   Garlic salt
- 2.5g   Ground white pepper
- 5g   Salt
- 2.5g   Five spice powder

1 Drain the tofu or tempeh and cut into 6 × 2cm finger-shape sticks. Pat dry.

2 Place all the other ingredients in a bowl or plastic bag and mix together thoroughly and coat well.

3 Deep-fry the fingers in vegetable oil at 185°C for 5–7 minutes, until golden brown. Drain on kitchen paper and then serve with tomato and scallion salsa and rice.

NOTES

Also suitable for vegan diets. Alternatively, serve with a crisp salad. ❏

Dhal Curry 4 covers

- 100g   Onions
- 10ml   Vegetable oil
- 2–3g   Ground ginger
- 10g   Curry powder
- 5g   Turmeric
- 250ml   Light vegetable stock
- 5g   Ground Cumin
- 10g   Fresh coriander, chopped
- 1   Bay leaf
- 275g   Tomatoes
- 200g   Lentils
- 2 cloves Garlic
-         Salt

1 Wash and soak the lentils overnight. Remove any debris and drain. Peel and purée the garlic.

2 Peel and dice the onions. Skin, deseed and cut the tomatoes into concasse (small dice).

3 Sweat off the onions in a little oil until golden brown, then add the spices, ginger and garlic and cook for a further 2–3 minutes. Then add the lentils.

4 Add the stock and stir into the mixture. Add half of the coriander and the bay leaf. Bring to the boil and simmer for 45 minutes.

5 Add the tomato concasse and cook for another 10–15 minutes. Correct the seasoning.

6 Serve with the remaining coriander.

NOTES

Serve with cooked rice, mango chutney, naan bread, pop-padums and minted yoghurt.

Also suitable for vegan, low-cholesterol, coeliac and diabetic diets. ❏

Easter Cauliflower

- 30ml Vegetable oil
- 200g Shallots
- 2 Green chillies
- 5g Garlic purée
- 3cm Ginger
- 2.5g Turmeric
- 200g Plum tomatoes
- 5g Fresh mint
- 10g Fresh coriander
- 200ml Strong vegetable stock
- 1 medium Cauliflower
- Salt and pepper

1 Wash the cauliflower and cut into florets. Peel and very finely slice the shallots, chillies, ginger, mint and coriander.

2 Skin, deseed and cut the tomatoes into 2cm dice. Reserve the tomato liquid.

3 Heat the oil in a suitable pan and sauté off the shallots, chillies, garlic purée and ginger until tender.

4 Add the turmeric and cook out for 1 minute. Then add the tomatoes, mint and half of the coriander. Cook for 3–4 minutes.

5 Stir in the stock, then add the cauliflower florets and cook for approximately 10 minutes until al dente (just cooked with a bite).

6 Season to taste with salt and pepper and garnish with the remaining coriander.

NOTES

Serve with rice and minted yoghurt. Also suitable for vegan, coeliac and low-cholesterol diets. ❏

Falafel

- 850g Chickpeas (tinned acceptable)
- 80g Spring onions
- 25g Banana shallots
- 1 Egg, medium size
- 20g Garlic
- 10g Ground cumin
- 5g Turmeric
- 20g Fresh parsley, chopped
- 20ml Lemon juice
- 2.5g Cayenne pepper
- 113g Rice flour
- Salt and ground black pepper

1 Drain the chickpeas in a colander.

2 Peel and top and tail the spring onions, then roughly chop.

3 Peel and roughly chop the garlic and the shallots.

4 Put all the ingredients except for the rice flour in a food processor and blend into a fine purée. Season.

5 Slowly add the flour until it forms into a firm dough.

6 Divide into small balls. On a lightly floured surface roll and shape the balls.

7 Deep-fry in vegetable oil until golden brown. Drain on kitchen paper and serve with low-fat natural yoghurt and a fresh crisp salad.

NOTES

Also suitable for vegan diets. ❏

❑ Forest Salad ❑

Forest Salad   4 covers

- 100ml Olive oil
- 220g   Shitake, oyster and chanterelle mushrooms
- 10g   Thyme leaves
- 10g   Fresh parsley, chopped
- 10g   Fresh chives and tarragon, chopped
- ½ head Oak leaf lettuce
- ½ head Radicchio lettuce
- 20 leaves Rocket
- 113g   Cherry vine tomatoes

1 Toast the pine nuts until golden brown. Wash the tomatoes and cut in half. Wash the lettuce and cut into suitable pieces. Peel and slice the shallots.

2 Clean the mushrooms and cut into quarters.

3 Make a vinaigrette by whisking the extra virgin oil, balsamic vinegar and salt and pepper together until it emulsifies.

4 Place the olive oil in a suitable pan and sauté off the mushrooms then add the vinaigrette to the pan and stir in half of the herbs.

5 Arrange the lettuce, rocket, tomatoes, shallots and nuts (keep a few for garnish) on suitable serving dishes or plates then spoon the mushrooms over.

→

→
- 60g Banana shallots
- 20g Pine nuts

Vinaigrette
- 60ml Balsamic vinegar
- 90ml Extra virgin olive oil
- ■   Salt and ground black pepper

6 Garnish with the remaining herbs and nuts.

NOTES

Also suitable for vegan and low-cholesterol diets. ❑

Masur Dhal Soup (p.151)   4 covers

200g Split red lentils
- 560ml Light vegetable stock
- 80ml Milk
- 10g   Fresh coriander, chopped
- 80g   Onions
- ■   Salt and ground black pepper

1 Peel and chop the onions.

2 Wash the lentils and soak overnight. Remove any debris and drain.

3 Put the lentils and onions in the stock with the milk and half of the coriander and season. Bring to the boil and simmer for 30–40 minutes.

4 When cooked place in a liquidiser and purée. Check the seasoning and serve with the remaining chopped coriander. ❑

Mixed Bean and Raisin Salad   4 covers

- 120g Cannellini beans (cooked or tinned)
- 80g   Borlotto beans (cooked or tinned)
- 150g Russet apples
- 100g Celery
- 40g   Raisins
- 5g   Lemon juice
- 5g   Fresh parsley, chopped
- 5g   Oregano leaves

1 Drain the beans and keep to one side. Peel and dice the celery.

2 De-core and dice the apples and soak in a little water and lemon juice.

3 Wash the raisins in warm water.

4 Mix all the beans, apples, celery and raisins together.

5 To make the dressing whisk the olive oil, mustard, vinegar and seasonings until all combined.

6 Add the dressing to the bean and raisin mixture and serve with crisp lettuce and herbs.

→

Dressing
- 60ml   *Olive oil*
- 5g   *Dijon mustard*
- 15g   *White wine vinegar*
- ■   *Salt and pepper*

→ | NOTES

If using dried beans, soak overnight in water.

Also suitable for vegan and low-cholesterol diets. ❏

Oyster Mushroom Country Stew   4 covers

- 100g   *Banana shallots*
- 5g   *Garlic purée*
- 40ml   *Sunflower oil*
- 2   *Peppers*
- 120g   *Dried chestnuts*
- 40ml   *White wine*
- 350ml *Vegetable stock*

1 Soak the dried chestnuts for at least 6 hours. Then place in the white wine and allow to soak for 30 minutes longer.

2 Peel the shallots and cut into 2cm dice. Skin, deseed and cut the peppers and tomatoes into 2cm dice. Top and tail the courgettes then cut into 2cm dice.

→

❏ Oyster Mushroom Country Stew ❏

→

- 5g Fresh basil, shredded
- 300g Courgettes
- 10g Pesto (gluten free/vegetarian)
- 350g Oyster mushrooms
- 630g Beef tomatoes
- ■ Salt and ground black pepper

3 Clean the mushrooms and cut into suitable pieces.

4 Sweat off the shallots and garlic purée in the oil for 2–3 minutes until limp. Add the peppers, then the chestnuts in white wine. Stir well and cook for 4–5 minutes, then add half of the stock and cook for a further 20 minutes.

5 Add half of the basil. Then add the remaining stock, the courgettes, pesto, mushrooms and tomatoes. Cook for 20 minutes. Check the seasoning and serve in a suitable dish, garnished with the remaining basil.

NOTES

Serve with boiled new potatoes or rice.

Also suitable for vegan and low-cholesterol diets. ❑

Shitake Mushroom Soup   4 covers

- 227g Shitake mushrooms
- 20ml Vegetable oil
- 600ml Vegetable stock
- 20g Garlic purée
- 113g Bamboo shoots
- 20ml Shoyu
- 150g Tofu
- 4 Spring onions
- ■ Salt and pepper

1 Clean and wash the mushrooms then slice thinly. Drain the tofu and cut into 1–2cm dice.

2 Peel and finely dice the spring onions. Wash and finely slice the bamboo shoots.

3 Sauté the mushrooms off in a little vegetable oil.

4 Add the stock and garlic purée and bring to the boil. Simmer for 10–15 minutes.

5 Add the remaining ingredients and simmer for a further 6–7 minutes.

6 Skim the surface for any debris and season. ❑

Spiced Moong Dal   4 covers

- 500ml Vegetable stock
- 140g Split yellow mung beans
- 2.5g Turmeric
- 50g Carrots
- 2.5g Garlic purée

1 Wash and soak the yellow split peas overnight. Remove any debris then drain.

2 Peel and finely dice the ginger, carrots and chilli.

3 Bring the stock, beans, turmeric and carrots to the boil and simmer for 10–12 minutes.

→

- ■ *2cm*   *Ginger*
- ■ *1 small Chilli*
- ■ *10g*   *Margarine*
- ■   *Salt and ground black pepper*

→

4 In a suitable pan sweat off the garlic purée, ginger and chilli in the margarine without colour

5 Add the cooked garlic, ginger and chilli to the lentils and cook for a further 15 minutes.

6 Garnish with fresh herbs. ❑

Spiced Peas   4 covers

- ■ *30ml*   *Sunflower oil*
- ■ *10g*   *Black mustard seeds*
- ■ *10g*   *Yellow split peas*
- ■ *10g*   *White split peas*
- ■ *2*   *Red chillies*
- ■ *1 clove Garlic*
- ■ *5g*   *Turmeric*
- ■ *5g*   *Fenugreek*
- ■ *300g*   *Basmati rice*
- ■ *450ml Vegetable stock*
- ■ *20ml*   *Lemon juice*
- ■ *10g*   *Fresh coriander, chopped*
- ■   *Salt and ground black pepper*

1 Peel and purée the garlic and top, tail and dice the chillies, removing the seeds.

2 Place the oil in a suitable pot with a tight-fitting lid and add the mustard seeds. Cook with the lid on until all the seeds have popped without burning, then add the peas and cook until lightly golden brown.

3 Add the chillies, garlic purée, turmeric and fenugreek and sauté for 1–2 minutes then add the rice and stir thoroughly to prevent burning.

4 Add the stock and lemon juice and cover with a lid. Cook for around 10–15 minutes then remove the lid, check the seasoning, stir and cook out until the rice is just cooked.

5 Serve in a suitable dish with the chopped coriander. ❑

Tempeh Nuggets (p.302)   4 covers

- ■ *500g*   *Tempeh*
- ■ *10g*   *Fresh coriander, finely chopped*
- ■ *20g*   *Sesame seeds*
- ■ *2.5g*   *Paprika*
- ■ *227g*   *Rice flour*
- ■ *Pinch Cayenne pepper*
- ■ *500ml Soda water*
- ■   *Salt and ground black pepper*

1 Drain the tempeh and cut into 3cm dice and then pat dry.

2 Put the coriander, sesame seeds, paprika, flour and cayenne into a suitable bowl and mix together.

3 Whisk in the soda water until a double-cream consistency has been achieved.

4 Dip the tempeh cubes into the batter and deep-fry for 8 minutes at 180°C until golden brown. Drain onto kitchen paper.

→

❑ Tempeh Nuggets ❑

→ | 5 Serve with a spicy tomato and scallion salsa and rice.

NOTES

Can also be served with a garlic, chilli and tamari dip and boiled rice. ❑

Teriyaki Tofu   4 covers

■ *500g* *Fresh tofu*
■ *20ml* *Sesame oil*
■ *70g* *Carrots*
■ *100g* *Cucumber*
■ *4* *Spring onions*

1 Drain the tofu and cut into 2–3cm cubes.

2 Peel the carrots, cucumber and spring onions. Wash, pick and drain the lettuce.

→

→

- 4 sprigs Lamb's lettuce
- ■   Chinese lettuce
- ■   Choi san
- ■   Red mustard lettuce

Teriyaki sauce
- 170ml Pineapple juice
- 142ml Tamari
- 50g   Demerara sugar
- 40cm Ginger root, grated
- 5g   Garlic purée

3 Cut the carrots into a very fine julienne (fine strips), de-core the cucumber and slice. Feather three-quarters of the top end of the spring onions.

4 Bring the pineapple juice, tamari and sugar to the boil then squeeze the grated ginger into the mixture.

5 Add the garlic purée and cook for a further 1–2 minutes. Allow the sauce to cool.

6 Add the tofu to the sauce and marinate for 30 minutes.

7 Remove the tofu from the marinade and pat dry. Strain the sauce and warm through in a suitable pan on the stove. Heat the oil in a pan and fry off the tofu colouring on all sides.

8 Serve with the teriyaki sauce, shredded carrot, sliced cucumber, spring onion and lettuce.

NOTES

Serve with a minted yoghurt dip. This recipe is also suitable for vegan diets. ❏

Tofu Fruit Mousse (p.293)   4 covers

- 400g Tofu (silken)
- 120g Bananas
- 400g Kiwi fruit
- 70g   Clear honey
- 10g   Maple syrup
- ½   Vanilla pod (seeds only)

1 Peel the bananas and the kiwi fruit. Use only the freshest fruit.

2 Place all the ingredients in a liquidiser and blend together with drained tofu.

3 Add a little water if desired to let down the thickness of the mixture.

NOTES

Add a liqueur for more flavour. Check the ingredients on the label carefully. ❏

Tomato-scented Lentil Soup

4 covers

- *100g* Onions
- *50g* Carrots
- *10ml* Vegetable oil
- *200g* Lentils
- *1l* Vegetable stock
- *120g* Tomatoes
- *5g* Tomato purée
- *1* Bay leaf
- *10g* Fresh thyme and parsley, chopped
- *8g* Garlic purée
- Salt and black pepper

1 Peel and chop the onions and carrots.

2 Skin, deseed and chop the tomatoes. Reserve the liquid.

3 Sweat the onions and carrots off in a little oil with garlic purée for 2–3 minutes then add the lentils.

4 Add the stock, tomatoes, tomato purée, tomato liquid, the bay leaf and half the herbs.

5 Bring to the boil and simmer for 60 minutes.

6 Remove the bay leaf, then liquidise. Reheat, season and garnish with the remaining chopped herbs.

NOTES

Also suitable for vegan and low-cholesterol diets. ❏

recipes for diabetic diets

- *100g*   *Carrots*
- *100g*   *Cauliflower*
- *2cm*   *Ginger*
- *5g*   *Chilli powder*
- *5g*   *Garlic purée*
- *10ml*   *Vegetable oil*
- *8*   *Baby corn*
- *8*   *Spring onions*
- *75g*   *Mange tout*
- *100g*   *Courgettes*
- *10g*   *Peanut butter (vegetarian)*
- *30ml*   *Shoyu*
- *300ml*   *Vegetable stock*
- *250g*   *Egg noodles*
- *1 large*   *Red chilli*
- *10g*   *Fresh basil, chopped*

1 Cook the noodles off in salted boiling water for 3–4 minutes and refresh under cold running water. Drain and reserve.

2 Peel and purée the ginger and peel and slice the carrots and spring onions. Wash and slice the courgettes and top and tail the mange tout. Remove the stalk and seeds from the chilli and slice. Wash the cauliflower and cut into florets.

3 Sweat off the carrots, cauliflower, ginger, chilli powder and garlic purée in a hot pan with the oil for 1–2 minutes, then add the baby corn, spring onions, mange tout and courgettes. Continue to stir-fry for 2–3 minutes.

4 Stir in the peanut butter, shoyu and stock and simmer for 2–3 minutes.

5 Add the drained noodles and chilli to the sauce and vegetables.

6 Divide into four portions and serve with chopped basil. ❑

❑ Top: Spiicy Egg Noodles   Bottom: Seitan with Szechwan and Lime ❑

Caribbean Mousse
4 covers

- 10g Margarine
- 130ml Evaporated milk
- 14g Diabetic chocolate
- 55g Sugar replacement
- 2.5ml Vanilla essence
- 1 Free-range egg yolk
- Pinch Salt
- 1 Banana
- 50g Desiccated coconut

1 Line four moulds with silicon paper and then lightly brush with melted margarine. Coat in the coconut and keep in the fridge.

2 Grate the chocolate, toast the remaining coconut, and peel and slice the banana.

3 Bring 30ml evaporated milk to a very gentle simmer. Place in a bain-marie and stir in the chocolate, then add the sugar replacement and vanilla essence.

4 Keep the remaining milk in the fridge.

5 Whisk the egg yolk then pour the chocolate mixture over slowly while whisking until fully incorporated. Return to the bain-marie and whisk in the salt until it thickens. Remove and allow to cool.

6 Very carefully fold the chilled milk, the banana slices and half of the coconut into the mixture.

7 Divide equally between the moulds, dust the top with the remaining coconut and place in the fridge until firm. Remove by warming the sides of the mould and remove the silicon paper.

NOTES

Serve with a fruit purée. When cooking with raw eggs always be aware of the risk posed by salmonella poisoning. ❏

Cheese Scones
4 covers

- 227g Plain flour
- 5g Baking powder
- Pinch Salt
- 85g Margarine
- 113g Cheddar cheese, grated (vegetarian)
- 80–90ml Milk to mix

1 Sieve the flour, baking powder and salt.

2 Rub in the margarine and grated cheese.

3 Bind together with the milk to form a dough.

4 Divide into equal portions – 8 large or 16 small.

5 Bake in a preheated oven at 200°C/Gas Mark 6 for 15–20 minutes until golden brown. ❏

→

Chocolate Crisps   4 covers

- *454g* *Vegetarian and diabetic chocolate*
- *227g* *Margarine*
- *227g* *Cornflakes*
- *227g* *Desiccated coconut (toasted)*

1 Melt the chocolate in a basin over hot water and stir in the margarine.

2 When the margarine is fully incorporated add the cornflakes and coconut.

3 Divide into 4 or 8 portions, place in cases and allow to cool and set. ❑

❑ Chololate Crisps ❑

- Pinch   Salt
- 110g   Wholemeal flour
- 1   Free-range egg, medium
- 265ml   Semi-skimmed milk
- 10ml   Vegetable oil or margarine
- 55g   Sugar replacement

1 Sieve the salt and flour into a suitable bowl then add the sugar replacement, egg and milk and fold into the flour, fully incorporating to make a smooth batter.

2 Place the oil in a thoroughly clean and hot pan until it is smoking.

3 Pour in a small amount of the batter, enough to cover the base of the pan.

4 When the top looks a little dry and the bottom golden brown, loosen the edges and turn over in one go and cook that side for 20–30 seconds.

5 Turn out onto kitchen paper and reserve.

→

❏ Diabetic Fruit Crêpes ❏

Raspberry Filling

- *250g Raspberries*
- *10g Corn flour*
- *15g Sugar replacement*
- *125ml Skimmed milk*
- *5ml Lime juice*
- *5ml Vanilla essence*

→

1 Take half of the berries and roughly chop.

2 Mix together the corn flour, sugar replacement and then add the milk to make a smooth paste.

3 Mix in the lime juice and slowly bring to a simmer. As it begins to thicken add the vanilla essence.

4 Remove from the heat and fold in the remaining berries. Divide equally between the crêpes.

NOTES

The raspberries can be substituted by strawberries, black-currants or blackberries. ❏

Papaya with Sticky Rice Pudding   4 covers

- *400g Jasmine rice*
- *330ml Coconut milk*
- *Pinch Ground cinnamon*
- *1 Star anise*
- *Pinch Salt*
- *120g Sugar replacement*
- *2 Papaya, large*
- *2.5g Sesame seeds, toasted*
- *4 sprigs Fresh mint*

1 Soak the rice in water overnight. Then drain and steam for 20–30 minutes until the rice is cooked. Place in a bowl.

2 In a separate bowl place the coconut milk, cinnamon, star anise, salt and the sugar replacement. Mix thoroughly and warm slightly.

3 Mix the hot rice with the liquid, this should allow the rice to still absorb the liquid, and then let it stand for 30–40 minutes.

4 Peel, deseed and dice the papaya and mix into the rice when it has cooled a little. Remove the star anise.

5 Divide into four portions and garnish with toasted sesame seeds and sprigs of fresh mint.

NOTES

Serve a sauce with this dessert by warming 100ml coconut milk, adding 25g sugar replacement, pinch of cinnamon, ½ star anise, and a pinch of salt. Stir all the ingredients, strain and serve. ❏

useful addresses

Birmingham College of Food,
Tourism and Creative Studies
Business and Community Unit
(Vegetarian Cookery Courses)
Summer Row
Birmingham B3 1JB
marketing@bcftcs.ac.uk

Coeliac UK
PO Box 349
High Wycombe
Bucks HP11 2GN
Tel: 01494 437278
www.coeliac.co.uk

Master Foods Services,
Customer Careline, (Ebly)
National Office
Waltham-on-the-wolds
Melton Mowbray
Leicestershire LE 14 4RS.
www.ootpeditor@ootp.co.uk

The NHS Cancer Plan
www.doh.gov.uk/cancer/
executivesum.htm

RSPCA
Freedom Foods
Enquiries Service
Causeway, Horsham
West Sussex RH12 1HG
Tel: 0870 333 5999
www.rspca.org.uk

Soil Association
Bristol House, 40–56 Victoria Street
Bristol BS1 6BY
Tel: 0117 929 0661
www.soilassociation.org

Suma Foods
Dean Clough, Halifax HX3 5AN
Tel: 01422 345513
www.suma.co.uk

Vegan Society
47 Highlands Road
Leatherhead, Surrey

The Vegetarian Society
Parkdale, Dunham Road, Altrincham
Cheshire

APPENDIX 1: Guide for Coeliac's

- Almonds are gluten-free. They are expensive, but ground almonds work well in cakes, breads and sweet dishes.
- Arrowroot is gluten-free. Starch extracted from the roots is used as a thickening agent.
- Barley should be avoided in all its forms.
- Buckwheat is gluten-free; and gives a delicious nutty flavour when used with gluten-free flours in baked products.
- Bulgar should be avoided as this is soaked and dried wheat.
- Carageenan is gluten-free and obtained from seaweed and used as a thickening agent.
- Corn is gluten-free in all forms, whether as corn-on-the-cob, corn-meal, cornflour or cornstarch. Also called Maize.
- Couscous should be avoided as it is prepared from wheat.
- Durum is not gluten-free and should be avoided.
- Flax is gluten-free, and occasionally used as a source of fibre. Also known as Linseed.
- Gram is naturally gluten-free, but could be contaminated. Produced from chick peas.
- Kamut is a member of the wheat family and NOT gluten-free.
- Millet is gluten-free, and better known for feeding budgerigars. Species of the grass family.
- Oats should be avoided unless your doctor specifically allows them.
- Pasta should be avoided as it is made from wheat flour.
- Pulses are gluten-free, and include peas, beans and lentils.
- Pulse flours are naturally gluten-free, although often contaminated with wheat flour in processing.
- Potato is gluten-free, but check some potato products e.g. waffles and hash-browns.
- Quinoa is gluten-free, and can be useful in cooking.
- Rice is gluten-free. This includes white rice, brown rice and wild rice.
- Rye should be avoided.
- Sago is gluten-free, and usually used in puddings, but can be difficult to work with in other recipes.
- Semolina should be avoided as it is 100% wheat.
- Sesame is gluten-free. Seeds are used although flour is now available.
- Sorghum is gluten-free, although rarely used in the UK.
- Spelt is not gluten-free, and should be avoided.
- Tapioca is gluten-free, and used as a thickener for puddings. Also called Cassava and Manioc. Produced from the tubers of the Tapioca Plant grown in India.
- Teff – gluten-free (relation of millet).
- Triticale should be avoided as it is a hybrid of wheat and rye.
- Urd is gluten-free, but could be contaminated. Produced from lentils.
- Wheat should be avoided in all varieties and forms.
- Wheatstarch is gluten-free, as long as it is specially prepared for Coeliacs and complies with the Codex Alimentarius gluten-free standard. Commercial wheatstarch should be avoided.

index

recipe index

Page numbers in *italics* refer to illustrations. Letters in brackets, on the recipe title only, refer to diets identified in the recipe notes as follows: V -vegan, L – low-cholesterol, C – coeliac, N – nut-free, D – diabetic.

mixed, and raisin salad 298-9
and noodle salad 140
pasta salad 145-6
salad 116
soya, kebabs 238, *239*
tomatoes and onion tart 260-61
triple, and fungi salad 155
Tuscan, and basil ragout 262, *263*
white, stew with sundried tomatoes 273
béchamel sauce 108, 214
black olive and chilli salad 117
bow pasta salad with hazel and pine nuts 117
bramley apple, peach and apricot strudel 280-81
brandy date cake 278, *279*, 280
bread pudding, olive and garlic 185-6
breakfast rashers, veggi 159, *159*
broccoli
    and leek strudel 190-91
    pancake fillings 115
    and pasta 218
broths
    EBLY vegetable 125
    enoki and watercress *120*, 126
    seaweed Japanese style *151*, 229-30
brown vegetable stock 109
buckwheat, roasted, salad garnished with aramé [V, L] 228
bulgar wheat
    and griddled vegetable salad 118-19, *118*
    Mexican style [V, L, D] 170, *188*
    and nut pilaff 170
    tabouli [V, L, D] 171
    and tomato salad [V, L, D] 119
burgers, mixed nut 198, 200

cabbage, hot red, and russet apples [V, L, D, C, N] 187, *207*
cakes
    Arabic 277
    brandy date 278, *279*, 280
    chocolate and coconut fudge 281
    coconut 282
    cranberry and orange 282, *283*
cannelloni with sweet pepper ragout 171-3, *172*
capelletti pasta combo [V, L, D, N] 173
capers, linguine with olives 194, *195*
Caribbean mousse [D] 307
carrots
    and cashew nut salad 121
    orange and nut soup *120*, *120*
cashew nuts

and carrot salad 121
and carrot salad [V, D, C, L] 121
mushroom and leek platt 212-13
seitan with lemon and fennel 231, 233
casseroles
    bean cup 169
    Mediterranean-style bean 198, *199*
    new potato and wheat grain 215
cauliflower, Easter 296
cepe mushroom soup [C] 293
chapattis [V, C] 294
chard rolls [V, C, L] 174
cheese
    see also cheeses by name
    avocado and spinach salad 292, *293*
    blue, dressing 150
    sauce 184
    scones [D] 307
    smoked tofu and EBLY 236
chestnuts, red wine with Paris mushrooms 226-7, *226*
chiabatta, and goat's cheese 122, *123*
chickpeas
    curry 175-6, *223*
    spiced, salad 238, 240
    and taco sauce [V, C] 174-5
chillies
    bean and mushroom soup [V, D, L] 121-2
    and black olive salad 117
    low-fat vegetarian beans 196
    potatoes [C] 294
    quick five-bean 224-5
    wheat 272
Chinese-style chow mein [V, C] 176
Chinese-style stir-fried mushrooms [V, D, C] 177-8, *177*
chocolate
    and coconut fudge cake [V] 281
    crisps [D] 308, *308*
    orange mousse 286
    orange roll 286-7
chow mein, Chinese-style 176
cider, shitake mushrooms with greens 234, *235*
classic stew with seitan 178
coconut
    cake 282
    chocolate fudge cake 281
    spinach ensemble 162-3, *163*
    toasted, buns 311
coffee, hazelnut and rice salad 124
coriander, and almond spiced couscous 162-3
couscous
    Moroccan-style 200

and orange salad 141-2
spiced
    almond and coriander 162-3
    and oyster mushrooms 235, 240
walnut and fig 269
cranberry and orange cake 282, 283
cream, sour, baked mushrooms with and
    nuts 165
creamed spinach parcels [V, D, L] 178-9,
    180
creams, roasted EBLY 228
crêpes, diabetic fruit 309-10, 309
crisp deep-fried tofu with spicy peanut dip
    179
crumbles
    lemongrass and potato 192, 193
    mushroom, herb and nut 211-12
    watercress, nettle and vegetable 269-70,
        271
cucumber, peanuts and pine salad 146
curries
    banana and apple 166-7, 167
    chickpea 175-6, 223
    dhal 295
    masaman 196-7
    red – paste 196-7
    Thai green with tempeh 253-4, 253
    vegetable 264-5
curry pastes
    green 254
    red 196-7
curry sauce 181

dates
    brandy cake 278, 279, 280
    seitan with tagine and honey [V] 234,
        271
deep-fried soya sticks [V, C] 295
deep-fried tofu in spicy peanut sauce 181,
    182
dhal curry [V, L, C, D] 295
diabetic fruit crêpes 309-10, 309
dressings 116, 124, 127, 129-30, 131, 142,
    143, 147, 152, 155, 156, 160
    balsamic 237
    blue cheese 150
    green 236
    lemon vinaigrette 210
    red wine vinegar 114
    vegetarian mayonnaise 157
    vinaigrette 141, 298

Easter cauliflower [C] 296
Eastern mushroom and tofu kebabs 182

EBLY
    field mushrooms filled with spinach and
        glazed cheese sauce 184
    hot buttered, with herbs 187
    Mediterranean 197
    Mediterranean salad 134, 134
    and orange custard with caramelised sugar
        283
    pilaff 183
    roasted, cream 228
    smoked tofu and cheese 236
    tamari 249
    vegetable broth 125
    and wild rice salad 124
eggs, egg-free scrambled [V, C] 125, 159
enoki
    oriental, and snow pea salad 143, 144
    and watercress broth [V, D, L] 120, 126

fajitas, mushroom and pepper 204, 205
falafel 296
    with a mint and chilli sauce [V] 126-7
farfalloni with shitake mushrooms 183-4
fennel
    orange and grapefruit salad 142-3
    seitan with lemon and cashews 231, 233
feta cheese, and Greek style tomato salad
    130-31
fettuccini
    mushroom 210
    mushroom and sundried tomato 208, 209
field mushrooms filled with spinach, EBLY
    and glazed cheese sauce 184
figs
    Moroccan-style, and millet 200-1, 201
    and walnut couscous 269
filled Chinese rolls and tomato sauce [V, L,
    D] 185, 255
filo parcels, sweet and sour 247
flans
    mushroom, leek and pea 212-13
    mushroom and nut 203-4
    tomatoes and spring onion oat 259
forest salad [V, C, L] 297-8, 297
fricassees, wheat and vegetable 270, 272
fruit and muesli [V, L] 284

garlic
    croûtons with a garden salad 127, 128
    linguine with roasted peppers 195, 205
    and olive bread pudding 185-6
    pasta and mushroom salad 129
Genoa garden salad 128, 129-30
glazes 162

goats' cheese, chiabatta 122, *123*
gorgonzola sauce 220
gorgozola, with penne pasta 220
grapefruit
    and avocado salad [V, C] 130, *133*
    pink, orange and fennel salad 142-3
gravies, vegetarian 112-13
Greek style tomato and feta salad 130-31
Greek-style stuffed vine leaves 186-7
green dressing 236
grilled polenta with Niçoise style salad 131

haricot and leek salad [V, D, C] 132
hazelnuts
    coffee and rice salad 124
    and mushroom pâté 139
    strawberry and cassia torte 289-90, *289*
herbs
    see also herbs by name
    hot buttered EBLY 187
    Mediterranean, aubergines and tomato
        sauce 164
    mushroom and nut crumble 211-12
honey, seitan with tagine and dates 234, *271*
hot buttered EBLY with herbs 187
hot red cabbage and russet apples [V, L, D,
    C, N] 187, *207*

Jamacan-style jerk [V] *188*, 189

kebabs
    Eastern mushrooms and tofu 182
    seitan 230
    soya bean 238, *239*
kedgeree, vegetarian 157, *159*

laver bread, samphire and mushroom lasagne
    189-90, *268*
leeks
    and broccoli strudel [V] 190-91
    and haricot salad 132
    mushroom and cashew nut platt 212-13
    mushroom and pea flan 213-14
    and parsnip pie 191-2
lemongrass, and potato crumble 192, *193*
lenmon, seitan with fennel and cashews 231,
    233
lentils
    daal [V] 193-4
    and rice salad 152
    soup, tomato-scented 304
limes, seitan with Szechwan 233, *306*
linguine
    with olives and capers 194, *195*

with roasted peppers and garlic [V, D, L]
    195, *205*
low-fat vegetarian chilli beans 196

macadamia nuts, pineapple and smoked tofu
    salad 147, *148*
mangoes
    and orange salad 142
    and papaya slice [V, L, D] 284, *285*
    and rambutan lime salsa [V, L, D, C, N]
        132, *133*
marinades 230
    Szechwan 233
marjoram and oregano, potato salad 149
masaman curry 196-7
masur dhal soup [C] *151*, 298
mayonnaise, vegetarian 157
Mediterranean EBLY 197
Mediterranean EBLY salad 134, *134*
Mediterranean mushroom salad [V, D, L]
    135-6, *135*
Mediterranean-style bean casserole [V, C, L,
    D] 198, *199*
mesur dhal soup *151*
Mexican-style stuffed mushrooms [D, L] 136
millet
    basil scented salad 115-16
    Moroccan-style, and fig 200-1, *201*
    salad [V] 136-7, *138*
mint and chilli sauce 126
miso soup 137
mixed bean and raisin salad 298-9
mixed nut burgers 198, 200
moong dal, spiced 300-1
Moroccan-style couscous 200
Moroccan-style millet and fig 200-1, *201*
Moroccan-style peaches and pears [V, D, L,
    C] 202
mousse
    Caribbean 307
    chocolate orange 286
    tofu fruit *279*, 303
muesli and fruit 284
muffins, orange and pecan 285
mushrooms
    baked, with sour cream and nuts 165
    and black olive pizza 202-3, *258*
    cepe, soup [C] 293
    chilli and bean soup 121-2
    Chinese-style stir-fried 177-8, *177*
    Eastern and tofu kebabs 182
    fetuccini 210
    field, filled with spinach, EBLY and
        glazed cheese sauce 184

wild
  and aramé paella 275-6, *275*
  and EBLY salad 124
  and mushroom soup 139
ricotta and vegetable pie 227
risottos, tempeh 251-2, *251*
roasted buckwheat salad garnished with
  aramé [V, L] 228
roasted EBLY cream 228
rogan josh, pumpkin and potato 222, *223*
rose apple and apple strudel 290, *291*

salad dressings *see* dressings
salads
  avocadoes, cheese and spinach 292, *293*
  basil scented millet 115-16
  bean 116
  black olive and chilli 117
  bulgar wheat and griddled vegetable
    118-19, *118*
  bulgar wheat and tomato 119
  cashew nut and carrot 121
  coffee, hazelnut and rice 124
  EBLY and wild rice 124
  forest 297-8, *297*
  garden
    with garlic croûtons 127, *128*
    Genoa *128*, 129-30
  grapefruit and avocado 130, *133*
  Greek style tomato and feta 130-31
  haricot and leek 132
  Mediterranean EBLY 134, *134*
  Mediterranean mushroom 135-6, *135*
  millet 136-7, *138*
  mixed, with toasted sunflower seeds and
    orange *123*, 160
  mixed bean and raisin 298-9
  Niçoise, with grilled polenta 131
  noodle and bean 140
  orange, pink grapefruit and fennel 142-3
  orange and couscous 141-2
  orange and mango 142
  oriental enoki and snow pea 143, *144*
  oriental vegetable 217
  pasta
    bean 145-6
    garlic and mushroom 129
    with hazel and pine nuts 117
  peanut, cucumber and pine 146
  pineapple, macadamia and smoked tofu
    147, *148*
  potato, oregano and marjoram 149
  radish and pea with blue cheese dressing
    150

rice
  nutty 141
  pepper flavoured 146-7
rice and lentil 152
roasted buckwheat garnished with aramé
  228
spiced chickpea 238, 240
summer, with a crunch 114
triple bean and fungi 155
tropical spinach 156
vegetable and fungi basil 156
salsas
  lime, mango and rambutan 132,
    133
  mushroom 173
  spicy vegetable 154
  tomato and scallion 155
samphire
  laver bread and mushroom lasagne
    189-90, *268*
  and quinoa 225, *263*
satay sauce 110
sauce supreme 110-11
sauces
  almond 219-20
  anise 161
  BBQ 166
  béchamel 108, 214
  cheese 184
  chickpea and taco 174-5
  gorgonzola 220
  mint and chilli 126
  mushroom 274
  peanut curry 181
  plum and honey 168
  red pepper 109
  satay 110
  spicy peanut 181, *182*
  spicy tomato 111
  sundried tomato 161
  supreme 110
  sweet and sour 247, 248
  teriyaki 253, 303
  tomato 164, 185
  velouté 113, 191-2
sausages, vegetarian 158, *159*
sauté tempeh with rice and nuts [V, L, C, D]
  229
scones, cheese 307
seaweed broth Japanese style [V, L, D, C]
  151, 229-30
seeds, sunflower, warm mixed green salad
  and orange 160
seitan